TUITION RISING

Ronald G. Ehrenberg

TUITION RISING

Why College Costs So Much

With a New Preface

HARVARD UNIVERSITY PRESS

Cambridge, Massachusetts, and London, England

First Harvard University Press paperback edition, 2002

Library of Congress Cataloging-in-Publication Data

Ehrenberg, Ronald G.
 Tuition rising : why college costs so much / Ronald G. Ehrenberg.
  p. cm.
 Includes bibliographical references and index.
 ISBN 0-674-00328-4 (cloth)
 ISBN 0-674-00988-6 (pbk.)
 1. College costs—United States. 2. Education, Higher—Economic aspects—United States.
 3. Universities and colleges—United States—Administration. I. Title.
 LB2342 .E42 2000
 378.3'8'0973—dc21   00-035086

To my wife Randy, with all my love

Contents

Preface, 2002

I wrote *Tuition Rising* for a general audience. No familiarity with economic concepts is required, and the use of notes and citations to references is kept to a minimum. Readers interested in delving more deeply into the issues that I address can go to my home page on the World Wide Web, <http://*www.people.cornell.edu/pages/rge2*>. Posted there are links to a reading list for the course on the economics of higher education that I teach at Cornell and an annotated list of sources that I prepared for readers of this book.

Since the hardcover edition was published, tuition at the selective private colleges and universities has continued to rise faster than the rate of inflation. Increases at the selective privates for the years 2000–01 and 2001–02 averaged about 2 percentage points more than the rate of inflation, which falls into the range for the previous fifty years reported in *Tuition Rising*.

The booming stock market of the late 1990s also saw the endowments of the institutions continue to rise. Indeed, Harvard University's endowment reached more than $19 billion on June 30, 2000. One year later, after a period of declining stock market prices, it was still valued at $18.3 billion.

Faced with unprecedented increases in wealth and growing public concern about their rate of tuition increases, the wealthiest selective privates increased the generosity of their financial aid policies, with Princeton announcing in February 2001 the elimination of all loans from its financial aid packages. To attract top students, a number of less wealthy selective private institutions increasingly moved in the direction of providing "merit aid" to applicants, which exacerbated concerns about whether these selective institutions would remain accessible to students from a wide variety of socioeconomic backgrounds. Not wanting to move in this direction, a group of presidents from twenty-eight other selective privates issued a joint statement in

July 2001 pledging to provide financial aid solely on the basis of need and to determine need in a consistent manner across institutions.

Nevertheless, it is not certain that the selective privates as a group will remain accessible to students from low- and lower-middle–income families. The decline in the stock market during the year ending June 30, 2001, which was followed by substantial market disruption and fall after the attacks of September 11, 2001, made it more difficult for the selective private institutions to continue to increase spending from their endowments. The recession that started in 2001 also had an adverse impact on their fund raising for current operations, and the corresponding decline in income of many parents of college-age students increased the financial need of many applicants. As a result of these pressures, many selective private institutions increased their tuitions by 5 percent or more for the 2002–03 academic year, which was more than 3 percent greater than the rate of inflation; this, in turn, still further increased students' financial need. Thus it became increasingly difficult for many selective private institutions to maintain the generosity of their financial aid packages, let alone to continue to enhance them.

Tuition Rising concludes that unless the selective privates as a group maintain their accessibility to students from a wide diversity of backgrounds, by moderating their rates of tuition increases or expanding their provision of need-based financial aid, public concern about tuition hikes is likely to increase. This concern will probably be magnified by the double-digit increases in tuition that occurred at a number of public institutions in 2002–03, as these institutions sought to offset the decline in state appropriations that accompanied the recession.

PART **I**

SETTING THE STAGE

CHAPTER 1

Why Do Costs Keep Rising at Selective Private Colleges and Universities?

The American system of higher education is the envy of the rest of the world. A mixed system of over thirty-six hundred public and private institutions, it provides access to higher education for a large proportion of our population. Its diversity is extraordinary. At one end of the spectrum are two-year institutions that provide both vocational training and academic instruction to prepare students for entry into four-year colleges. At the other end are the large multi-product research universities that provide four-year undergraduate education in a wide variety of liberal arts and applied areas; offer graduate education for professions such as law, medicine, business, and education; and undertake research and educate doctoral students.

Among this latter group are America's selective private research universities. Examples include the Ivy League institutions—Brown, Columbia, Cornell, Dartmouth, Harvard, Pennsylvania, Princeton, and Yale—as well as the Massachusetts Institute of Technology (MIT), Duke, Johns Hopkins, Northwestern, Chicago, Stanford, and the California Institute of Technology (Cal Tech). Small in number, they have a unique place in American higher education, exert a unique influence on it, and often get their names in the news.

Along with their selective private liberal arts college counterparts, such as Amherst, Bryn Mawr, Carleton, Claremont, Macalester, Oberlin, Smith, Swarthmore, Wesleyan, and Williams, these institutions educate a disproportionate share of the leaders of American industry and government. They are "selective" in the sense that they have far more applicants each year than they have room to enroll in their freshman classes. As a result, they have considerable discretion in deciding whom to admit. Many of the best and brightest high school students in the nation compete for positions in their classes, and the average quality of their undergraduate students, as measured by test scores and high school grades, is the highest in the nation.

Along with their public research university counterparts, such as Michigan, Wisconsin, Berkeley, the University of California at Los Angeles (UCLA), and North Carolina, the selective private research universities are world-class centers of the production of new knowledge and new researchers. By far the vast majority of Nobel Prize winners were educated at or teach at them. Their excellence attracts Ph.D. students from around the world. Indeed, in 1997, noncitizens earned about 29 percent of all the doctoral degrees that they granted. In key scientific and engineering fields, the percentages were much higher. For example, 53 percent of the doctoral degrees awarded in engineering and 49 percent of those awarded in the mathematical and computer sciences fields in 1997 went to noncitizens.[1] One noted economist and academic administrator has even asserted that two thirds to three quarters of the best research universities in the world are located in the United States and that similar claims of achievement can be made for very few other sectors of the American economy.[2]

In recent years, the selective private research universities and liberal arts colleges have come under attack. Their endowments, or stocks of financial assets, have soared to unprecedented heights because of the increase in stock market prices during the 1990s and the large flow of annual gifts that they continually receive. Harvard University alone had an endowment of almost $11 billion on June 30, 1997, and received over $425 million dollars in gifts in the academic year ending on that date. The large private research universities now regularly announce capital campaigns with multiyear goals of over $1 billion. Although some of the money received from such campaigns is used to fund current operations and building projects, a stated objective is always to increase the size of the institution's endowment.

As their endowment levels have increased, so too have the levels of tuition that they charge undergraduate students. In 1997–98, tuition and fee levels at the selective private colleges and universities averaged well over $20,000 a year. The tuition levels at these institutions have continually increased at rates that exceed the rate of increase in consumer prices. Faced with tuitions increasing at rates that exceed the growth of prices and often of their incomes, many American families with children nearing college age worry that they can no longer afford to send their children to these selective private institutions. Many are angry that the institutions have the audacity to increase their tuition at all, given that the institutions are becoming increasingly wealthy.

Indeed, concern over the increase in tuition levels at these and other academic institutions led to Congress's establishing a National Commission on the Cost of Higher Education in 1997 to conduct a comprehensive review of college costs and prices and to make recommendations on how to hold costs down. The prevailing public view when this commission was established seemed to be that these institutions and others were letting their costs grow without concern for the public welfare. Over and over the question was raised, Why can't these selective private academic institutions behave more like business firms and hold down their costs?

To keep things in perspective, I should point out that only about 5.5 percent of students enrolled at four-year colleges in 1997–98 were enrolled at colleges that charged more than $20,000 a year. Nationwide, average tuition and fee levels were $13,785 and $3,111, respectively, for students enrolled at four-year private and public institutions. Inasmuch as the vast majority of students attend public institutions, about three quarters of all students attending four-year institutions were paying tuition and fees of less than $8,000 a year.

Although these selective institutions are an important component of the American college and university system, they educate only a small share of our undergraduate college students. Moreover, focusing on their stated level of tuition and fees, their "list prices," ignores the large amount of need-based financial aid that they distribute to students in an effort to make education at these institutions accessible to all talented students, regardless of the students' family backgrounds.

Why Public Concern Increased in the 1990s

A true, and to some a depressing, fact is that selective private institutions have almost always increased their tuition levels each year by more than the rate of increase in consumer prices. Over thirty years ago William Bowen documented that educational costs per student rose by an average of 2 to 3 percentage points more than the rate of increase in consumer prices each year at a set of selective private universities during the 1905–1965 period.[3] This rise was attributed partly to the increased specialization of knowledge and the growth of new fields of study, as well as to the increasing emphasis at these institutions on graduate training and research. But first and foremost, it was attributed to the fact that the nature of the educational process did not permit selective private academic institutions to share in the productivity gains that were occurring in the rest of the economy.

The real earnings of workers increase as their productivity levels increase. During the period that Bowen studied, because of changes in technology and increased use of capital equipment, the productivity and hence the real earnings of Americans rose by about 2.5 percent a year. However, the productivity of faculty at these selective private institutions, as measured by the number of students that they educated each year, did not change very much, primarily because low student-faculty ratios were felt to be essential to high-quality college education. As a result, these institutions did not receive extra revenue each year from gains in faculty members' productivity, which in turn could then be distributed back to the faculty in the form of salary increases.

The institutions thus faced a choice. On the one hand, they could allow faculty salaries to decline relative to salaries of individuals in other professions. On the other hand, they could raise tuition sufficiently to provide faculty salary increases in line with the raises other employees in the economy were receiving. The former strategy would make it difficult to attract and retain high-quality faculty, so invariably the latter strategy was pursued.

What has happened to tuition levels at selective private universities since the period that Bowen studied can be illustrated by looking at the experiences of Cornell University. As I will discuss in more detail below, several of Cornell's colleges receive some direct support from the state of New York. This enables them to charge a considerably lower tuition to residents of the state than is charged in the rest of the university. The tuition numbers discussed here are for tuition in the other Cornell colleges, which I will refer to throughout as the endowed colleges.

Between 1966–67 and 1997–98, the annual tuition increase at Cornell averaged 2.8 percentage points more than the rate of increase in consumer prices during the year. In three of these years, the rate of tuition increase was actually lower than the rate of increase in consumer prices. In one year, tuition increased by 9 percentage points more than consumer prices. But similar to tuition from 1905 to 1965, tuition rose, on average, by 2 to 3 percentage points more a year than did consumer prices during this period.

What is of most concern to parents is how these tuition increases influence their ability to help finance their children's education. During most of the twentieth century family incomes also increased, on average, by 2 to 3 percentage points more each year than did consumer prices. Such increases in purchasing power, or real income gains, arose both because productivity gains caused earnings to rise by more than the rate of inflation and because women were increasingly entering the labor force and finding employment. As a result, tuition increases that were greater than increases in consumer prices did not reduce the accessibility of the selective private institutions because family income gains kept up with these tuition increases.

Figure 1.1 illustrates whether this continued to be true at Cornell during the 1966–67 to 1997–98 period. It plots the ratio of Cornell's tuition and fees to the median income of families in the United States. Between 1966–67 and 1979–80, this ratio remained roughly constant, fluctuating between 26 and 28 percent. This means that even though on average Cornell's tuition increases exceeded the rate of increase in consumer prices during the thirteen-year period, family incomes grew by enough to keep the relationship between Cornell's tuition and the income of the median family in the United States constant.

In contrast, starting in 1980 Cornell's tuition increases began to exceed the growth of family incomes in the United States. Between 1980–81 and 1992–93, Cornell's tuition rose from 28 percent to 49 percent of the median American family's income. The relationship between tuition and family income had been drastically changed, and a Cornell education was much more expensive in relative terms at the end of the period than it was at the start. Although part of the reason for this was that the university increased

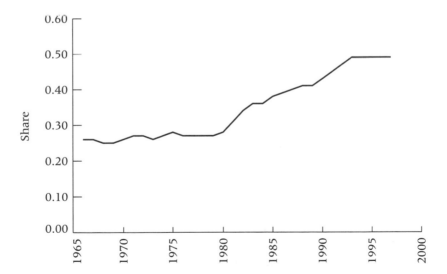

Figure 1.1. Endowed Cornell tuition and fees as a share of median family income in the United States, 1956–1998.

the spread between its tuition increases and the increases in the consumer price index, the major reason was that family incomes did not keep up, on average, with the increase in consumer prices during the period. In real terms, the median family in the United States was worse off at the end of the period than it was at the start.

The reasons why median family income did not grow in real terms during the period are complex. Contributing factors include increased foreign competition, deregulation of several key industries, and a decline in the strength of the union movement. However, by the mid-1990s median family income again began to grow in real terms in the United States. Hence even though Cornell's annual tuition increases continued to exceed the growth of consumer prices, as Figure 1.1 indicates, its tuition level relative to median family income stabilized after 1993.

Cornell's experience was not unique. Data collected by the College Board for all private institutions in the United States show a similar pattern: costs of attendance remaining stable relative to family incomes through 1980, rising substantially throughout the 1980s and early 1990s, and then leveling off at a substantially higher ratio.[4]

Figure 1.1 simplifies things greatly. The typical family sending a child to a selective institution has an income level far above the median family income level in the United States. During the period shown in the figure the income levels for many such families have grown at more rapid rates than has median family income. Selective private institutions also provide substantial levels of need-based grant aid to students to enable students to attend their institutions independent of the students' families' ability to pay. Federal grant aid also reduces family costs for lower-income students, and federal subsidized loans are available for students from lower- and middle-income families. On balance, however, it took a much greater share of a family's income to send a student to a selective private university in 1993 than it did in 1980.

So unhappiness with the way that the selective private institutions were behaving with respect to their tuition levels was growing. When the institutions continued to raise tuition by more than the rate of inflation after 1993, and at the same time the value of the institutions' endowments started to soar, public outrage grew. That tuition levels had stabilized relative to family income by then did not prevent the outrage; families were unhappy at how much they had to pay.

Interestingly, this outrage and unhappiness did not reduce the numbers of applicants to the selective institutions. Over time their applicants continued to increase, and it became more difficult to obtain admission at many of them. Just as the economic benefit to attending college increased during the 1980s and 1990s, so too did the economic benefits from attending these institutions rather than other academic institutions. Numerous studies indicate that the economic gains to students from attending selective private institutions, both as undergraduates and as graduate professional degree students, are substantial.[5]

That they are should not be surprising. These institutions are the ones that devote the most resources to educating their students and the ones at which students pay the smallest share of their educational costs. Virtually all students at public and private nonprofit academic institutions have their educational costs subsidized. At the private institutions the subsidies come primarily from endowment income, annual giving, and government funding for student aid, as well as from private contributions and government funding from earlier years that covered the costs of the academic buildings and equipment on the campuses. At the public institutions, the subsidies come from the same sources (although endowment income and annual giving are typically lower) and from direct state appropriations.

Figure 1.2, which is based on the work of Gordon Winston, illustrates this point. An institution spends a certain amount educating each student. These costs include the direct operating costs that show up on the institution's books as well as the implicit value of the services provided by all of the

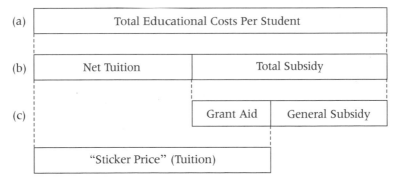

Figure 1.2. The relationships between educational costs per student, tuition levels, and subsidies received by students in American higher education. (Source: Adapted from Gordon C. Winston and Ivan C. Yen, "Cost, Prices, Subsidies, and Hierarchy: The Economic Structure of U.S. Higher Education," The Williams Project on the Economics of Higher Education discussion paper 32 Williams College, Williamstown, Mass. [revised December 1998].)

institution's academic facilities and equipment (panel a). These costs are financed by net tuition payments from students and the total subsidies that students receive (panel b). Net tuition payments are simply the stated tuition levels minus the grant aid given back to students. Hence the total subsidy that students receive consists of two parts; grant aid that goes only to grant recipients and a general subsidy that every student receives (panel c).

Using national data for the 1994–95 academic year, Winston has demonstrated that these general subsidies are enormous at the selective private institutions. For example, calculations generously done for me by him for the fifteen private liberal arts colleges that *U.S. News & World Report* (hereafter *USNWR*) ranked the highest in its 1999 ranking of national liberal arts colleges, indicated that while their average "sticker price," or stated tuition level, was $18,057 in 1994–95, the institutions spent an average of $33,449 educating each student that academic year. Thus the average general subsidy received by each student was $14,739. Once one adds in grant aid, which averaged $5,822 per student, the average student attending these institutions received a total educational subsidy of $20,561 in 1994–95 (see Table 1.1).

Table 1.1 Educational costs per student, tuition levels, and student subsidies at top private liberal arts colleges in 1994–95.

	Top 15 private liberal arts colleges[a]	All institutions[b]
(1) Total educational costs per student	$33,449	$12,265
− (2) "Sticker price"—tuition	$18,710	$5,919
(3) General subsidy per student	$14,739	$6,346
+ (4) Average grant aid per student	$5,822	$2,144
(5) Total educational subsidy per student	$20,561	$8,490

Source: Unpublished tabulations provided by Gordon Winston and Jared Carbone from the U.S. Department of Education 1995 Integrated Postsecondary Education Data System (IPEDS) (Washington, D.C., 1995) and Gordon C. Winston and Ivan C. Yen, "Cost, Prices, Subsidies, and Hierarchy: The Economic Structure of U.S. Higher Education," The Williams Project on the Economics of Higher Education discussion paper 32, Williams College, Williamstown, Mass. (revised December 1998), table 1.

a. The 15 highest-rated national liberal arts colleges in *1999 America's Best Colleges* (Washington, D.C.: *USNWR*, August 1998).

b. Includes 2,739 institutions, of which 1,420 are public and 1,319 are private.

Similar computations can be made for our nation's top private research universities. There is more ambiguity in such calculations because the research universities produce multiple things—undergraduate education, professional education, graduate education, and research—and it is difficult to assign various costs precisely to these different areas. But when such calculations were done, Winston found subsidies of similar magnitudes for the top selective private research universities.

For comparison purposes, he estimated that the average educational subsidy received by college students nationwide that year was $8490.[6] Students who attend the selective private colleges and universities get a lot more resources devoted to their education than they would get at other institutions. They also get a lot more than they pay for.

Why Selective Private Colleges and Universities Can't Hold Down Their Costs

The objective of executives of major American corporations is to maximize the market value of their corporations. To maintain profit margins in the face of domestic and foreign competition, they have increasingly come to analyze their companies' operations to find ways to increase their efficiency and to cut costs. Why can't the selective private colleges and universities behave the same way?

Administrators of selective private colleges and universities also want to maximize the value of their institutions. However, for them value is not measured by economic profits. As nonprofit organizations, their institutions show no profits on their accounting books. Rather, maximizing value to these administrators means making their institutions the very best that they can be in almost every area of their activities. These administrators are like cookie monsters searching for cookies. They seek out all the resources that they can get their hands on and then devour them. They put these resources to use funding activities that the institution feels are important and that will make some aspect of its operations better.

The selective private colleges and the universities are all concerned with the quality of the education that they deliver to their undergraduate and graduate students. Each selective private institution wants more faculty members to permit smaller class sizes and to allow it to expand into new exciting fields of study. Each wants classrooms equipped with the most modern technology. Each wants to have discretionary resources to pay for field trips and other off-campus educational experiences for its students, and to use to bring the most interesting speakers to campus to engage the students in the important issues of the day. Each wants to have more funds for faculty salaries to allow it to attract and retain the very best faculty in the nation.

At both types of institution, but especially at the research universities, emphasis is placed not only on disseminating knowledge and engaging students in critical thinking, but also on creating new knowledge. Facilities for research are expensive, and faculty members need time to devote to research so that they can remain at the frontiers of their fields. Although some research, especially in science and engineering fields, is funded externally by the government, corporations, and foundations, much research at universities is funded by the universities themselves, primarily in the form of low teaching loads for their faculty members. There is continual pressure at the institutions to reduce faculty members' teaching loads to permit more time for research. This pressure leads to what Robert Zemsky has called the "academic ratchet": the gradual decline of teaching loads and the escalation of educational costs.[7]

The value of university research to society is enormous. To take but a few recent examples from Cornell, faculty have worked on genetic reengineering of crops to make them resistant to disease, on developing new materials that are both stronger and lighter, and on showing that nutritional education programs can play a major role in reducing cardiac health problems. The benefits that undergraduate and graduate students get from studying with faculty members who are at the frontiers of their disciplines and conducting such important research cannot be overstated. All the Nobel Prize winners at Cornell regularly teach introductory undergraduate courses.

As anyone who has been an administrator at one of these institutions knows, innovative and creative faculty members regularly present the administration with new ideas for improving the quality of the teaching and research that goes on at the institution. In the main these are wonderful ideas, and a major role that administrators play is deciding how to allocate limited resources to foster these initiatives. The more resources that the administrators can get their hands on, the fewer hard decisions they have to make and the better the institution can be.

The quality of education at a selective private college or university depends heavily on the type of students who attend the institution. A bright and diverse undergraduate student body facilitates the educational experiences of students and allows the faculty to concentrate on developing critical thinking skills in students rather than on remedial education. A student body of high academic quality allows all classes to move at rapid rates and much learning to be accomplished.

With over thirty-six hundred higher educational institutions for students to choose from, one might expect that higher education would be an extremely competitive business. It is, and the freedom that less selective private institutions have to raise their tuition levels is much more limited. Indeed a growing, but still small, number of private institutions with excess capacity have begun to reduce their tuition levels in the hope of attracting more students and improving their financial pictures. These institutions do have to worry about keeping costs down and improving their efficiency.

However, the selective private institutions live almost entirely in a world of their own. As their tuition levels have increased, so too have the number of applications they receive. Over the last forty years, the fraction of our nation's top academic students, as measured by their test scores, that chooses to enroll in these selective institutions has increased.

Various observers have attributed this trend to the growing availability of need-based financial aid, which opened up attendance at these institutions to students from lower- and middle-income families. Others have noted the reductions in transportation and communication costs that have taken place over the last forty years, which increasingly have led to the expansion of attendance at them by students from all parts of the nation. Each has become a truly national institution. Still others attribute this trend to the growing income inequality that has occurred in the United States since 1980. Just as there has been a widening in the distribution of earnings between high school and college graduates, there has been, in the view of many, an increase in the economic benefit of attending a selective private college or university rather than another academic institution.

As top academic students become more concentrated in these institutions, many large companies have concentrated a greater share of their recruiting efforts for new college graduates at the selective private institutions. This in turn provides increased impetus for the next generation of top high school students to attend these schools.

The desire of the selective private colleges and universities to be the very best that they can be has thus been reinforced by what Phillip Cook and Robert Frank have called our winner-take-all society.[8] As top academic students have become increasingly concentrated in these institutions, it becomes increasingly important to each of the institutions in this group to maintain its status within the group so that it can continue to attract these students.

The result is what a number of observers have called the arms race of spending at the selective private institutions. Their competition has expanded beyond spending to improve the academic quality of the institutions to spending to enhance all aspects of students' college experiences. Construction of apartment-style living units to replace traditional dormitories and of improved dining facilities with expanded food selections, as well as the construction of new athletic facilities for varsity athletes, intramural sports, and recreational uses, is occurring at many of these institutions. To maintain its status in the upper echelon of American higher educational institutions, each institution believes it has to spend more.

Students who attend these selective private institutions benefit from the improved academic and living environments that the institutions offer. But the net result of the process is that the cost of attending the institutions keeps increasing. As long as lengthy lines of highly qualified applicants keep knocking at its door and accepting its offers of admission, no institution has a strong incentive to unilaterally end the spending race.

Other Forces That Add to Cost Pressures

As if this were not enough, I am going to argue throughout this book that there are other forces that put added cost pressures on the selective private colleges and universities. The first is the system of shared governance that exists between trustees, administrators, and faculty. Faculty members have a unique role in this system because they are the creators of new knowledge and have primary responsibility for the educational mission of the institution. But the system of shared governance almost guarantees that the institutions will be slow to react to cost pressures and that internal politics will play an important role in decisions. In addition, I will show that faculty involved in shared governance sometimes find it difficult to distinguish between what is best for the institution as a whole and what is best for the existing faculty members.

The second force is the federal government. A consent decree entered into between a group of the selective private institutions and the U.S Department of Justice in 1991 prohibits the institutions from taking joint actions that limit competition. This decree was aimed at stimulating competition in financial aid offers and increasing the total dollar amount of grant aid that the institutions distribute to students. However, it is likely that this decree caused tuition increases at these institutions to be higher than would otherwise have been the case. The institutions also believe that the consent decree prevents them from coming to agreement on voluntary joint actions that might help to slow down the arms race, and I will illustrate this point later on.

I will also show that changes in the way the federal government supports research have directly increased the costs of the private research universities. Finally, I will show that changes in the funding levels of the federal government's major grant program for students from lower-income families have increasingly led financial aid to become an institutional responsibility, a development that has put more pressure on tuition levels at selective private colleges and universities.

The third force consists of a variety of external actors that put pressure on the university and increase its costs. Alumni are key to the support of these institutions through the funds they contribute, the students they help to recruit, the internship opportunities they provide for current students, and the assistance they give new graduates of the institutions who are searching for employment. However, the alumni also have strong preferences about what should be valued at the institutions, and by forcefully communicating these preferences, they discourage the institutions from cutting almost anything. The threat of withholding contributions is a powerful one, and administrators sometimes add to the cost structure of the institution to avoid angering key alumni. Similarly, they occasionally accept gifts that increase the institutions' costs.

The institutions also face cost pressures from local government and interest groups, such as environmentalists and historic preservationists. The institutions are always adding new facilities and renovating old ones. To obtain the required construction permits from the local government requires complex discussions and negotiations. Ultimately, these may lead to the institution's having to make increased financial payments to local government to compensate it for the tax-exempt status of the university.

Pressure from environmentalists and historic preservationists may slow down academic institutions' projects and increase their costs much more than similar pressure would increase the cost of for-profit firms undertaking similar types of projects. The reason is twofold. First, unlike business firms, most of the selective academic institutions do not have the option of packing up and moving to a new location. Second, because they are nonprofits themselves and receive very favorable treatment under tax laws, they are expected to make decisions that are in the public interest. As I will show, this expectation often leads them to choose options that are more costly than others would be.

One last external actor that influences selective college and university costs is the set of publications that now annually do rankings of these institutions' undergraduate and graduate programs. When published rankings influence potential students' perceptions of the quality of institutions, the institutions have a strong incentive to try to influence the rankings. To the extent that the rankings are based partly on how much an institution spends on each student, as is the popular *USNWR* ranking of undergraduate institutions, no administrator in his or her right mind would take actions to cut costs unless he or she had to. To the extent that they are based on subjective evaluations of students, as is the influential *Business Week* ranking of business school programs, and students' satisfaction is based on the quality of the facilities in which a program is housed, pressure to build new and better facilities increases.

Each selective private research university consists of a number of colleges. A final set of factors that affects the ability of these universities and their public research university counterparts to hold down costs is how they organize the budget relationships between the central university administration and the individual colleges, the incentives they give the colleges to raise their own funds, and how they select and evaluate the academic leaders of each of their colleges. I will show that these organizational factors influence the ability of the central administration of a university to get its constituent colleges to share resources, to cooperate in pursuing university-wide objectives, and to behave efficiently.

A Word about Cornell University

Much of what follows draws heavily on my experience as a senior administrator at Cornell University. Founded in 1865 by Ezra Cornell, it is both a selective private university and the land grant university of New York state. Although it is a private university, it also receives state appropriations that help support four of its colleges. It is one of the national leaders in terms of the level of external research funding received by its faculty and the number of doctoral degrees granted each year, and its undergraduate colleges are also among the most selective in the nation. Because of its state funding and land-grant mission, it operates credit and noncredit programs throughout New York state that are directed at a wide range of the state's population. These are conducted by extension associates from its agricultural, cooperative, and industrial and labor relations extension divisions.

Ezra Cornell is widely reputed to have said, "I would found an institution in which any man can find instruction in any study." Over the years many people associated with Cornell have interpreted this statement literally. This makes it difficult for the university ever to contemplate eliminating any subject of study from its curriculum. The roughly 13,000 undergraduate students and 6,000 graduate and professional students that are enrolled on its main campus in Ithaca, New York, study for degrees in ten different colleges. Over 600 additional students are enrolled in medical degree and graduate degree programs in biomedical fields at its medical college, which is located in New York City.

Together, the Ithaca and New York City campuses had a combined operating budget of almost $1.5 billion in 1997–98, with slightly over $1.0 billion of this total being spent on the Ithaca campus. With an operating budget of this magnitude, any action taken by the university that would save it $1 million a year represents less than 0.1 percent reduction in its costs. Hence many such reductions are necessary if the university is to substantially reduce its costs.

The university's revenue comes from a variety of sources. In 1997–98, approximately 33 percent of the Ithaca campus budget came from tuition and fees. Endowment income, as well as interest on short-term balances that the university holds, generated about 7 percent of the budget, and an equivalent amount came from current-year gifts to the university.[9] About 21 percent of the budget came from sponsored programs, primarily in the form of externally generated support for faculty members' research.

Another 13 percent came from direct appropriations from New York state, primarily to support research, teaching, and extension activities at Cornell's four state-assisted colleges. Support from state government is much lower for other selective private research universities. The support Cornell receives from New York state permits it to charge substantially lower undergraduate tuition levels to New York state residents enrolled in the four colleges than it charges to undergraduates enrolled in the rest of the university. For example, in 1997–98, New York state residents paid tuition and fees of $9,300 to attend these four colleges as undergraduates, while undergraduate tuition and fees in the endowed part of the university came to $21,840. Because of the lower level of tuition in the four state-assisted colleges, Cornell's tuition and fee revenue represents a smaller share of its overall budget than that revenue at most selective private universities.

A final major revenue source for the university is enterprise income, which constituted about 10 percent of the university's revenue in 1997–98. The enterprises include housing, dining, the campus store, and utilities. Enterprises are expected to at least break even, and only rarely do they yield revenues that can be used to support the academic programs of the university.

The current operating budget of a university does not contain all of the expenditures that the institution plans on making during a year. What is left out of the current operating budget is most of the expenditures that the institution plans to make renovating and expanding existing facilities, as well as constructing new ones. These are included in the institution's capital budget. During 1997–98, Cornell spent over $90 million on those activities. These were financed by state appropriations, private gifts, anticipated future revenues from external grants and contracts, and anticipated future revenues from enterprises.

Finally, in 1997–98, Cornell employed 9,120 employees, of which 1,532, or less than 17 percent, were in regular faculty positions with professorial titles. Although its faculty members constitute a minority of the employees of the university, they have a disproportionate influence on most decisions.

CHAPTER 2

Who Is in Charge of the University?

Shared Governance

When I was a Cornell vice president, one of my responsibilities was to supervise Cornell's army, navy, and air force ROTC units. The commanders of the units are high-level military officers, usually colonels. The commanders and I met biweekly to discuss the issues they faced. One of their major concerns was that several Cornell colleges were unwilling to give students academic credit within their colleges for taking courses that ROTC offered.

ROTC courses do count toward the overall number of credits that students needed to graduate from the university. However, each college at Cornell requires students enrolled in the college to take a large number of courses within that college. If ROTC courses could not be counted as within-college courses, students enrolled in ROTC faced an unhappy choice. Either they could eliminate all out-of-college courses other than ROTC ones from their schedules, thereby depriving them of valuable educational opportunities, or they could take their required ROTC courses in addition to the usual number of courses. In practice, given Cornell students' intellectual curiosity, most chose the latter option. The ROTC commanders worried that the heavier workload that their cadets assumed would discourage some prospective students from enrolling in ROTC.

They were aghast when I explained to them that decisions on awarding credit for courses were made by the faculty of each college. Although I could and would ask the dean of a college to meet with them to discuss the issue, I could not order him to do so. Even if he agreed with their position that college credit was warranted for an ROTC course, he could not order the faculty of the college to award credit for any course. He could request that the curriculum committee of the college consider the issue, but he could not compel them to do so.

Military commanders are used to a system of top-down control, and it took each new commander a few months to comprehend that colleges and universities do not operate the way the armed services do. Critics of how academic institutions operate sometimes contend that no one is in charge. Sometimes, and especially with regard to some issues, that description is not far from the truth. But for the most part academic institutions operate under a system of governance that shares responsibility between trustees, administrators, faculty, staff, and, increasingly, students.

Trustees have the fiduciary responsibility and final authority for all that goes on at the institution. However, trustees are busy people with lives and careers of their own, and once they have hired a president, they typically delegate most of their legal authority to the president. After discussions with the president and other senior administrators, they focus on establishing financial policies (such as how much to spend from the endowment, how the endowment should be invested, what the total budget should be for the university, how much tuition and faculty and staff salaries should be raised, and what the institution's level of debt should be), sanctioning the design and construction of new facilities, approving major policies for the university (such as whether financial aid should be based on a student's need or merit, whether more funding should go to athletics), and giving final approval on academic matters (the creation of new colleges or degree programs, the award of tenure to faculty).

Most trustees know that they are not experts on academic issues. Hence although they formally retain final approval in academic matters, in practice they rarely override an administrative academic recommendation. Cornell's trustees recently reaffirmed, for example, that their major role in tenure and promotion decisions was to consider broad policy issues. Examples of such issues include whether teaching was being given the same weight as research in tenure evaluations and whether the tenure system was helping or hindering the university's efforts to diversify its faculty in terms of race, gender, and ethnicity. Trustees do not see their role as making judgments about the merits of the research of individual faculty members being considered for tenure. Such judgments are more appropriately made by international experts from the faculty members' disciplines.

Faculty members play a unique role in universities. They are the creators of new knowledge and the key participants, along with students, in the educational process. Students are attracted to selective universities because of the universities' reputations, and these reputations in large part derive from the quality of the faculty. This fact has led more than one faculty member to claim that the faculty is the university. This is an overstatement, but there is no denying that because of their importance, the faculty plays a key role in the governance of universities.

On educational matters, the faculty rules supreme. The faculty of each college determines the graduation requirements for students enrolled in that college, and the departments in each college determine the course requirements for majors. New courses are typically approved by departmental and college committees. University-wide faculty issues, such as the establishment of new colleges or programs, are often discussed and decided by an elected faculty senate or a council of faculty representatives and then sent to the president and the trustees for final approval.

Once administrators allot resources for the creation of a faculty position, the recruitment of new faculty members is almost entirely done by the faculty. Although administrators may define the nature of the position (such as the rank or subject matter area), it is the faculty who search for new colleagues and then make recommendations to the administrators for appointments. Similarly, although administrators may overrule positive faculty recommendations in promotion and tenure cases, it is extremely rare for anyone to receive tenure without the support of the faculty in the department and college.

The phrase "trying to lead the faculty is like trying to herd cats" has often been used to describe one of the challenges of being a university administrator. In many respects, faculty members are more like independent entrepreneurs than employees. What makes each important to the university is the faculty member's creativity, and creative people often are independent minded and march to a different drummer. Fostering individual creativity and initiative, while trying to assure that an excellent education is provided for all students, is a real challenge for administrators.

One distinguished social scientist from another university suggested to me that "faculty members are like campers at campgrounds. They pitch their tents and camp, but if they decide they don't like the weather or the campground, they pack up the tents and move to another location." He meant that because of the increasing specialization of academia many faculty members at major research universities now view their profession, not their university, as the primary entity to which they are attached. In many fields, universities actively compete for faculty, and if faculty members at an institution grow disgruntled, they may well have the opportunity to move elsewhere.

To prevent such loss of faculty, administrators devote a lot of time to creating and nurturing an academic environment in which faculty members feel appreciated and supported. Their task is occasionally complicated by faculty members who express the attitude that what is best for me personally is always best for the university as a whole. When this happens, administrators must smile and decide if the importance of a faculty member to the institution justifies giving that faculty member what he or she wants.

Because of the unique role that faculty members play in the university, they expect to be consulted about any university decision that affects their working environment, and often are annoyed if they don't have the final word. Faculty members at major research universities regularly discuss with administrators what the size of the faculty salary increase pool should be. They become involved in discussions about proposed changes in faculty benefits and express concern with whether decisions made by the university to devote resources to nonacademic purposes (such as improved varsity athletics) are diminishing the academic base of the university. They worry about whether and where new buildings should be built. It is hard to think of any decision made by the university in which faculty members do not feel that they have a legitimate interest in participating in the decision process.

Academic administrators usually realize the importance of consulting with the faculty. This consultation process often leads to what appears to be an endless series of meetings and discussions. The university is a deliberative organization where rational debate is highly valued, and decisions are typically not reached quickly on major, or even minor, issues.

In rare cases a president can lead a selective institution without seriously consulting the faculty on many issues and in the face of strong opposition from them. John Silber was president of Boston University for twenty-five years, and during that time he had the unwavering support of the board of trustees. This enabled him to achieve considerable change at the institution, even though many faculty members sometimes objected to his actions. His experience, however, is the exception rather than the rule.

On many campuses, the governance structure includes employees who are not faculty members, so that their positions can be heard on issues that are important to them. Rarely, however, do other employees have a voice in campus decisions equal to that of the faculty.

Students also have an important voice in campus governance. To some observers, it seems strange that consumers of an academic institution's product, its students, should play any role in governance. After all, they are only passing through the institution and will be gone in roughly four years. But there are several compelling reasons why students should play a role in university governance.

One objective of selective institutions is to prepare students for future leadership positions. Participating in campus governance allows them to gain needed experience. Another objective, not as often publicly mentioned by the institutions, is to strengthen the ties between the institution and its students so that after they graduate they will become active alumni and contribute to the well-being of the institution and its future students. Involvement in university governance often is an effective way of creating such ties. Finally, given the activism of many students, the failure to provide an official outlet for students to express their views on issues the university faces may lead to them to express these views in other ways. But of course involving students in university governance does not necessarily prevent demonstrations and student sit-ins in the president's office.

Good academic administrators fully understand the importance of the faculty to the university. As one high-level administrator said to me while I was a Cornell vice president, "They are the producers; we are the enablers." A major role of academic administrators is to try to obtain resources to facilitate the realization of good ideas that faculty members have generated. As a result, central administrators and college deans on many campuses increasingly find themselves involved in fund raising and external relations.

Many academic administrators themselves come from the ranks of the faculty at the university. However, once they become administrators, their faculty colleagues often have a tendency to view them as the enemy and their effectiveness may suffer. My credibility as an academic administrator, for example, depended heavily on the belief of my colleagues on the faculty that I was one of them and that I planned to return to my faculty position at some unspecified date. But if faculty members believe that an administrator's return is imminent, they will try to outlast the administrator rather than cooperating in the initiatives that he or she suggests. Hence, to maintain my effectiveness, I regularly had to claim to colleagues that I expected to stay in the position of vice president for longer than I actually had planned. Even academic administrators with the utmost integrity sometimes have to tell white lies to their faculty colleagues.

Why Public Institutions Control Costs Better Than Private Institutions

In the academic year 1978–79, the average full professor at public doctorate-granting universities in the United States earned about 91 percent of what the typical professor at private doctorate-granting universities earned. As

Figure 2.1 indicates, this percentage fell steadily during the 1980s and early 1990s until it stabilized at about 78 to 80 percent during the rest of the 1990s. So in the 1990s there was an even greater discrepancy between the salaries of professors at public universities and their counterparts at private universities than there was in the late 1970s. This fall in relative salaries made it more difficult for the public universities to hire and retain top faculty and invariably led to some decline in the public universities' academic quality.

How could this decline occur? The answer has to do with a fundamental difference between the governance of public and private institutions that makes it much easier for the public institutions to hold down their costs. Boards of trustees at public universities answer to the executive and legislative branches of state government. In contrast, in the short run boards of trustees at private universities answer directly only to themselves.

Trustees of a selective private university have the ultimate authority for all that goes on at the university. Many are alumni, and all want to see the in-

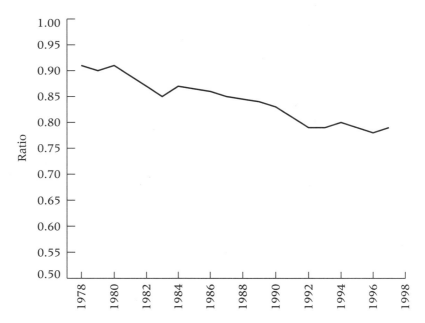

Figure 2.1. Ratio of the average salary of professors at public doctorate-granting institutions to the average salary of professors at private doctorate-granting institutions, fall 1978 to fall 1997.

stitution prosper. They want to be supportive of the president they hired unless something happens that causes them to lose confidence in him or her. Many trustees prefer that tuition be held as low as possible so that their university will be accessible to a wide a range of students. However, if the president of the university recommends a budget increase that exceeds inflation to provide funds for increased financial aid, to attract and retain top faculty, or to build a new biology teaching building, the trustees will probably go along with the president.

If times are bad, the trustees will probably require belt-tightening to achieve financial equilibrium. But cutting costs for the sake of cutting costs is rarely their objective. Thus although they have final authority over the setting of the university's budget and tuition levels, they often give the university administration considerable latitude in these areas.

In contrast, trustees of public universities are often political appointees of the governor or state legislature. They may have the same desire to see their university prosper that trustees at private universities have. However, they operate under the constraint that they do not always have final authority over the setting of the university's budget or the tuition levels that it charges for its various degree programs.

In some states, for example Virginia, the governor and the legislature must approve both the tuition levels and the size of the state appropriation for state universities. In other states, such as New York, the trustees have final authority over tuition levels, while the legislature and the governor determine the size of the state appropriation for the state universities.

However, to say that the trustees of some state universities have final authority over tuition levels does not mean that they actually get to exercise this authority in an unfettered manner. If the trustees have been informed that the governor wants to hold tuition constant, for them to raise tuition might be both political suicide for them and very costly for the university. The trustees would then face the wrath of the governor, which might lead either to their immediate dismissal or their failure to be reappointed when their terms expire. In addition, the governor and legislature might respond by cutting the institution's state appropriation by an amount equivalent to the revenue increase that the tuition increase was expected to generate. So if the governor and the legislature say no tuition increase, typically the trustees of a state university do not oppose them.

Why would the executive and legislative branches of state government be less responsive to the needs of public universities and be more likely to want to hold tuition down than the appointed trustees of these universities? Put simply, state government faces many competing demands for its funds and must make tradeoffs among them. Many state governments also believe that it is essential to keep tuition levels low at public universities to maintain their accessibility to citizens in the state.[1]

As a result, administrators at public universities have often been faced in recent years with smaller levels of funding and lower levels of tuition increases than they would prefer. If such actions by state governments require them to cut budgets or give faculty members smaller salary increases than the administrators had hoped to do, the administrators can always blame the state government.

In contrast, when administrators at private universities face tight budgets, if they recommend budget cutbacks or smaller salary increases than the faculty expects, all blame will fall upon them. They will be accused of not making a sufficiently strong case to the trustees of the need for higher tuition to maintain the quality of the university. So, rather than risk losing the support of the faculty, administrators typically compromise and recommend raising tuition more than they desire in order to provide some budget relief. After all, the typical administrative term is not that long, and once an administrator loses the support of the faculty, it is hard to regain it.

The Central Administration and the College's Behavior

Does it make sense to talk about the typical American research university as a single institution whose individual colleges and auxiliary enterprises (such as housing and dining) work together in harmony to pursue a set of university-wide objectives, such as controlling costs? Over twenty-five years ago, Michael D. Cohen and James C. March described universities as "organized anarchies," with all of the colleges (and departments within colleges and faculty within departments) pursuing independent objectives.[2] I have concluded from my experiences that universities themselves contribute to this anarchy and to their inability to hold down costs by the way they organize their budgetary relationships, by the incentives that they provide to their colleges to raise their own funds, and by the way that they select and evaluate the academic deans of their individual colleges.

Consider the institutional structure of a typical university. In the center are its executive officers, its senior central administrators. The equivalent of the chief executive officer of a corporation is the president, or on some campuses the chancellor, of the university. Selected by the board of trustees, the president has overall responsibility for leadership of the university. Today most presidents are heavily involved in external activities such as fund raising, government relations, and alumni relations.

The chief academic officer of the university is called the provost, or on some campuses, the vice president or vice chancellor for academic affairs. Typically, the provost has been delegated authority by the president to preside over all of the academic operations of the university. He or she is often referred to as "first among equals" when the relationship of the provost to the senior administrators in charge of the nonacademic parts of the university is described. The latter include the vice presidents or the vice chancellors in charge of finance, facilities, student services, development, government relations, and the like. On some campuses, many of these senior administrators report to the provost, and at these institutions the provost plays a role equivalent to that of the president of a corporation. All of the academic deans, save perhaps the dean of the medical college if a medical college is part of the institution, typically report to the provost.

The central administrative and support services include the office of the registrar, the office of the bursar, the athletics department, student housing and dining services, the utilities department, student services, the office of grant administration, the campus store, the office of information technology, the office for telecommunications, and the libraries. Some of these, such as student housing and dining and utilities may be organized as enterprises that charge prices for their services and if so they are usually expected to at least break even. It is often claimed that such enterprise units do not impose any costs on the rest of the university. As I will show, nothing could be further from the truth.

The rest of the university is made up of the individual undergraduate colleges, professional schools, and graduate colleges. In some universities, the graduate school, where Ph.D. study is undertaken, is formally a separate college. In others, graduate study takes place within the separate colleges. Many research universities also contain several large research centers in which sponsored research is undertaken. To keep things simple, I will ignore the research centers in this discussion.

The financial relationships between the university's central administration and its various colleges determine to a large extent whether the colleges are likely to cooperate in pursuing university-wide objectives, such as holding down costs. Revenue comes into the university from sources such as tuition, government appropriations, endowment income, annual giving, enterprise income, research funding, and continuing and executive education. At one extreme, all revenue (with the possible exception of some external gifts and external research grants) flows directly to the central administration, which after covering all central university costs, then allocates the remaining revenue to the colleges.

At the other extreme, the university operates as a set of "tubs." Each college keeps all of the tuition and other sources of revenue that it generates and then remits to the central administration funds to cover the college's allocated share of central costs. This approach is often called a Responsibility Center Management (RCM) approach to budgeting.[3] The colleges are responsible for all of the direct and indirect costs that they incur, including the costs of facilities, maintenance, and operations. The tub model is thought to provide each college with incentives to worry about generating revenues and to use its own resources efficiently. However, it provides no incentives for a college to participate in activities that minimize the overall costs of the university, but do not minimize its own costs.

Sometimes under a RCM approach, each college remits to the center more than the funds necessary to cover its allocated share of the central administrative and support costs. The extra amount that a college remits may be thought of as a "franchise fee" that it pays for being part of the university and using the university's name. The central administration then can reallocate back to the colleges all of the franchise fees that it has collected on a one-time or a continuing basis to further institution-wide objectives.

A similar method, which avoids many questions about the level of central administrative and support costs and how they are allocated to different units, is one in which each college remits to the central administration a share of its total expenditures. The share may vary depending upon whether the expenditures are for on-campus instruction, sponsored research, or other programs, such as executive education. No explicit allocation of central costs to the different units is made when this approach is used. The central administration typically sets (or negotiates with the colleges) the "expenditure tax rates" that it uses at levels that provide it more revenue than it needs to cover central administration and support costs. The extra revenue that it receives can then be reallocated back to the colleges on the basis of university priorities.

The central administration often engages in fund raising to pay for current operations to fund the maintenance and construction of buildings, and to increase the endowment. In recent years, fund raising has also become a responsibility of the individual colleges at many universities. Access to donors may, however, be rationed by the central administration, which tries both to match donors' interests with the colleges' needs and to stress institutional priorities.

In some universities, the central administration places a "tax" on gifts given directly to the individual colleges. This tax may take the form of a share of the gift, a share of the first-year income that the gift provides, or, in the case of a contribution to the endowment, a share of the endowment return. Development officers hate such taxes, which they believe discourage donors from giving. Some central administrators find them useful to further the objectives of the university, which may differ from the objectives of the donors, and to cover costs that the gifts may impose on the university as a whole.

Similarly, the university would like the annual giving and the endowment it raises to be unrestricted in purpose, but the donors often have very specific objectives. To the extent that a donor's objective coincides with an institutional priority, the donation may prove to be unrestricted in practice even though it was intended for a very specific purpose, because it may free up for other uses the internal funds that the institution would have used for the purpose in the absence of the donation.

This is but a simplified presentation of the budgetary processes at major universities. Nevertheless, it clearly suggests that the more a central administration can gain control over the allocation of the university's resources, the greater the power that it has to encourage cooperative behavior and efficient operations.

By way of example, at Cornell University, the provost has some direct control over the budgets of only three of the ten colleges that are located on the Ithaca campus. These three are the College of Arts and Sciences, the College of Engineering, and the College of Architecture, Art, and Planning, and they are referred to as the general-purpose colleges. The other seven colleges are treated as tubs, either by statute (the four state-assisted statutory units at Cornell—the School of Industrial and Labor Relations, the College of Agriculture and Life Sciences, the College of Human Ecology, and the College of Veterinary Medicine) or by trustee designation (the School of Law, the Johnson Graduate School of Management, and the School of Hotel Administration). Through a complicated cost-accounting scheme, the tubs are billed only for the average costs of the central and support services provided to them, as well as for the difference between the credit hours that their students take in the three general-purpose colleges and the credit hours that students from the general-purpose colleges take in each of them. The central administration also directly controls only a very small fraction of the spending that the endowment produces, except for endowment funds used for financial aid. Finally, the central administration does not tax the annual giving and endowment income that the tublike colleges obtain.

It should come as no surprise to the reader that given these arrangements, Cornell has historically often operated like a system of fiefdoms rather than one university. Not surprisingly, as I will describe throughout the book, it has often been unable to avoid unnecessary duplication and to establish university-wide priorities.

This problem is exacerbated by the method by which deans, the chief academic officers of the colleges, are selected. At Cornell and many other universities, the search for a college dean is conducted by a committee that consists primarily of faculty members, and sometimes students and alumni, from the college. In addition, a few faculty and administrators from outside the college are often on the committee. Although the president or provost nominally picks the dean from a small group of finalists recommended by the committee, in the main it is the views of the search committee that carry the day. The president and provost know, from discussions with the committee of each candidate's strengths and weaknesses, which candidate the committee and hence the faculty of the college favor.

Once the deans are installed, a primary role for many is external relations, including fund raising, and they build up strong external constituent support. Hence it is unlikely for a dean to be censured or fired for focusing on the goals of the particular college and not worrying about the overall goals of the university, including the elimination of redundancies across the colleges. Indeed, in many cases, once a dean is appointed in the absence of discontent from the faculty or alumni of the college, the president and provost substantially lose the ability to influence the dean's behavior.

In recent years, several incidents have confirmed this point. During the summer of 1997, the president of Columbia University bowed to strong criticisms from alumni and reappointed a college dean only a few days after dismissing him.[4] Similarly, in April of 1998, the president of Georgetown University bowed to alumni criticisms—which included resignations from advisory boards and threats to withhold contributions—and reversed a decision not to reappoint a popular law school dean. It is believed that the dean's unwillingness to share the law school's revenue with the university precipitated the initial decision, but the university has never confirmed this.[5]

In his memoir of his life in Washington, former Secretary of Labor Robert Reich wrote:

> Cabinet officers have nothing in common except the first word in our titles . . . even the formal titles belie reality. Each of us has a special responsibility for one slice of America . . . I make a list of the real Cabinet . . .
>
>   Secretary of the Interior—Secretary of the West
>   Secretary of the Treasury—Secretary of Wall Street
>   Secretary of HUD—Secretary of Big Cities
>   Secretary of Agriculture—Secretary of Small Towns
>   Secretary of Commerce—Secretary of Corporate America
>   Secretary of Labor—Secretary of Blue-Collar America
> And so forth . . . No wonder we rarely meet.[6]

If one substitutes the words "Dean of . . ." or "Vice President of . . ." for Reich's words "Secretary of . . ." and a college or administrative unit name for his Cabinet department name, my sense is that his description often applies to Cornell and other large universities. Conversations that I have had with senior administrators at numerous public and private universities support this view. Hence the notion that we can treat these each of these institutions as a single entity pursuing university wide-objectives and striving to keep costs down seems in many cases far-fetched.

PART II

WEALTH AND THE
QUEST FOR PRESTIGE

CHAPTER 3

Endowment Policies,
Development Policies,
and the Color of Money

The Nature of Endowments

Many academic institutions hold large stocks of financial assets, or endowments, to generate income for both current and future operations. Technically the term "endowment" refers to assets that, at the time they were initially given to the university, were specified by the donor to be held by the institution in perpetuity. Hence, only the total return (income plus capital gains) that they generate may be spent by the university. In practice, universities also treat other funds, often called "funds functioning as endowment" as if they were endowment funds and seek to spend only out of the total return from these assets as well.

It is useful to think of endowments, and many institutions treat them this way, as being akin to mutual funds. A donor contributes a certain amount of money to the university, and the university invests these funds in a portfolio that consists of domestic and foreign stocks, bonds, real estate, and other income-earning assets. The donor's contribution buys a certain number of shares in the endowment, and over time the legal requirement is that the number of shares cannot be reduced. In good years, the endowment produces a positive total return in the form of dividend, interest, and rental income, as well as capital appreciation (due to unrealized and realized capital gains on the underlying assets). The institution spends part of the total return on current operations and returns part of it to the endowment. It does the latter by not realizing all the capital gains (not selling all the assets that have appreciated) or by using some of the realized return to invest in more assets and hence more shares in the endowment.

In bad years, the total return on the endowment may actually be negative, if the assets in the endowment fall in value by more than the income they generate. Inasmuch as the institution funds some of its current operations out of the endowment, it would be difficult financially if no spending could occur in a year because the total return was negative. To guard against this eventuality, most institutions use "spending rules" that base their spending on the performance of the endowment over a number of years.

The magnitude of the endowments that some institutions have is truly mind-boggling. Table 3.1 displays the market value of the endowments at the eighteen private universities that had the largest endowments on June 30, 1997. Harvard led the list with an endowment whose market value was almost $11 billion. A year later, Harvard's endowment exceeded $13 billion.

Table 3.1   Market value of endowments and endowments per student at private universities with the largest endowments, June 30, 1997.

Institution	Endowment (billions of dollars)	Endowment per student (dollars)	Income per student generated by the endowment at a 4% payout rate
Harvard	10.920	610,140	24,406
Yale	5.742	525,920	21,037
Princeton	4.941	775,743	31,110
Stanford	4.475	346,593	13,863
Emory	4.273	420,452	16,818
MIT	3.046	309,969	12,399
Columbia	3.039	172,754	6,910
Washington Univ.	2.798	279,822	11,193
Pennsylvania	2.535	131,132	5,245
Rice	2.321	578,127	23,125
Cornell	2.125	111,295	4,451
Chicago	2.031	180,129	7,205
Northwestern	1.799	118,427	4,737
Vanderbilt	1.340	136,532	5,461
Dartmouth	1.278	248,638	9,946
Johns Hopkins	1.157	104,367	4,175
Duke	1.134	101,521	4,060
Brown	.949	128,182	5,127

Source: The Chronicle of Higher Education Almanac at <http://www.Chronicle.com/weekly/almanac/1998/facts/money.htm> and *Cornell University 1998–99 Financial Plan: Operating and Capital* (Ithaca: Cornell University, May 1998), appendix K. Reprinted with permission from the National Association of College and University Business Officers (NACUBO).

Even the institution that was in eighteenth place on the list, Brown, had an endowment that was close to $1 billion. With the exception of Rice University, which resolutely pursues a low tuition policy, these institutions all had tuition levels that were close to, or exceeded, $20,000 that year. Seeing universities with such vast wealth, politicians and the public often ask why their tuitions are so high and why they are continually increasing at rates that exceed the inflation rate.

The absolute value of a university's endowment probably is not the best measure of a university's financial wealth, because these institutions vary widely in scale. One way to control for the scale of the institution is to divide each institution's endowment value by the number of students enrolled at the institution to get a measure of the institution's wealth per student. These numbers are provided in the second column of Table 3.1.

Viewed in these terms, Harvard was no longer the wealthiest institution in 1997. Princeton, which has a relatively small student body, had an endowment that totaled almost $800,000 per student. Harvard was second at slightly over $600,000 per student. Although Cornell had an endowment that was about two thirds larger than Dartmouth's, on a per-student basis Dartmouth's endowment was more than twice that of Cornell's because Cornell is a much larger institution. Focusing on per-student endowment levels gives a different picture of which institutions are financially well off.

How much did these endowments actually contribute to each university's well-being? For reasons that will shortly become clear, universities typically aim to spend about 4 to 4.5 percent of the value of their endowments each year on current operations.[1] Taking the lower figure to be conservative and multiplying it by the endowment per student level at each institution, we can estimate the "spending" per student that the endowment at each university would have produced in 1997, if each institution had followed a 4 percent endowment spending policy. These estimates are listed in the last column of the table.

The income per student that these endowments generated varied from over $31,000 at Princeton down to about $4,000 per student at Duke. To get a sense of what these numbers mean, it is useful to know that the tuition level at Duke was slightly over $22,000 in 1997–98. If we add Duke's tuition to its endowment spending per student, the total of $26,000 is less than Princeton's endowment income per student was that year. Since Princeton had a tuition of over $23,000 that year, its tuition plus endowment spending per student was over $54,000. Is it any wonder that Princeton has smaller class sizes, pays its faculty much more, and has more generous financial aid policies than Duke?

The great disparity that exists in the endowment spending per student generated by the endowments at these institutions suggests that it is wrong to treat the institutions as if they were nearly identical. Indeed, even if we restrict the comparisons to the eight Ivy League institutions, we see vast differences. Harvard, Yale, and Princeton each would have generated more than $20,000 in expenditures per student from their endowments in 1997–98, if they followed a 4 percent endowment spending rule. In contrast, Cornell, Brown, and Pennsylvania would all have generated less than $5,200 per year. Is it any wonder that Harvard, Yale, and Princeton are generally regarded as the top schools in the Ivy League? Money does matter.

Lest one feel sorry for the "poorer" institutions on this list, I am making comparisons here only among institutions in the upper tail of the wealth distribution of all private universities. To say that the rich are not all equal in wealth does not negate the fact that they are all a lot better off than the private universities that are less wealthy.

Endowment Spending Policies

A recent study of the endowment spending policies at 317 academic institutions indicated that in 1996 they paid the units on their campuses that "owned" their endowments an average of 4.3 percent of the average value of their endowments over a period of several years. The median rate for these institutions was only 4.1 percent.[2] When potential donors hear that endowment payout rates are in the range of 4 percent, they often are outraged. After all, the stock market averaged double-digit returns every year during most of the 1990s. Several potential donors at Cornell went so far as to tell Cornell that it would be better off if, instead of presenting endowment gifts to the university, they invested the funds themselves and annually gave Cornell gifts based on their earnings from those investments.

Such a view represents a misunderstanding of what the payout from an endowment represents. The payout from an endowment is not the total rate of return on the endowment's assets during the year. Indeed, the average total return on university endowments during the fiscal year that ended June 30, 1996, was 17.2 percent.[3] Rather, the payout is the amount that the university has decided to spend from the endowment during the year. On average, universities spend less than the total return their endowments earn.

The reason is that they seek to preserve the real value, or purchasing power, of the spending that their endowments produce over time. For example, if the rate of inflation is about 5 percent a year, the endowment must produce 5 percent more spending each year to enable the university to continue to purchase the same market basket of goods with endowment spending that it did the year before. Hence, some portion of the total return that the university earns must be plowed back into the endowment to enable its spending to increase over time and to provide protection against inflation.

Where does the roughly 4 to 4.5 percent payout rate that many academic institutions aim for come from? It is a mistake to look at the total return on investments and the rate of inflation in any single year because these vary widely over time. Table 3.2 illustrates this point with respect to financial assets. The average percentage total returns on five different investment portfolios that vary in the degree of risk that is associated with them are presented for the 1956 to 1997 period. The most conservative of the five portfolios, one that was balanced between stocks, bonds, and cash, yielded an average total rate of return of 7.9 percent over the forty-year period. The total rate of return in individual years varied from a high of 20.8 percent to a low of −2.1 percent, and in three of the years the total return was negative.

As the portfolios become more heavily invested in stocks, the average total return on the portfolio increases, as does the risk involved. So, for the riskiest portfolio, the one invested 100 percent in stocks, the average total rate of return over the forty-year period was 11.6 percent. However, the range of annual returns varied from 43.4 to −26.5 percent, with the annual rate of return being negative in almost one quarter of the years (nine of the forty years). Indeed, for each of the portfolios that had at least 40 percent of their assets in stocks, the portfolio experienced negative rates of return in at least eight of the forty years. The fact that negative total annual returns can and do occur helps to explain why the academic institutions never base their spending decisions simply on the current year's total return. To do so would mean that spending from the endowment would fall to zero in years when the return was negative, and that would cause fluctuations in the institution's budget that would prove unacceptable. As a result, most institutions, at least implicitly, base their spending on some average of what their endowment's total return is over time.

Which of the five portfolios represents best how a university is likely to structure its investments? The answer varies both over time and across institutions. Rich institutions can afford to take more risk than poorer ones. The

Table 3.2 Average percentage total return on different investment portfolios, 1956–1997.

Strategy	% allocation stocks/bonds/cash	Average annual % total return	Best/worst annual return %	Number of years with negative total return
Most conservative	25/40/35	7.9	20.8/−2.1	3
Moderately conservative	40/40/20	8.8	22.5/−7.5	8
Moderate	60/30/10	9.8	27.6/−14.1	8
Moderately aggressive	80/20/0	10.8	33.2/−20.5	9
Most aggressive	100/0/0	11.6	43.4/−26.5	9

Source: Business Week, November 9, 1998, p. 118.
Note: The calculations assume reinvestment of all dividends and annual balancing to keep portfolio allocation constant.

share of investments that an institution has in different forms of assets is likely to depend upon the institution's perceptions of the likely returns on the different forms of investments. Most large institutions have committees of trustees that give advice to internal or external managers of their endowment portfolios about how their funds should be invested. Many smaller institutions pool their assets into one large investment vehicle called the Commonfund to take advantage of the reduced management cost and increased professional expertise that they can achieve through the pooling of resources.

In the fiscal year that ended June 30, 1998, the university endowment that had the highest rate of return had 85 percent of its investments in domestic stocks and most of the rest in domestic bonds. The endowment that performed the worst had 67 percent of its portfolio in domestic bonds. Most institutions were somewhere in between in how they invested their funds. A 1998 survey of over four hundred institutions showed that 63.5 percent of the assets in their portfolios were invested in stocks, 24.5 percent were invested in bonds, 4.2 percent were invested in cash, and the remaining 7.8 percent were invested in real estate and other assets.[4] It is likely when stock market prices decline, portfolio holdings will be reallocated to include more bonds and fewer stocks. This suggests that the portfolio described as moderate in Table 3.2 may be reflective of how many institutions actually are invested, on average, over time. The average total annual rate of return on such a portfolio over the forty-year period was 9.8 percent.

During the same period of time, the annual rate of inflation in the consumer price index (CPI) varied between 0.7 and 13.5 percent. The average rate of inflation during the period was 4.4 percent. Academic institutions do not buy the same market basket of goods that consumers do, and in many years the rate of increase in prices faced by these institutions, called the Higher Education Price Index (HEPI), exceeded the rate of increase in consumer prices. Indeed, over the thirty-seven year period when both rates were computed, the HEPI increased by almost 0.8 percentage points more a year than did the CPI.[5]

Hence, to maintain the purchasing power of their endowments and to protect against future inflation, academic institutions had to reinvest in their endowments on average at least 4.4 percentage points and perhaps as much as 5.2 percentage points of the total annual endowment return. When we subtract these amounts from the average 9.8 percent total return that was probably earned on endowments, we come up with between 4.6 and 5.4

percent that is potentially available to support the current operations of the academic institution.

Unfortunately, these amounts are not all actually available to support the academic programs of a university because there are administrative expenses associated with managing the investments, tracking expenditures made from the endowment funds, and providing reports to donors. At Cornell, these costs have been running about 0.7 percent of the endowment value each year. If this rate is typical of other institutions, the payout to "owners" of the endowment would be reduced to roughly 3.9 to 4.8 percent. This range brackets the mean and median payout rates of 4.3 and 4.1 percent that existed in 1996.

Decisions must be made by universities on how much to spend out of their endowments each year. If they spent a constant fraction of their endowment value and the endowment went up in value by 20 percent one year and then fell in value by 20 percent the next year, they would see their spending from the endowment first increase, and then decrease, by 20 percent. Such wide fluctuations in spending do not make sense for an academic institution, because it would have to scramble to find funds to make up for the loss of funding from the endowment in the second year. So instead most institutions, almost two thirds in one recent study, base their spending decisions on the average value of their endowments over a number of years, often three.[6] Using an average value of the endowment will reduce the annual fluctuations in endowment spending that occur during periods when the endowment values are fluctuating.

Other universities try to achieve the same goal by initially setting their endowment spending at a sum that is a fraction of the average of the endowment values for some prior number of years and then increasing this spending at an annual rate that they believe can be maintained over time. For example, for a number of years during the 1990s Cornell sought to increase spending from its endowment by 5.6 percent a year. This was the amount by which the university believed its average annual total rate of return on the endowment (minus administrative charges and investment expenses) would exceed the fraction of the three-year average of the endowment that it was initially paying out to "owners" of the endowment.

The good news for academic institutions in the 1990s was that the decade was one of unprecedented returns on financial assets. After a −2.9 percent total return in 1994, the average total rates of return on academic institutions' endowments during the next four years were 15.5 percent, 17.2 percent, 20.5 percent, and 18.2 percent. The average return during these four years of almost 17.9 percent far exceeded the 9.8 percent average total return expected on the "moderate" portfolio in Table 3.2. In addition, the rate of price inflation during those four years was very low, averaging less than 3 percent. Hence, academic institutions earned about 15 percent per year in real terms on their endowment portfolios during those four years.

Not surprisingly, the endowment payout as a fraction of the current value of the endowment fell substantially at institutions, such as Cornell, that were increasing their endowment spending at a fixed rate that was far less than the rate at which the endowment was increasing in value. For example, at Cornell, each share of the endowment paid out $1.93 to its owners in the year that ended June 30, 1990. This represented 4.1 percent of the value of the endowment as of June 30, 1990. By June 30, 1997, the payout had grown at about 5.6 percent a year to $2.43 a share. By then, however, the end of fiscal year value of each share in the endowment had grown to $83.01. As a result, the payout had fallen to less than 3 percent a year of the endowment value in the year ending June 30, 1997.

Endowment payouts also fell rapidly at institutions that based their payouts on an average of the endowment value over a number of years because of the rapid increase in endowment values. Put simply, because they were using average values of the endowment over several years to compute their payout rate and because their endowment values were growing at rapid rates, the payout as a fraction of the current endowment was substantially lower than the payout as a fraction of the average value of the endowment over a number of years. It was not unusual to observe payout rates as a function of current endowment values that were less than 3 percent.

The public became increasingly outraged that the payout rates at these institutions were so low relative to their endowment values at a time when many of the institutions were raising their tuition levels by substantially more than the rate of inflation. This anger "encouraged" the trustees of these institutions to change their spending policies, and many announced a substantial increase in their endowment payouts. Although some announced that the increase would permit them to hire more faculty and provide better research support for them, most asserted that a major reason for the increased payout was to enable the institutions to substantially improve their financial aid programs. Princeton, Yale, Stanford, Johns Hopkins, and Harvard all announced with great fanfare major improvements in their financial aid programs during 1997 and 1998. In the case of Princeton and

Harvard, the improvements eventually will add more than $6 million a year to each institution's operating budget.[7]

Improved financial aid programs will increase the accessibility of these institutions to low- and middle-income students, which most people believe is socially desirable. Concomitantly, they will reduce public concern about the rates at which tuition is increasing at the institutions. Having substantial endowment resources that can be used for increased financial aid helps a university continue to increase its tuition levels.

Development and the Color of Money

Academic institutions add to their endowments by soliciting gifts from alumni, foundations, and corporations. They also solicit gifts to provide funding for current operations and for capital projects. The amount that the leading private research universities with the largest endowments raised in 1996–97 is shown in the first column of Table 3.3. Harvard led the pack, receiving $427.6 million in gifts that year, followed by Stanford, Cornell, Duke, and Yale.

The extent that institutions depend upon alumni for their annual fund raising varies widely across institutions. Alumni giving totals for the year appear in the second column of the table. Cornell and Duke each received about $220 million in total gifts that year. But while Cornell received over half of its giving from alumni (111.5/220.6), Duke received less than 20 percent of its gifts from alumni (37/220).

Total alumni giving figures mask the fact that the number of living alumni varies widely across these institutions. Alumni giving per alumnus figures are shown in the third column of Table 3.3. Princeton, the richest school in terms of endowment per student (see Table 3.1), is the school that also received the most dollars per alumnus that year, $1,075. Other schools receiving over $800 per alumnus were Harvard, Stanford, Yale, and Dartmouth. The average dollars received per alumnus is the average amount that each alumnus who makes a contribution to a school donates multiplied by the percentage of alumni who make contributions in a year. In 1996–97, this percentage varied across the institutions from 19 to 50 percent.

It is interesting to compare annual fund raising per student with the spending that each institution received from its endowment in the year. Column 4 of Table 3.3 displays the annual fund raising per student. Harvard topped the list at $23,024, followed by Stanford, Princeton, Duke, and Yale.

Table 3.3 Annual fund raising at the private universities with the largest endowments, 1996–97.

Institution	(1) Total (millions of $)	(2) Alumni giving (millions of $)	(3) Alumni giving per alumnus (dollars)	(4) Total giving per student (dollars)
Harvard	427.6	210.7	844	23,024
Stanford	312.3	139.1	987	20,784
Cornell	220.6	111.5	675	11,327
Duke	220.0	37.0	379	18,433
Yale	203.2	107.2	916	18,330
Columbia	201.7	55.3	336	9,965
Pennsylvania	174.5	58.1	279	7,981
Johns Hopkins	164.6	49.4	563	9,949
MIT	137.4	49.0	559	13,812
Princeton	133.8	69.3	1,075	20,726
Chicago	129.2	47.0	473	10,503
Northwestern	124.6	52.3	342	9,196
Dartmouth	100.0	46.7	942	16,747
Washington Univ.	92.8	39.9	437	8,032
Vanderbilt	78.0	22.9	253	7,616
Brown	67.4	22.6	335	8,841
Rice	51.6	22.6	670	12,316

Source: Benchmarking Fund-Raising Excellence (Charlottesville: Office of the Vice President for Development, University of Virginia, July 1998). All figures are based on data provided by the Council for Aid to Education in *1997 Voluntary Support of Education* (New York, 1998), data from pp. 7–12.

My own institution, Cornell, while ranked third overall in terms of total gifts, ranked ninth in the group in terms of total giving per student. Except for Duke, the top five schools in terms of fund raising per student were all among the top schools in endowments per student.

The universities use these gifts in a number of ways. They do not all help fund current operations. Some are used to increase the endowment. Other gifts help finance capital projects. During fiscal years 1996 to 1998, about 40 percent of all gifts at Cornell were used to help support current operations, about 50 percent were directed at increasing the endowment, and the rest were used for the construction and renovation of facilities.

The costs of university development efforts are substantial. Successful development officers know that they cannot simply ask potential donors for large sums of money. Rather, over long periods of time they build relationships between the institution and potential donors by involving them in the activities of the institution. Only after potential donors are committed to these relationships do major fund-raising appeals take place. Hence, much of what development officers do is an "investment activity." Efforts at building relationships and commitment today may pay off financially only years in the future. These relationships are often very personal in nature, and it is thus very important to a university that its development staff stay with it for a long time. However, as more and more institutions realize the importance of fund-raising efforts, a fierce market for talented development officers has arisen and there is much mobility in the profession.[8]

Despite the fact that much of what development officers do is to cultivate relationships that will pay off only in the future, university administrators and trustees often evaluate their efforts by focusing on what the development office has generated in new gifts and commitments in a year, its actual dollars raised, relative to the costs of those efforts in the year. This approach of course ignores the fact that some dollars raised in a year are a result of development efforts undertaken in previous years, and that some development efforts in the current year will not bear substantial returns until many years later. Nonetheless, dividing the total costs of the development effort in a year by the total funds raised in that year does provide a measure of "performance" that is often used to gauge the success of the development office..

Based on three surveys of academic institutions that it conducted in the late 1980s, the Council for the Advancement and Support of Education concluded that the average cost of each gift dollar raised by academic institutions during the time period was around 16 cents. The median cost was about 11 cents.[9] At Cornell University, the cost has been even lower. Between 1990 and 1995, the university raised over $1.5 billion at an average cost of 8 cents per dollar raised.[10]

One would think that if each dollar raised cost the university only 8 cents all the faculty, administration, and trustees at the university would be delighted. Cornell's trustees certainly were, and they "urged" the institution to increase its funding of the development office. In doing so, they were expressing their belief that the marginal cost of raising additional funds would not be substantially higher than the average costs of 8 cents per dollar incurred in the past.

However, faculty and administrators at the university did not view the

$1.5 billion raised as an unmixed blessing. Many of the academic units felt poorer, rather than richer, in the short run for several reasons. First, university development at Cornell is funded through a tax on the units. And while the units were paying 8 cents for each dollar raised, those dollars that went into the endowment yielded them only 4 cents of income per dollar in the initial year. In addition, much of the endowment raised during the campaign I am talking about came in the form of pledges that were to be honored over a number of years. Hence, during the campaign and for a few years thereafter, the units often received even less than 4 cents of income per year in return for the 8 cents of costs they had paid.

Second, and perhaps more important, much of the money used to pay for the development campaign came out of the general operating budgets of the colleges. The funds raised, whether for the endowment or for current operations, often came to the university to fund new activities that were not part of the previous operations of the colleges. Put another way, "the color" of the money being raised was often different from the color of the money that was being used to support the fund-raising efforts. Thus the colleges often found that they were short of funds to support their ongoing efforts.

Finally, inevitably gifts came that did not fully fund the activities they were meant to support. For example, an endowment for a new faculty position should, in principle, provide funds for support staff and office and laboratory space for the new faculty member. However, that rarely occurred.

Events such as these have led to concern that raising money may leave an institution financially worse off rather than better off. Prudent institutions therefore often try to raise endowment and operating funds to support activities in which they would have been engaged even in the absence of the fund raising. For example, Cornell has tried very hard to focus its recent fund-raising campaigns on endowing chairs for existing faculty positions (not increasing the overall faculty size) and on raising money for financial aid to undergraduates and graduate students. To the extent that such efforts are successful, the new endowments effectively provide budget relief. They free up the funds that the institution would have expended on the targeted activities. Even if such gifts come to the university restricted for these purposes, they effectively are unrestricted gifts because the funds that they free up can be used for other purposes.

If donors' priorities do not match an institution's priorities, their gifts may not provide budget relief. During the 1990–1995 Cornell campaign, the university received endowments for three chairs in ornithology. Cornell has an outstanding laboratory of ornithology, and these gifts promise to enhance the university's national stature in the area. However, only one of these chairs funded an existing faculty position; the other two were for new faculty positions. Unless the university was prepared to reduce the size of the faculty by two positions elsewhere (it wasn't), the net effect of these three chairs was to increase the size of the faculty.

Because of Cornell's budget structure, if two positions had been eliminated and concomitant budget savings had been realized, the savings would have benefited only the College of Agriculture and Life Sciences, to which the Laboratory of Ornithology reports. One senior administrator at the institution often mused to me that during the campaign the English Department, arguably one of the top two or three departments in the College of Arts and Sciences, received only one chair. He asked: What do three new endowed chairs for ornithology and only one for English say about the priorities of the university? The answer is that with a budget structure that prevents the university from transferring resources from the College of Agriculture to the College of Arts and Sciences, there was no possibility that the new chairs in ornithology would free up resources to enhance the English department.

The priorities of donors are thus very important in determining which units benefit during fund-raising campaigns. The university often tries to "shape" donors' priorities by limiting the access of units to major donors and "reserving" them for institutional priorities. How effective an institution can be in denying different units access to donors is an open question. In one case at Cornell, a donor had committed substantial funds to the university and the university believed that it had persuaded the donor the funds could best be used to endow chairs for faculty members in the College of Arts and Sciences. Before the funds were formally allocated to that college, an athletic administrator had a conversation with the donor during a university event about the importance to athletics of obtaining funding for a facility for varsity athletes. The donor was a former varsity athlete and he decided that part of his gift should go to fund the facility. The dean of the College of Arts and Sciences was not very happy.

Did the athletic administrator "violate" the rule that one should not approach major donors without first receiving university permission? That is hard to say, because only he and the donor were present when their conversation took place. The administrator may have "innocently" been describing his program and have had no intention of "hitting up" the donor for funds. Even if he had, would a university want to go back to the donor and say that the donor could not direct his funds where the donor desired, especially if the donor was a regular major benefactor of the institution? Moreover, if the athletic administrator had solicited someone that he should not have, what "penalty" might the university impose upon him? Would alumni who are supportive of athletics be happy to learn that an athletic administrator had been penalized in any way for doing what he had been hired to do, namely improving athletic facilities available to varsity athletes?

CHAPTER 4

Undergraduate and Graduate Program Rankings

Undergraduate Program Rankings

In their quest for prestige, colleges and universities strive to get the best published rankings of their undergraduate and graduate programs that they can. The ranking of an institution's undergraduate program influences the quantity and academic quality of the applicants, as well as the likelihood that high-quality applicants who are accepted will enroll. The same is true for graduate program rankings. These rankings also influence the willingness of research-oriented faculty to accept positions at a university, because high-quality graduate students enhance the teaching and research of faculty involved in graduate education.

College guides have for a long time been providing information about the characteristics of different undergraduate institutions to help high school students decide to which institutions to apply. Such publications as *Barron's Profile of American Colleges* (now in its twenty-third edition), *The Fiske Guide to Colleges: 1999* (now in its fifteenth edition), *Peterson's 4 Year Colleges 1999* (now in its twenty-ninth edition), and *The Insider's Guide to Colleges, 1999* (now in its twenty-fifth edition) have been around for decades. In the last few years, the number of guides has dramatically increased. A recent search of the Amazon.com Web site turned up over three hundred different guides.

In addition to providing detailed data and narratives about each college, the long-standing college guides group institutions into broad categories. *Barron's*, for example, ranks each institution by the selectivity of its entering freshman class (measured by their entrance test scores), grouping institutions into broad categories such as most selective, highly selective, nonselective, and open enrollment. No attempt is made, however, to make fine distinctions between institutions within each group. Similarly, *The Fiske Guide to Colleges* awards up to five stars to each institution on three dimensions; academics, social life, and quality of life.

During the decade of the 1990s "ratings game" accelerated when *USNWR*

Table 4.1   *USNWR*'s top twenty-five national universities, 1999.

Rank	University
1	Harvard University
1	Princeton University
1	Yale University
4	Massachusetts Inst. of Technology
4	Stanford University
6	Cornell University
6	Duke University
6	University of Pennsylvania
9	California Inst. of Technology
10	Brown University
10	Columbia University
10	Dartmouth College
10	Northwestern University
14	Johns Hopkins University
14	University of Chicago
16	Emory University
16	Washington University-Saint Louis
18	Rice University
18	University of Notre Dame
20	Georgetown University
20	Vanderbilt University
22	University of California-Berkeley
22	University of Virginia
24	U. of North Carolina-Chapel Hill
25	Tufts University
25	Univ. of California-Los Angeles
25	Univ. of Michigan-Ann Arbor

Source: 1999 America's Best Colleges (Washington, D.C.: *USNWR,* August 1998), p. 36. Copyright © 1998, *U.S. News & World Report.*

entered the market with an annual ranking of undergraduate institutions. This is published in a fall issue of the magazine and then, with more detail, as a separate volume. Institutions are divided into broad categories, such as national universities, national liberal arts colleges, regional universities, and regional liberal arts colleges. *USNWR* then constructs a single numerical ranking of the institutions in each category based on a set of objective and subjective factors that I will describe shortly.

Before the advent of the *USNWR* rankings, administrators, faculty, students, and alumni had to worry only about in which selectivity group their institution was placed. Once classified in a group, the institution was accorded roughly the same "prestige" as all other institutions in the group. With the advent of the *USNWR* rankings, they must now worry about how their institution is numerically ranked relative to its close competitors.

Table 4.1 displays the rankings that *USNWR* reported for the top twenty-five national research universities in 1999, the category in which Cornell University is classified. Cornell finished tied for sixth that year, which left the university administration feeling elated because during the previous eleven years that *USNWR* had published their ratings, Cornell had never ranked so close to the top. As Figure 4.1 indicates, between 1988 and 1998 Cornell's rankings among top national universities fluctuated between a high of ninth place and a low of fifteenth place. The university's rank during most of the 1990s, although sometimes increasing, seemed overall to be getting worse. This decline was puzzling because by objective measures, such as student quality, Cornell was constantly improving.

Even though colleges and universities constantly criticize the rankings and urge potential students and their parents to ignore them, every institution pays very close attention to the ratings and tries to take actions to improve its own ranking. A recent study that James Monks and I conducted

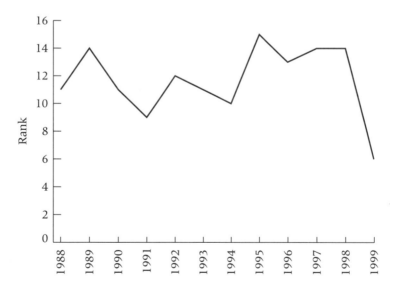

Figure 4.1. *USNWR*'s ranking of Cornell University among national universities, 1988–1999.

suggests that they are wise to do so. A worsening in a selective private institution's ranking appears to reduce the number and academic quality of the institution's applicants, as well as the probability that applicants who are accepted will enroll there.[1]

Virtually all of the objective data used in the ranking formula are self-reported by institutions, and this has led some institutions to challenge the rankings' accuracy. Stanford University, for example, hired an auditing firm to validate its own data. Stanford then posted on its Web site its audited information, along with other facts that *USNWR* ignored that the university thought were important measures of institutional quality (such as the number of prestigious awards won by the faculty).

The factors that *USNWR* uses in its formula, and the arbitrary weight that it assigns to each to compute the overall ranking, have changed over time. This leads to the possibility that institution A may be ranked higher than institution B one year, but lower the next year, even if nothing has changed at either institution, simply because the weights assigned to different factors have changed. Indeed, once one realizes that different students may value the characteristics of universities differently, the notion that one can come up with a single number that summarizes the overall ranking of an academic institution seems quite silly. For example, my son who plays the trumpet may care only about the music program at an institution, while your daughter, who is interested in science, may care only about the laboratory facilities. Nonetheless, the rankings are there, and since institutions fear that they influence behavior, they pay attention to them.

Table 4.2 summarizes the formula that *USNWR* used to compute its 1999 ranking. A weight of 25 percent is assigned to the academic reputation of an institution, as measured by a survey of presidents, provosts, and deans of admissions of colleges and universities. Cornell consistently has done well on this measure, ranking in the top seven or eight institutions in most years. *USNWR* acknowledges that reputation per se is important because it influences the subsequent educational and employment opportunities of graduates of an institution.

Student selectivity is measured by the fraction of freshman applicants that the institution accepts (low is good), the fraction of accepted applicants that choose to enroll, or its yield (high is good), the fraction of entering students that come from the top 10 percent of their high school classes, and entering students admission test scores. Student selectivity is given a weight of 15 percent by *USNWR* in the rating.

However, increasingly, high schools fail to report their students' class rank

Table 4.2 *USNWR*'s 1999 college rankings: criteria and weights.

Ranking category	National universities and liberal arts colleges category weight	Subfactor	National universities and national liberal arts colleges subfactor
Academic reputation	25%	Academic reputation survey	100%
Student selectivity	15%	Acceptance rate	15%
		Yield	10%
		High school class standing, top 10%	35%
		SAT/ACT scores	40%
Faculty resources	20%	Faculty compensation	35%
		Faculty with Ph.D.'s	15%
		Full-time faculty	5%
		Student/faculty ratio	5%
		Class size, 1–19 students	30%
		Class size, 50+ students	10%
Retention rate	20%	Graduation rate	80%
		Freshman retention rate	20%
Financial resources	10%	Educational expenditures per student	100%
Alumni giving	5%	Alumni giving rate	100%
Graduation rate performance	5%	Graduation rate performance	100%

Source: 1999 America's Best Colleges (Washington, D.C.: *USNWR*, August 1998), pp. 33–35. Copyright © 1998, *U.S. News & World Report*.

to colleges. For example, in a recent year, while over 80 percent of the freshmen whose class rank was reported to Cornell were in the top 10 percent of their high school classes, about 35 percent of entering freshman students' high schools ranks were not reported. Hence, the inclusion of the class rank variable in the *USNWR* rating scheme can be called into question.

In addition, an institution can influence its acceptance rate and yield through altering the proportion of applicants that it admits through an early-decision process. In recent years Cornell and many other selective institutions have increased the share of their classes that they admit this way. Under an early-decision process, an applicant applies to one institution by early November of the applicant's senior year of high school. At most institutions, the applicant is required to sign a statement that he or she will enroll if admitted and will withdraw any other college applications that have been submitted. The institution gives the applicant a decision by December 15. The decision takes the form of an acceptance, a rejection, or a deferral of the applicant to the regular decision process. If admitted, the applicant has a brief period of time to notify the institution that the offer of admission has been accepted and that applications pending at other institutions have been withdrawn.

Expanding the fraction of an institution's class admitted via the early-decision route lowers the institution's acceptance rate and increases its yield, because early-decision applicants accept offers of admission with a probability of close to one. Thus to attain any given class size, the institution can admit fewer students overall. In addition, its yield automatically will rise.

To see this, consider the following example. Suppose that initially a university has 10,000 freshman applicants, it admits 4,000 of them, and 2,000 of those admitted applicants enroll. Its acceptance rate will be 40 percent (4,000/10,000) and its yield will be 50 percent (2,000/4,000). Now suppose it offers an early-decision option, that 2,000 of its 10,000 applicants choose this route, and that it accepts 1,000 of these early-decision applicants, all of whom enroll. If its yield on regular accepted applicants remains at 50 percent, to maintain an enrollment level of 2,000 students, it now need admit only 2,000 of the remaining 8,000 applicants. Hence its acceptance rate will fall to 30 percent (3,000/10,000), and its yield will rise to 67 percent (2,000/3,000).

Although such "gaming" of the system may increase an institution's *USNWR* rating, it is not clear that increasing the number of students admitted through the early-decision process is socially desirable. As a greater proportion of high school students are admitted to selective institutions via the early-decision route, the pressure increases on all high school seniors who are interested in attending these institutions to apply to one of them via this route. Students may be forced to make such decisions without having had the time to acquire sufficient information about the characteristics of a number of institutions and to evaluate which institution would really be best for them.

Faculty resources is a factor measured by average faculty salary levels, the fraction of faculty with Ph.D.'s, the fraction of faculty who are full-time, the student/faculty ratio, and the fractions of classes that have less than twenty students enrolled (high is good) and fifty or more students enrolled (high is bad). Faculty resources is given a weight of 20 percent in the *USNWR* ranking scheme.

Institutions, such as Cornell, that are located in areas where the cost of living is low do not have to pay as high salaries to attract and retain faculty as institutions located in areas where the cost of living is high. Before I became a Cornell administrator, I was able to convince *USNWR* that it should adjust salaries for cost-of-living differences across areas before including salaries in its faculty resources measure to avoid penalizing institutions located in areas where the cost of living is low.

The class size measures indicate the proportions of classes of given sizes, not the proportion of students enrolled in classes of given sizes. To see the problem with the measures, consider the following simple example. Suppose an institution had only two classes, one with 2,000 students and one with 2 students. The institution would report to *USNWR* that 50 percent of its classes had less than 20 students and 50 percent had more than 50 students. However, 99.9 percent of its students would actually be enrolled in large classes and only 0.1 percent would be enrolled in small classes.

Suppose now that the institution felt guilty about the very large class and divided it into 40 classes of 50 students each. Most people would judge this change to be educationally desirable. Unfortunately, the percentage of small classes with less than 20 students reported to *USNWR* would fall to 2.5 percent (1/41) and the percentage of classes with 50 or more students would rise to 97.5 percent (40/41). These changes would hurt the institution's rating, and hence the rating system would discourage the institution from making an educationally desirable change.

The institution's retention rate, as measured by the fraction of its entering freshman students who graduate within six years and the fraction of its freshman class that enrolls again as sophomores (high is good in both cases), is given a weight of 20 percent in the rating scheme. Institutions that attract better-prepared students and students with securer finances will obviously do better on these measures. A graduation rate performance measure that attempts to control for differences in the academic background of students and the resources the university spends educating them is given a weight of 5 percent in the rating scheme.

Financial resources, which is measured by the dollars that the institution spends educating its students, has a weight of 10 percent. We saw that in the mid-1990s Cornell was not doing very well relative to its competitors on this measure. One reason for this is that Cornell's endowment per student is lower than that of many of its private competitors. A second reason is that faculty salaries are a major component of educational expenditures. Sadly, I was unsuccessful in my efforts to convince *USNWR* that it should adjust the educational expenditure measure for area differences in the cost of living as it had adjusted faculty salaries.

Still a third reason is that many of Cornell's competitors have medical schools on their campuses. Inasmuch as expenditures per student are typically much higher for medical education than for undergraduates, using an overall expenditure per student measure, as *USNWR* does, favors institutions with medical colleges. The Cornell University Medical College (CUMC) is located in New York City, not on the Ithaca campus, and it had not occurred to my predecessors that Cornell administrators should average the CUMC numbers in with the Ithaca campus numbers that Cornell submits to *USNWR*. This did occur to a member of my staff, and *USNWR* allowed the university to make this adjustment, which raised Cornell's reported expenditures per student.

A final reason is that in Cornell's four state-assisted statutory colleges the costs for employee benefits (over 30 percent of salary) are paid directly by New York state and do not appear in the Cornell financial accounts. Because all other universities include all of their employee benefit costs in their expenditure per student measure, Cornell was at a disadvantage. We were able to get *USNWR* to agree to allow us to impute Cornell statutory employees' benefit costs and then to add these imputed costs to the expenditures per student number that we submitted to *USNWR*.

These adjustments improved Cornell's relative position. Virtually all institutions are similarly engaged in the process of examining their data very carefully to see if there are legitimate adjustments they can make in the data they report to *USNWR* that will improve their position in the ranking. Of course, no institution ever looks to see if anything it reported unintentionally overstates its position. One may well wonder if the resources an institution devotes to checking and adjusting its data could more productively be saved or devoted to educating students.

Indeed, the use of expenditures per student in the *USNWR* ranking scheme places academic institutions in a very difficult position. On the one hand, the institutions would like to reduce their costs to keep tuition increases down. On the other hand, if any institution unilaterally did so, it would adversely affect its ranking because the ranking is based on how much it spends. You can imagine the reaction of the Cornell trustees' finance committee when I explained to them that Cornell could not unilaterally aggressively cut costs because of what this would do to the university's rankings and, in turn, to its ability to attract high-quality students.

The final factor in the *USNWR* ranking is alumni satisfaction, which is measured by the percentage of living alumni who have made contributions to the institution during a recent two-year period. Historically, Cornell has always ranked very high in the generosity of its alumni. For example, in 1996–97 Cornell ranked third in the nation in total contributions from alumni. The $111 million that it raised from alumni that year was exceeded only by the amounts that Harvard and Stanford raised from their alumni. However, the percentage of Cornell's alumni who contribute was ranked eightieth among national universities by *USNWR* in 1997, a position that hurt the university's overall rating that year.

Cornell ranked low on that measure for three reasons. First, the university's Development Office had included all individuals who ever enrolled as undergraduates at the university as alumni, regardless of whether they went on to graduate. Taking the time to restrict alumni to graduates, which is what the *USNWR* measure was supposed to be based upon, raised the university's ranking to fortieth in 1998. This was a substantial improvement, but it still was a "drag" on the overall *USNWR* rating of the university.

Second, because almost half of Cornell's undergraduates attend the state-assisted colleges and pay "state" tuition levels that are considerably lower than the endowed tuition levels, many graduates of statutory colleges have assumed that there is little need for them to make contributions to the university—they erroneously have thought that New York state was fully supporting these colleges. It is only over the last fifteen years, as state support has declined, that the university has made a substantial effort to increase contributions from statutory college alumni.

Finally, Cornell long ago realized that the marginal cost of raising each dollar was lower if it concentrated its attention on cultivating long-term relationships with a relatively small number of alumni who had, or were expected to have, the potential to make large contributions to the university. Put another way, the total volume of alumni giving that the university receives by following this strategy is thought to be higher than the volume it would receive if more of the resources it devotes to fund raising were spent trying to increase the number of small donors. Paradoxically, for the university to do substantially better on the *USNWR* ranking in the category of alumni satisfaction, it would have to redirect its fund-raising resources to follow a strategy that did not make financial sense for it.

Although alumni satisfaction "counts" for only 5 percent of a university's overall ranking, the best minds in Cornell's administration thought long and hard about how to improve performance on this measure. Picking up on a suggestion made by a member of my staff, I half seriously suggested that we should find a donor that was capable of giving $125,000. We could then divide this into one-dollar bills, stick each bill into an envelope, and address the envelopes to the roughly 125,000 living undergraduate alumni for whom Cornell had mailing addresses, and ask each to return the dollar to the university in the enclosed self-addressed stamped envelope. If even a small fraction did, the university would substantially improve its ranking on this measure. This idea (like many of my ideas) was never taken seriously by my colleagues—perhaps because the postage costs and the costs of preparing the mailings were thought to exceed the expected benefits to the university from improving its position on the alumni giving measure.

There still remains the issue of how Cornell was able to leap from a tie for fourteenth place in the national university ratings in *USNWR* in 1998 to a tie for sixth place in the 1999 ratings. Anyone connected with the university will, of course, confirm that *USNWR* was finally recognizing the excellence that Cornell has always shown. However, the underlying characteristics of the university did not change very much between those two years, and the dramatic shift in Cornell's position was caused by two changes that had nothing to do with the true academic quality of the institution.

First, Cornell excluded from its count of living alumni those alumni for whom it did not have good mailing addresses. This change caused Cornell's percentage of alumni who contribute to the university to jump from fortieth to sixteenth place. This adjustment was warranted given what *UNSWR* actually asks institutions to provide. One would hope, of course, that institutions do not increasingly strategically "lose" the addresses of alumni who have never contributed to improve their performance on this measure.

Second, and more important, Cornell's leap had to do with the mechanical way in which *USNWR* calculates the ratings. In particular, there was a subtle change in the methodology between 1998 and 1999 in how the financial resources measure was calculated, which most readers probably didn't even notice. In particular, in explaining how the rankings are computed, *USNWR* indicated.

> This year, because of changes in reporting rules for private colleges and universities, we are measuring financial resources by the average spending per student on instruction, research, public service, academic support, student services, institutional support, and operations and maintenance . . . In prior years, financial resources were broken down into two components: educational expenditures and other expenditures. (Educational expenditures were calculated as the sum of per-student spending for instruction, student services, academic support, and institutional support (computers, library and administration). The other component, "other expenditures," included spending on financial aid, research, operations, maintenance, and public service.) This year, these components could not be measured separately because private colleges began reporting different financial information than public colleges . . . in order to conform to changes in accounting and financial reporting standards issued by the Financial Accounting Standards Board.[2]

Put simply, because of a change in accounting standards imposed on private institutions, *USNWR* shifted from using educational expenditures per student to total expenditures per student as its measure of financial resources. The major additional expenditures included were for research, public service, and operations and maintenance. This shift was delightful for a university that typically ranks ninth in the nation in terms of total research expenditures, trailing behind primarily public universities that are not included among the very top national universities in the *USNWR* ranking. MIT is the single private university that ranks higher than Cornell did in the *UNSWR* ranking and has larger research expenditures. The shift was also gratifying because Cornell has a statutory component that engages in extension and public service activities throughout New York state. Cornell received almost $18 million in appropriation for these purposes from New York state in the academic year 1995–96 and also generated almost $55 million in funds from the federal government and external sponsors to enhance these activities. All of the institutions ranked above Cornell in the 1998 *USNWR* survey were private institutions that devote a much smaller share, if any, of their budgets to public service and extension activities. How fortunate the shift was for a university like Cornell that devotes more funds than many of its competitors to maintaining its buildings and campus.

Very few Cornell administrators realized that this change in variable definition was a major reason for the drastic improvement of the *USNWR* ranking of the university between 1998 and 1999. Although the university may claim that *USNWR* has finally recognized the true worth of the institution, Cornell's dramatic rise highlights the problems inherent in a mechanical ranking scheme that changes its components and the weight assigned to each component over time.

USNWR generates lots of revenue for itself with its college ranking issues, but it is clear that its ranking scheme makes little sense. That some institutions alter their policies for reasons that make little sense educationally to raise their rankings is a travesty.

A postscript: *USNWR* slightly modified the formula that it used to compute its 2000 ranking of institutions. The changed formula was at least partially responsible for Cornell's falling to eleventh place among national universities in that ranking. Over a three-year period, the university had risen from fourteenth to sixth place and then fallen back to eleventh place in the *USNWR* ranking. Does the reader think that the academic quality of Cornell really either increased or decreased relative to other leading universities' academic quality during this period?

Rankings of Graduate Professional Programs

Rankings also are undertaken of graduate professional (law, medicine, business) programs, and institutions also follow them with great concern. The most influential rankings of Master of Business Administration (MBA) programs are now those undertaken by *Business Week* (henceforth *BW*), which began in 1988. These rankings are based upon a multiplicity of factors, including academic reputation, reputation among business leaders and corporate recruiters, the test scores of entering students, and the placement success of graduates. As with the undergraduate program rankings, the specific factors included in the rankings often change over time, as do the weights applied to the various factors.

When *BW* announced that it was going to develop a ranking of MBA programs, feature them in a special issue, and base its initial 1988 ranking partially on an alumni satisfaction survey, an enterprising Cornell dean called or wrote all second-year MBA students and recent MBA graduates of Cornell's Johnson Graduate School of Management (JGSM). He told them that if they gave high marks to the school, JGSM's ratings would improve and this, in turn, would enhance the value of their degrees. The alumni responded magnificently and JGSM ranked fifth in the initial 1988 *BW* ratings.

This in turn led to an improvement in the quality of the students that JGSM was able to attract the next year. Unfortunately, JGSM was not that highly ranked by employers, and so when the newly attracted students graduated, they did not all receive the type of positions that they had expected. This led to some alumni discontent, which adversely affected future ratings, and as deans at other business schools began to play the same "game," the ranking of JGSM in the *BW* survey fell into the middle of the second ten schools. When the 1996 *BW* results were announced, JGSM had slipped still further to eighteenth place.

One of the reasons for this fall was that a number of other universities had invested enormous sums of money to improve the quality of their business school facilities. New buildings impress prospective students and provide them with a sense of the success that they aspire to attain in the corporate world. They also demonstrate to corporate recruiters that the institution understands what success in the corporate world is all about.

Great consternation arose among JGSM's alumni, faculty, and student body, as well as among the Cornell trustees associated with the school. JGSM became almost exclusively preoccupied with improving the rankings of its MBA program. Other activities that it might have undertaken that promised benefits for the rest of the university were not given high priority. Efforts by a group of business and operations research professors to set up a one-year computational finance program, housed jointly in JGSM and Cornell's College of Engineering, never had much hope of succeeding because the JGSM faculty worried that such a program would adversely affect their school's MBA program rankings. They thought that their MBA students (who tend to have several years of post-college work experience) would resent being placed in courses with the recent college graduates who were expected to enroll in the computational finance program. The failure to establish this program caused a leading expert in computational finance from the operations research department to leave the university.

Discussions had been under way for years about the renovation of a historic building, Sage Hall, to provide larger and state of the art facilities for JGSM. By the summer of 1996, the university administration had transferred all residents of the building to other quarters and was awaiting some assurance that money to cover the full cost of the renovation would be raised before it agreed to start construction. The fall in the rankings and the resulting pressures placed on the administration by concerned parties sped up the start of the renovation and no expense was spared in making the building a showplace. When the building reopened in the summer of 1998, sufficient funding had not yet been obtained to cover all the renovation costs, and JGSM had to bear the substantial interest costs of the resulting debt in its operating budget.

When I left my vice president's position, Cornell's provost held a "retirement" luncheon for me. The luncheon was held in a small room in the renovated building and lasted for about two hours. Perhaps the interest costs on the debt that JGSM had to cover explains why the provost received a bill from JGSM for $500 for the rental of the room (this fee did not include the caterer's charges). I have often wondered if the provost actually paid that bill.

There was a debt for renovation of the building even though the senior administration of the university had opened up its major donor list to JGSM and the president and provost had asked many friends of the university whose primary interest was not JGSM to lend their support. Hence this expensive renovation undoubtedly diverted some contributions to JGSM that otherwise would have gone to other parts of the university.

It would have been very surprising if JGSM did not improve in the 1998 *BW* ranking of business schools, and indeed it jumped all the way up to eighth place. The dramatic rise was primarily due to a huge increase in the ratings given JGSM by its graduates, which were attributed to the new building and to an increased responsiveness of faculty and staff to students' concerns. But by the time the next *BW* ranking of business schools appears in the year 2000, some other institutions will be building new facilities for their business schools, and Cornell will probably fall back into the pack. Having the newest, most modern facilities is only a short-run phenomenon.

Why universities believe they need expensive new facilities to attract top MBA students who will then go out into the world and earn starting salaries of over $100,000 a year is not hard to understand. It is yet another example of the winner-take-all phenomenon and it is representative of the lengths to which universities will go to remain preeminent. One might, of course, question why having a highly ranked graduate business school should be a major priority of a highly ranked research university. I can think of three possible reasons:

1. The belief that it is important that the university provide high-quality training for the individuals who will go on to lead major American and international corporations, as well as to start their own new businesses.
2. The belief that the research being conducted at major business schools is of fundamental importance to our society.
3. The belief that graduates of these schools often turn out to be among the wealthiest alumni of universities and thus have the means to give future financial resources to the university. Their positions also enable them to be a source of internships for future students at the university and of career opportunities for future graduates.

I leave it to the reader to deduce the importance placed on each of these three reasons by the administrators at America's universities.

The 1998 *BW* rankings were remarkable because *BW* determined that students at five schools, Dartmouth, Duke, Purdue, the University of Texas at Austin, and the University of Washington tried to "game" the rankings by urging fellow students to give their high school ratings on the student survey. To the extent that a school's *BW* ranking influences the future earnings of its graduates, such attempts to pack the ballot box make a lot of sense, and one can only wonder why students at other business schools had not caught on, or at least had not gotten caught.

Responding in righteous indignation, *BW* penalized these five schools by placing less weight on their 1998 student survey results, substituting in part the results from the 1994 and 1996 student surveys for these schools. So much for the *BW* ranking being an objective one. *BW* has still not learned what major league baseball learned long ago. When fans, rather than professional sportswriters, pick the all-star team, strange things can happen.

Doctoral Program Rankings

Sometimes rankings of academic programs at a university can be used to help make decisions about the allocation of resources at the institution and to improve the quality of the educational experience. Doctoral program rankings are a good example of this kind of influence.

The most influential rankings of doctoral programs are those that have been conducted by the National Research Council (NRC) approximately every decade. The NRC rankings are based solely on a large national survey of faculty within each field who are asked to rank programs in their field both in terms of the scholarly quality of the faculty connected with each program and in terms of the program's effectiveness in training graduate students. These rankings heavily influence the ability of departments to attract high-quality faculty and graduate students.

Table 4.3 displays the rankings that thirty-six Cornell arts and science and engineering programs received in the most recent NRC ranking, which took place in the mid-1990s.[3] What should be apparent is that the perceived quality of Cornell's faculty in the forty fields is somewhat uneven. The university is very strong in the arts and the humanities, in engineering, and in the physical sciences and mathematics. Virtually all of Cornell's programs in these fields are ranked among the top ten nationwide. But the faculty in the behavioral and social science fields are typically ranked in the ten to twenty range. With one exception, Cornell's programs in the biological science fields are ranked twenty-second or worse. Although there are well over two hundred universities in the United States that grant Ph.D. degrees, Cornell is not satisfied with being in the top twenty or thirty in a field, and it defines a strong program as being among the top ten nationwide.

University administrators want each program to be as strong as possible. Strong faculty members attract strong graduate students. Strong graduate students play important roles in the research and undergraduate teaching programs of most departments and help attract new faculty. But most universities cannot afford to maintain the strength of all their existing strong programs and also devote more resources to improving all of their weaker programs. They must be selective.

In deciding where to allocate its money, a university needs to understand why its weak programs are weak. A common argument often heard from the weaker departments is that they are weak because they do not have enough faculty positions; if the university would only give them more positions, they could hire great scholars and move up in the rankings. But since no department in any university is likely to be willing to acknowledge that it has more resources than it needs, it is difficult for administrators to respond to such arguments unless they have some objective evidence that the arguments are valid.

Table 4.3   National Research Council faculty quality ratings for Cornell University doctoral programs, 1993.

Program	National rank	Program	National rank
Arts and Humanities		Physical Sciences and Mathematics	
Art history	23	Astrophysics/astronomy	9
Classics	12	Chemistry	6
Comparative literature	6	Computer science	5
English	7	Geosciences	9 (tie)
French	8	Mathematics	15
German	3	Physics	6
Linguistics	9	Statistics/biostatistics	4
Music	11 (tie)		
Philosophy	9		
Spanish	8		
Biological Sciences		Social and Behavioral Sciences	
Biochem. and molecular biol.	22	Anthropology	31
Cell and developmental biololgy	35 (tie)	Economics	18
Ecology, evolution, and behavior	4	History	13
Molecular and general genetics	23	Political science	15
Neurosciences	24	Psychology	14
Pharmacology	65	Sociology	35
Physiology	31		
Engineering			
Aerospace engineering	6		
Chemical engineering	13		
Civil engineering	6		
Electrical engineering	7		
Material sciences	3		
Mechanical engineering	7		

Source: Marvin Goldberger, Brendan A. Maher, and Pamela Ebert Flattau, ed., *Research-Doctorate Programs in the United States: Continuity and Change* (Washington, D.C.: National Academy Press, 1995), pp. 150, 160, 171, 179, 189.

Fortunately, although the NRC rankings are based solely on the subjective assessments of faculty members nationwide, objective data that one might reasonably believe should be related to faculty members' perceptions of departments' quality were also collected and published by the NRC. We know, for example, the number of faculty members in each program, the number of graduate students the programs have enrolled, the number of new Ph.D.'s that they produce each year, the average time it takes their students to earn the degree, and certain things about the faculty members' scholarly productivity. Measures of productivity include the number of publications the faculty have generated, the number of times other authors cite their work, and the number of distinguished awards that faculty members in the program have received. It is possible for researchers to assume that there is a causal relationship between these objective measures and the subjective rankings that the departments received and then to statistically estimate the role that each of these objective factors plays in influencing national doctoral program rankings in each field.

Peter Hurst and I did this and subsequently published our results in an article that appeared in *Change* magazine in 1996.[4] What we found helped guide resource allocations at Cornell, and I present two examples here.

Many administrators at the university were "down on" Cornell's Sociology Department. In addition to being among the poorest-ranked social science programs at Cornell, sociology is not a field that currently is thought by many to be making major intellectual breakthroughs and discoveries that will benefit society. Undergraduate student interest in the department's curriculum was low, at least partly because many of the topics previously taught in sociology departments are now taught in women's and ethnic studies departments. As a result, sociology's undergraduate student course enrollments were low and it ranked among the lowest departments in the College of Arts and Sciences in terms of enrollments generated per faculty member per year. In addition, at the time the rankings came out, the department could best be described as fractious, and it was difficult to see how progress could be made.

Given tight resources at the university, the dean of the college wondered if it was worth his, and my, efforts to try to improve the Sociology Department by allocating it a few more faculty positions and by trying to draw on the resources of the rest of the university. More sociologists were employed in departments outside the College of Arts and Sciences, including Rural Sociology (Agriculture), Organizational Behavior (Industrial and Labor Relations), and Human Development (Human Ecology), than were employed in the Arts and Sciences Sociology Department itself. However, for historical reasons, including issues of "turf," very few of these faculty members were connected to the Sociology Department's graduate or undergraduate programs.

Faced with many competing demands for resources, the dean would have been perfectly justified in concluding that it was not worth his effort to try to improve the program and thus in letting the department wither away. A number of years earlier, Washington University in St. Louis had abolished its once-strong sociology program.

I showed the dean that Hurst's and my analyses indicated that the faculty members in the department were every bit as productive as scholars as the average faculty member in top-ten departments and that the primary reason for the department's low ranking was its small size. He then made a commitment to provide the department with resources so that it could expand. He and I also worked with several other deans to improve sociology university-wide at Cornell.

Biology was a different story. When the NRC rankings were published, many of Cornell's biologists could not believe that the national academic community ranked them so low. Our analyses indicated that these fields appeared to be ranked lower than we had hoped primarily because of the relatively low research output of the faculty. Contrary to faculty arguments, program size did not play an important role in explaining Cornell's relatively low rankings in biology.

After the almost obligatory ranting and raving that occurs whenever any academic group is criticized, Cornell's biologists began to think seriously about why their research productivity was lower than that of biologists in the top-ranked departments. Part of the explanation was that much biological research relates to biomedical topics and is conducted primarily in medical colleges. Research faculty in medical colleges have much lighter teaching responsibilities than biologists who teach at mixed undergraduate-graduate institutions, because biologists in medical colleges typically receive much of their support from external research grants. Thus biological researchers in medical colleges usually have more time to spend on research than their counterparts in colleges of arts and sciences and agriculture.

Most major biological research departments are in, or are connected closely to, a medical college. However, Cornell's medical college is located in New York City, and it was not even included in the NRC ranking of biology at the university. Although Cornell's biologists would like lighter teaching loads so that they could devote more time to research, so would our economists (or at least this economist). Given the university's concern for high-quality undergraduate instruction and its limited resources, reduced teaching loads for biologists (whose teaching loads are already light) was not an option.

Another reason the biologists' research productivity was ranked low was that although the NRC rankings purported to rank biology programs, they really ranked only basic biology programs. Excluded from the rankings were Cornell's applied biology departments, such as entomology, plant pathology, plant breeding, animal science, and nutrition, which the university believed were often among the best in the nation. Part of Cornell's response to the low NRC ratings was simply for the university to remind itself that the NRC rankings were not accurate indicators of all that went on in biology-related fields at the university.

Cornell's biologists volunteered to be one of the first faculties reviewed under a new program review system that had been established at the university. Many of them also came together and urged the university to devote resources to particular areas of biology in which Cornell already had substantial strength and which were likely to be important areas in the years ahead. Included among these areas was research at the interface of biology and chemistry and research relating to animal, plant, and human genomics. Prodded by the central administration, efforts also began to build much better links to the Cornell University Medical College.

Sociology and biology provide contrasting examples of how knowledge of the determinants of doctoral program rankings influenced the directions that the university took. In sociology, there was a direct relationship. The knowledge helped to forestall the demise of sociology at the university. In biology, the knowledge served as a catalyst that eventually caused the biologists to come to agreement that there was a problem and then to try to remedy it. Given the probable importance of biology in the century ahead, no administrator at Cornell ever suggested reducing the university's commitment to biology. The only question was how to make it better.

CHAPTER 5

Admissions and
Financial Aid Policies

The Costs of Recruiting and Enrolling Students

Selective private colleges and universities have considerable discretion as to which freshman applicants to admit. Table 5.1 presents data on the percentage of applicants that were admitted and then enrolled at a number of selective private colleges and universities that were ranked among the top twenty-five institutions by *USNWR* in 1999. Most enrolled less than 15 percent and many less than 10 percent of their applicants.

The proportion of applicants that enroll is the product of two other proportions, the proportion of applicants accepted for admission and the proportion of accepted applicants that enroll. The proportion of applicants that were accepted at each institution is displayed in Table 5.2. The institutions are listed in the order that *USNWR* ranked them in 1999. Not surprisingly, the highest-rated institutions have the most discretion over whom to admit. Among national universities, Harvard and Yale each admitted only 13 percent of their applicants, while the top national college, Amherst, admitted 20 percent of its applicants. All but three of these selective institutions were able to fill their classes by admitting less than half of their applicants.[1]

One might think that these institutions are so well known that potential applicants will flock to them and the institutions can be quite passive in their efforts to attract students. In fact, nothing could be further from the truth. The competition for top students has heated up, and selective colleges and universities spend considerable amounts of money recruiting applicants and then trying to persuade accepted applicants to enroll. Parents of bright high school sophomores or juniors are well aware of the voluminous mailings that their children receive from literally hundreds of colleges and universities, each trying to convince the students that it is the best place to attend.

Selective colleges and universities have staff members that travel around

Table 5.1   Proportions of freshman applicants to selected *USNWR* 1999 top twenty-five national universities and colleges that enrolled at each institution.

Universities		Colleges	
Harvard	.10	Amherst	.08
Princeton	.09	Swarthmore	.09
Yale	.11	Williams	.12
Stanford	.09	Haverford	.12
Cornell	.16	Wesleyan	.12
Duke	.12	Davidson	.14
Pennsylvania	.14	Washington and Lee	.14
Cal. Tech.	.07	Bates	.13
Brown	.10	Colgate	.13
Columbia	.09	Hamilton	.23
Dartmouth	.10	Colorado College	.16
Johns Hopkins	.12	Connecticut College	.12
Emory	.12	Macalester	.16
Washington (St. Louis)	.09	Oberlin	.16
Rice	.11		
Notre Dame	.21		
Georgetown	.11		
Vanderbilt	.16		
Tufts	.10		

Source: Author's calculations from data provided by the institutions on their World Wide Web pages. Typically, the data are for the freshman class entering in the fall of 1997 or the fall of 1998. Oberlin's data are for its Arts and Science College.

Note: The top twenty-five institutions excluded from the table are either public institutions or those whose data I could not locate.

the nation participating in "college" days at high schools and working with alumni to help generate applicants for them. Other staff members are busy preparing materials to attract students to the campus for visits, giving tours, answering questions, and interviewing potential applicants. Still others are busy keeping World Wide Web pages up to date and filled with lively material.

Requests for applications and descriptive materials come pouring into these institutions. Because there is no charge for them, potential applicants request materials from many more schools than the ones to which they

Table 5.2 Proportions of freshman applicants to selected *USNWR* 1999 top twenty-five national universities and colleges that were accepted at each institution.

Universities		Colleges	
Harvard	.13	Amherst	.20
Princeton	.13	Swarthmore	.23
Yale	.18	Williams	.26
Stanford	.15	Haverford	.34
Cornell	.34	Wesleyan	.33
Duke	.30	Davidson	.36
Pennsylvania	.31	Washington and Lee	.31
Cal. Tech.	.23	Bates	.34
Brown	.18	Colgate	.42
Columbia	.17	Hamilton	.42
Dartmouth	.22	Colorado College	.48
Johns Hopkins	.41	Connecticut College	.40
Emory	.46	Macalester	.54
Washington (St. Louis)	.40	Oberlin	.54
Rice	.27		
Notre Dame	.40		
Georgetown	.21		
Vanderbilt	.58		
Tufts	.32		

Source: 1999 America's Best Colleges (Washington, D.C.: *USNWR*, August 1998), pp. 36–37, 42–43. Copyright © 1998, *U.S. News & World Report*.

Note: Only institutions for which data were presented in Table 5.1 are included.

eventually apply. For example, although Cornell receives roughly 20,000 applications for its freshman class each year, it mails out application materials and descriptive brochures to over 110,000 high school seniors every year.

Once applications are received, they must be evaluated. Trained admission staff and faculty members pore through applications filled with grades, test scores, lists of activities, letters of recommendation, and personal statements. Their goal is to admit a class of students that has the intellectual qualifications to succeed at the institution and that also brings other desirable attributes to it. They strive to admit classes with sufficiently diverse interests and talents to ensure that an institution's orchestra and jazz band will have enough clarinet players, its women's softball team will have enough pitchers, and its student newspaper will have enough editors, reporters, and photographers. They also seek a class that is diverse along geographic, socio-economic, gender, and racial/ethnic lines so that students will benefit from associating with classmates who come from different backgrounds and who have different perspectives.

Once applicants have been admitted, there is the matter of persuading them to enroll. So an institution's admitted applicants are again swamped with materials telling them how much they are wanted and how wonderful the institution will be for them. Accepted applicants receive calls or letters from professional staff, students, and increasingly faculty, encouraging them to enroll. They are also invited to spend weekends visiting the campus.

When one adds up all the costs that selective private institutions incur in recruiting, admitting, and then enrolling their freshman classes, the num-bers are mind-boggling. Information provided to me from a confidential study of a set of selective private institutions indicates that in the fall of 1996 the average cost per student was about $1,700 in the universities and $2,500 in the colleges. These numbers actually underestimate the true average cost to the institutions because they do not include the value of the time spent by faculty and alumni in the admission process. The higher value for the col-leges reflects the ability of the universities to take advantage of certain econ-omies of scale.

It is true that the institutions recover some of these costs in the form of the application fees that they charge. The undergraduate application fee at Cor-nell in 1996 was $65 and was among the highest of any school. To use this figure, even if an institution had ten applicants for each student that it en-rolled, on average, the universities in the set would have spent over $1,000 and the colleges almost $2,000, to recruit, admit, and enroll each enter-ing first-year student. These amounts represent roughly 5 to 10 percent of the first-year gross revenue (before financial aid costs are subtracted) from tuitions that the institutions received from their first-year students that year.

One might wonder whether some of these funds would have been better spent on educating enrolled students. Put another way, just as it is often al-leged that pharmaceutical companies spend too much on advertising their existing drugs and not enough on research and development of new drugs, perhaps selective academic institutions are spending too much on recruiting students and not enough on educating them. If recruiting costs could be re-duced, it is even possible that these reductions could be passed on to stu-dents in the form of lower tuition fees.

No selective institution has an incentive to unilaterally reduce the funds it expends to attract its freshman class. Would it be possible for the selective institutions to voluntarily agree to limit their recruiting expenditures? Although some might think such an action socially desirable, it is in fact explicitly prohibited by a consent decree (to be discussed shortly), between the U.S. Department of Justice and a number of these institutions, that was entered into in 1991. The consent decree prohibits the institutions from taking any action that limits competition. It could easily be argued that placing restrictions on expenditures on information provided to potential students limits competition. Without the ability of the institutions to voluntarily agree to reduce recruitment costs, there is no chance that the savings that would accrue from such a reduction will be passed on to students in the form of lower tuition levels. So the consent decree, which was intended to stimulate competition and lower tuition, actually fosters one set of costs that helps to keep tuition high.

Realistically, even if the selective institutions were permitted to agree to limit recruitment costs, they would be unable to do so. The competitive pressure to enroll the top academic students is so great that no institution wants to give its competitors any leg up. Even the very top institutions are not immune from this pressure because increasingly institutions just a notch below the top ones are seeking to move into the top tier of institutions through aggressively recruiting top students, often with financial aid packages that are based upon merit rather than need.

To return to the drug analogy, consumers have an interest in seeing drug prices as low as possible. The federal government helps to achieve this goal by limiting the length of time that patents are effective for new drugs, but not by limiting the amount drug manufacturers can spend on advertising. Once a patent expires on a company's brand-name drug, other companies can make and sell generic equivalents. The competition from low-cost generic equivalents usually also leads to lower prices for the brand-name drug, as the original producer seeks to maintain a share of the market.

There are no patents to limit entry into the higher education industry (although there are regional and state certification boards). However, competition by new entrants with the selective private colleges and universities is severely limited by the amount of capital needed to create new institutions that are of equal quality. Cornell, for example, has an endowment that was worth more than $2 billion in 1998 and the value of its land and buildings exceeded that amount. Hence one would need well over $4 billion to provide the infrastructure and endowment for a selective university of comparable size.

Admittedly a few individuals, such as Bill Gates, could come up with that much money. Even then, however, one would not have a Cornell. The major reason is that Cornell has over 150,000 living alumni, who provide vital support for the university by helping to recruit potential students, providing students with summer jobs, helping to find new graduates post-college employment, and giving annual gifts to the institution. To take a personal example, both of my sons are Cornell graduates and attorneys in the Washington, D.C., area. Their connection with Cornell provided them both with help during their job search. Generations of successful alumni help to limit the competition that selective private institutions face from new entrants. A university's alumni are an important part of its "wealth."

The Birth and Death of Need-Based Financial Aid Policies

Before the early 1970s, high school graduates in the United States were guaranteed access to higher education through the provision of state supported low- or zero-tuition public institutions.[2] However, beginning in the 1970s, the federal government sought to provide students with the opportunity for choice as well as access. Through a combination of grants for low-income students (the Basic Educational Opportunity, or Pell, Grants), subsidized loans for low- and middle-income students, and funding to institutions to help defray the costs of hiring students to work while they were in school (the College Work Study program), the federal government tried to make attendance at higher-priced private institutions a real option for qualified high school students. The nation's most selective private colleges and universities embraced this policy, and virtually all adopted need-blind admissions policies, admitting students independently of their financial circumstances.

The Ivy League universities and a number of the other selective private institutions went further: they awarded financial aid based only on financial need and met the full financial "need" of each accepted student. After evaluating how much an applicant and his or her family should be able to contribute to the applicant's educational costs (based on the family's income and assets, the student's assets and expected summer earnings, and other family circumstances such as the number of siblings in college), the institution calculated a student's financial need as the difference between the total costs of the student's attending the institution (tuition, room, board, books, and other expenses) and any external grants (federal, state, private) that the student was eligible to receive. The applicant's need was then "met" by the institution's providing a package of scholarship (grant) aid and "self-help" aid. The self-help component of the package consisted of loans and the provision of employment during the academic year.

These federal and institutional policies proved extraordinarily successful. The selective private institutions enrolled many more talented students from middle- and lower-income families than they had in the past. Academic accomplishments, rather than family background, became increasingly important in admission decisions, and our nation's top students increasingly found their ways to these institutions. It is well documented that top students, as measured for example by Scholastic Aptitude Test (SAT) scores, became much more heavily concentrated in these institutions.[3]

Other forces contributed to this trend, including decreases in the cost of airline travel, caused by deregulation of the airlines, and decreases in long-distance telephone charges, which reduced the costs to students of attending institutions far from their homes. Increasingly, the selective private institutions drew their students from a national market rather than from regional ones. As top students became increasingly concentrated at selective private institutions, many major corporations began to concentrate their recruitment of graduating seniors at these institutions and their selective public counterparts. This move further enhanced the value of attendance at the selective private institutions and provided additional incentives for top students to want to enroll at them.

For a number of years Ivy League institutions and fourteen other northeastern selective private institutions formally met each spring to consider the financial circumstances of each applicant who had been admitted to more than one of the institutions. This group, which was known as the Overlap Group, compared information about each applicant's financial circumstances to make sure that the calculation of each admitted student's need was roughly the same at each institution to which the applicant had been admitted.

The members of the Overlap Group used a common formula to assess an accepted applicant's need. Hence if two of the institutions had the same total costs, an accepted applicant's need should be the same at the two institutions. The rationale for this policy was the institutions' desire for the applicants to choose the institution that was the best fit for them based on the programs of each institution, not on differences in financial aid. In sum, the policy sought to promote student choice based on educational grounds, not differences in costs.

Under this policy, if Brown discovered that an applicant's father had hidden $1 million in a Swiss bank, but Columbia, where the applicant also had been accepted, was unaware of this, the group would give Columbia the information. Columbia could then reduce its estimate of the applicant's need. Similarly, if Harvard learned that a father had lost his job and thus that his child's financial need was increased, and the applicant had also been accepted at Yale, Yale would also learn this information. Yale would thus be able increase its estimate of the applicant's need.

During the summer of 1989 the U.S. Justice Department became very concerned about the Overlap Group and began to investigate its practices. Its worry derived partly from the fact that tuition levels did not vary very much across the Ivy institutions. In 1991–92, for example, the range from the highest to the lowest tuition across the eight schools was only 5.5 percent (by 1998–99 the range was actually smaller). Although some may jump to the conclusion that similar "list prices" are prima facie evidence of collusive behavior, we should remember that in highly competitive environments competitive forces cause the prices of very similar products to tend to be the same.

Perhaps more disturbing to the Justice Department was that by agreeing on the financial need levels of applicants accepted at more than one of their institutions, the Overlap Group appeared to be restricting price competition for students with financial need. It is important to note that the Justice Department ignored that an applicant accepted at two institutions, and estimated to have the same financial need at both, would not necessarily receive the same level of grant aid at each. Each institution was free to meet its accepted students' need through whatever combination of grant aid and self-help that it chose. Because the amount of endowment per student varied widely across the institutions, it is no surprise that grant levels tended to be higher, and hence self-help levels lower, at the richer schools than at the poorer ones, for individuals with the same level of need. So a form of "price" competition for students with financial need was taking place.

In May 1991, the Justice Department proceeded to charge the Ivy League institutions and MIT with violating anti-trust laws against price fixing. MIT took its case to court, lost, and then had the decision reversed on appeal. However, the Ivy League institutions formally agreed, as part of a consent degree, to stop sharing data on financial aid data before making offers to students. Under the 1992 reauthorization of the Higher Education Act, they are allowed to come together as a group to discuss how they will define need and to agree to award grant aid only on the basis of need, but they cannot confer about any individual's need.

The Justice Department hoped that the consent decree would provide more grant aid to some needy students and indeed it did. To see why, suppose that Brown offers one hundred talented applicants an average of $10,000 of grant aid each based on the students' financial need. Suppose that these applicants come back to Brown and inform it that other selective private institutions have offered them an average of $15,000 of grant aid. What will Brown do?

One option is for Brown to discuss with each of the other institutions how it computed each of these individuals' need. But this option is explicitly precluded by the consent decree. A second option is for Brown to do nothing, in which case it will probably lose many of these talented students to its competitors. A third option is for Brown's Dean of Admissions and Financial Aid to report to her higher-ups that without better grant aid packages Brown will lose many of these students and that she recommends that the university needs to improve its offers for the accepted applicants in the group that it really wants. Some applicants will probably find that Brown will respond by increasing its offers of grant aid. This means that they will receive more grant aid and less self-help aid than other accepted applicants to Brown with identical financial need whom the university is equally desirous of attracting, but who did not inform it of a larger aid offer from another institution.

Do selective institutions actually respond when admitted applicants inform them that they have received better financial aid offers elsewhere? By the late 1990s, several, including Harvard and Carnegie-Mellon, actually were inviting accepted applicants to inform them about offers elsewhere. During 1997–98, Carnegie-Mellon had about 800 competitive offers faxed to it, and it responded by increasing the size of the grant that it offered in about 460 cases.[4] Dialing for dollars, the shopping around to get institutions to improve their financial aid offers, has become a widely practiced strategy by admitted students and their families.[5]

Fueled partially by the tremendous increase in stock market prices, and hence in endowment values, that occurred during the 1990s, many selective institutions also increased the generosity of their grant aid programs in 1998. To name a few, Harvard and MIT reduced the size of their self-help packages and increased their grant aid per recipient by $2,000 and $1,000 a year, respectively. Princeton went even further, replacing the loan component of the self-help package completely with grant aid for all individuals coming from families with family incomes less than $40,000 a year. Stanford, Yale, Cornell, Dartmouth, and Johns Hopkins were among others that announced in public press releases improvements in their programs. The competition for top academic students has dramatically heated up.

The richest institutions were, of course, in the best position to take advantage of enhanced endowment values. For example, as Table 3.1 indicates, if one assumes a 4 percent payout rate, in 1997 Princeton was generating about $30,000 and Pennsylvania about $5,000 per student in endowment spending. If each institution was able to increase its endowment spending by 20 percent the next year, Princeton's per student spending would have risen by $6,000, but Pennsylvania's by only $1,000. Thus rich institutions, such as Princeton, could fund the improvements in their financial aid programs solely out of endowment spending. But the relatively poorer ones, such as the University of Pennsylvania, could not afford to do so. To try to remain competitive they had to resort to new fund-raising campaigns to increase their endowments and annual giving for financial aid, as well as to use more of their tuition revenues for financial aid.

So in one respect the Justice Department was correct. Outlawing the Overlap Group has led to an increase in price competition for students and the size of financial packages going to some admitted applicants. Unfortunately, these extra funds have to come from endowment funds, annual giving, or tuition dollars. If they come from the first two, the funds available for other uses will be reduced (unless annual giving can be increased above the level that would have existed if the institution had not spent more on financial aid). In practice, some of the increased financial aid costs have been paid for by money from endowment funds and annual giving, but some of these costs have also been paid for out of tuition revenues. Doing the latter directly puts upward pressure on tuition because if the institution is unwilling or unable to cut other expenditures, it needs to find a way to replace the increased dollars taken for financial aid from its operating budget.

Thus while the consent decree has put more institutional grant aid in some students' pockets, it also has contributed to institutions' need to raise tuition levels by more than the rate of inflation. Consequently, some students and their families have financially benefited from the consent decree, but many others have been made worse off.

Federal and state governments have had even more direct effects on tuition levels through the policies that the governments have followed with respect to their grant aid programs for undergraduate students. To understand why, refer to Table 5.3, which provides information for the academic years 1987–88 and 1997–98 on the sources of grant aid received by Cornell undergraduates. During the period grant dollars received from the federal government grew by 46.6 percent. Grant dollars received from state programs, primarily the New York state Tuition Assistant Program (TAP) program, grew by 10.3 percent. When one adds in grant dollars received by Cornell undergraduates from other external sources (primarily private scholarships, funding from the military for ROTC students, and funding from foreign governments), which grew by 80.8 percent, the total grant aid that Cornell undergraduate students received from external sources grew by 39.8 percent during the decade.

In contrast, grant dollars going to Cornell undergraduate students from Cornell's own funds—endowment income, annual giving, or tuition dollars—rose from $20.5 million to $56.2 million, an increase of almost 174 percent. As a result, the share of financial aid grant dollars that came from the university's own funds rose from .618 to .760. Increasingly, financial aid grants were the responsibility of the university and increasingly its financial aid dollars came from its own tuition revenues. Hence the need for

Table 5.3   Sources of financial aid grant dollars for undergraduate students at Cornell University (in millions of dollars), 1987–88 and 1997–98.

Source	1987–88	1997–98	Cumulative percentage change
Federal government	5.143	7.538	46.6
State government	4.903	5.410	10.3
Other external	2.663	4.816	80.8
Total external	12.709	17.764	39.8
Total Cornell	20.521	56.217	173.9
Cornell share of grant dollars	.618	.760	

Source: Cornell University 1998–99 Financial Plan: Operating and Capital: In-Year Forecast (Ithaca: Cornell University, January 1999), p. 21.

more funds to provide grant aid to students was partially responsible for tuition's continuing to rise at rates greater than the rate of inflation during the period.

Why did grant aid for undergraduate students increase so rapidly during the period? Table 5.4 shows that during the period the CPI rose by 41.2 percent. Even if tuition had grown by only this rate during the period, Cornell would have had to increase its expenditures on financial aid at a more rapid rate to make up for the failure of grant aid from state governments to keep up with inflation.

Still another reason Cornell spent so much more on grant aid was the relatively slow growth of the amount of grant aid coming from the federal government. At first glance, it appears that federal grant aid grew by a greater percentage (46.0) than inflation. However, the number of Cornell undergraduate students grew by 2.5 percent during the period and the number of undergraduates eligible for federal grant aid grew even faster, because the university was successful in attracting more students from low-income and lower-middle-income families. As a result, federal grant aid per student actually grew by less than the consumer price index during the period, and

Table 5.4   Cumulative and annual percentage changes in prices, income, and Cornell tuition and fees, 1987–1997.

	Cumulative	Annual
Consumer price index	41.2	3.5
Mean family income of families (level in 1997)		
in the lowest fifth ($12,057)	41.7	3.5
in the second fifth ($28,252)	41.9	3.5
in the third fifth ($44,575)	44.2	3.7
in the fourth fifth ($65,363)	47.7	3.9
in the highest fifth ($134,285)	66.1	5.2
in the top 5 percent ($235,021) of the income distribution	85.6	6.3
Endowed Cornell tuition and fees	77.6	5.9
Higher education price index	46.0	3.9

Note: Consumer price index and mean family income data are for calendar years. Cornell tuition and the Higher Education Price Index are for the academic years 1987–88 to 1997–98.

this too made it necessary for Cornell's own expenditures of grant aid to increase at a more rapid rate.

Information on the growth of mean family income in the United States during the period, for families located at various places in the distribution of family incomes, is also found in Table 5.4. Mean family income grew at, or slightly faster, than the rate of increase in consumer prices for families in the lowest three fifths of the income distribution. Indicative of the trend toward increased income inequality in the United States, families in the highest two fifths of the income distribution experienced increases in their mean income that were considerably higher. Indeed, the mean income of individuals in the top 5 percent of the income distribution grew during the period by 85.6 percent, an increase that was about twice as large as the increase in consumer prices. Individuals at the top of the income distribution were much better off in real terms by the end of the ten-year period than they were in the beginning.

If the growth in grant dollars from the federal government had kept up with inflation, and Cornell had increased its tuition by the rate of inflation during the period, its expenditures on grant aid from its own resources would have grown at roughly the same, or even a slightly lower, rate. This would have happened because family incomes kept up with, or increased, relative to inflation and thus students' financial needs did not increase more rapidly than inflation.

But Cornell did not hold its rate of tuition increases down to the rate of consumer price inflation. The cumulative rate of increase in tuition in the endowed part of the university was 77.6 percent. On an annual basis, its average rate of increase in tuition was 5.9 percent, which was almost 2.5 percentage points a year higher than the rate of increase in consumer prices. This rate of tuition increase also exceeded the annual rate of growth in the Higher Education Price Index, which was 3.9 percent during the period.

Cornell's rate of growth of tuition, which was similar to the rate of growth of tuition at other selective private institutions, was greater than the rate of growth of family incomes for applicants from families other than those in the top 5 percent of the income distribution. Because students who have financial need invariably come from lower- and middle-income families, this rapid tuition increase caused the need of existing financial aid recipients to grow at rates faster than the rate of growth of consumer prices. Having tuition rising faster than family incomes also increased the proportions of Cornell students who were eligible for Cornell grant aid. Indeed, during the period, the fraction of undergraduate students receiving grant aid from the university rose from 29.4 to 37.4 percent.

Part of this increased grant aid came directly from the university's tuition revenue. The share of each dollar of tuition revenue that the university received in the endowed colleges that was "recycled" in the form of financial aid for undergraduate students rose, and by the end of the period it reached approximately 20 percent. So when the university raised tuition by enough to increase its revenues by say $10 million, that increase yielded only about $8 million to help operate the university. This created even more pressure to increase tuition. In the absence of resistance by students and their families to paying higher tuition, which would have been measured by lower yield rates on admitted students, there was little reason for the university not to keep increasing its tuition so rapidly. Inasmuch as Cornell's competitors were raising their tuition levels at roughly the same rate, Cornell's yield rates did not fall.

Of course if the federal government had increased its grant aid to students at a more rapid rate, less institutional aid would have been required for Cornell students, and tuition increases at it and at other selective institutions might have been somewhat more moderate. Although a strong case can be made that the federal government should increase its grant aid expenditures to Cornell students at a rate equal to the rate of inflation, why it should do so more rapidly is less clear. Certainly those of us who believe that increasing access to higher education for students from low-income families should be a high public policy priority can argue for increases in grant aid expenditures. But of course other public priorities, such as ensuring the solvency of the Social Security retirement and Medicare systems, also compete for federal funds.

The story was quite different at a number of less selective, smaller private institutions, which increasingly found that they were having difficulty filling the number of seats that they had available in their first-year classes. A number of these institutions, including Wells College (New York), Wesleyan College (North Carolina), and Muskingum College (Ohio), cut their tuition levels for entering first-year students by between 23 and 30 percent during the late 1990s. Each of these institutions saw its applications and enrollments grow, its financial aid bill decline, and the test scores of its entering students increase. Private institutions of somewhat lesser selectivity than the ones whose behavior I am discussing in this book increasingly understand that the demand for their product is sensitive to the tuition level (price) that they charge their student customers who receive no financial aid.[6]

Preferential Packaging and Merit Aid

Over time, as selective private institutions found it increasingly expensive to maintain a need-blind admission and need-based financial aid policies, the number of institutions rigorously adhering to these practices declined. Some institutions, including Brown University and Carleton, Lafayette, and Smith Colleges, while continuing to adhere for the most part to the policy, explicitly included lack of need as an important factor in admitting the last 5 to 10 percent of their classes. Other institutions, such as Washington University in St. Louis, began offering full-tuition merit scholarships to all applicants who scored above a certain level on the National Merit Scholarship examination. Still others, such as Syracuse University, began offering multiple categories of merit scholarships, with the level of grant aid offered declining as the "attractiveness" of the applicant to the institution declined.

Some selective private institutions found themselves losing students to public institutions. Concern by the University of Rochester that it was losing middle- and upper-middle-income students to nearby SUNY at Geneseo, led Rochester to adopt a policy of providing $5,000 in grant aid to any accepted applicant from a contiguous six-county area in New York state. This policy actually reduced Rochester's total financial aid costs because many applicants who accepted this offer were from families whose economic position excluded them from receiving need-based financial aid and who would not have chosen to attend Rochester in the absence of this grant aid. By enrolling more of these middle- and upper-middle-income students, Rochester was able to substantially decrease the number of students it admitted and enrolled who were eligible for need-based aid. Since the typical applicant to Rochester with financial need received substantially more than $10,000 a year in grant aid, the university saved money by this policy change. In the process, the university was also able to increase the test scores of its entering students, which in turn increased the university's prestige. So the policy change enhanced both the university's financial and its academic well-being.

Today there are only a handful of selective private institutions that fully maintain need-blind admission and need-based financial aid policies. Even among them, cracks in the policy have widened. For example, an institution may practice need-blind admission, but where it concentrates its recruiting efforts will influence the income distribution of its applicants. Institutions that recruit heavily from suburban high schools are likely to have applicant pools that have fewer lower-income students and thus are more likely to admit and to enroll classes that include fewer lower-income students and require less grant aid than institutions that recruit heavily in inner-city areas.

At Cornell, which is strongly committed to need-blind admission and need-based financial aid, the university realized in the early 1980s that the institution was losing accepted applicants to better-endowed competitors. These institutions had the financial resources to offer financial aid packages that contained more grant aid and less self-help aid than Cornell's packages. It disturbed Cornell administrators that top accepted applicants were choosing institutions of comparable, or perhaps even lower, quality because the applicants were receiving financial aid packages elsewhere that contained more grant aid. Cornell was not unique; this experience was being repeated at all lesser-endowed selective private institutions.

The concept of preferential packaging, or offering different combinations of grant aid and self-help aid to applicants with the same level of financial need, grew out of these experiences. The applicants these institutions were losing tended to be the ones who had the best options elsewhere, and these applicants in turn tended to be the best applicants, in terms of academic credentials, that the institutions had. The institutions pondered whether it would make sense to try to stem the loss of these applicants by offering them more grant aid. To keep their financial aid budgets in balance, they would of course have to offer other applicants less grant aid. Ultimately, many institutions decided that it would make sense, and preferential packaging became part of the financial aid competition.

To see why, consider two accepted applicants to Cornell with the same level of need. One is an excellent student who also has offers of admission and grant awards from a number of institutions, some as good or better than Cornell is. The second is not as good a student and his other acceptances all come from lesser institutions. It is logical to assume that the decision whether to attend Cornell for the student with fewer comparable alternatives would be much less sensitive to the size of Cornell's grant award than would the decision of the student with several good alternatives. Empirical analyses confirmed that this is the case.[7]

Economists have long known that if a seller faces buyers with different sensitivities to price and can "price-discriminate" and charge them different prices, the seller will maximize his profit if he charges a lower price to the buyer whose decision to buy is most sensitive to price. An example where such price discrimination occurs is in the pricing of airline tickets. Business travelers, who often make last-minute decisions about traveling and whose schedules are constrained, are much less sensitive to airline ticket prices than are vacation travelers. Thus airlines rationally charge lower prices to travelers who make reservations thirty days in advance and whose travel involves a Saturday-night stay.

If one views the university as a seller of positions in its freshman class, accepted applicants as buyers of these positions, and the net tuition (the tuition level minus the grant award) charged to an accepted applicant as the price of a position, then it follows that the university should charge a lower price and give more grant aid to the first accepted applicant. Thus the strategy of preferential packaging within a need class is nothing more than a form of price discrimination.

Over time, the extent to which preferential packaging was practiced grew. Johns Hopkins, a university long known for its success in getting science majors into medical school, discovered that the enrollment decisions of accepted applicants with interests in science were much less sensitive to financial aid awards than the enrollment decisions of accepted applicants with interests in the humanities. So it quite rationally decided to give students with the identical level of financial need larger grant awards if they were interested in the humanities rather than the sciences. The university also discovered that the enrollment decisions of accepted applicants who had visited the campus were less sensitive to the size of their financial aid award than were the enrollment decisions of accepted applicants who had not visited the campus. To the institution's credit, it decided not to give smaller financial aid awards to students who had visited the campus.[8]

Selective institutions, such as Cornell, found that they were increasingly losing top students not only to better-endowed selective private institutions that practiced need-based financial aid, but also to lesser private and public institutions that were explicitly providing merit awards that were unrelated to need. At Cornell, for example, the number of National Merit Scholarship winners that enrolled at the university declined from sixty-eight in 1990 to thirty-three in 1996. It was believed that most of the reduction occurred because National Merit Scholarship winners accepted at Cornell instead enrolled at lesser institutions that offered them additional merit aid. Fortunately, this decline did not affect the average SAT scores of entering Cornell students, which is one of the measures that *USNWR* and other rankers use to gauge the academic quality of an institution; Cornell's students' average SAT scores continued to rise during the period. The university was, however, very concerned that it was increasingly losing accepted applicants of high academic quality.

The university responded as well as it could within the context of maintaining a need-based financial aid policy. Funding was obtained from donors for a new Presidential Research Scholar program. This program guaranteed 2 percent of accepted students research apprenticeships, starting in their freshman year. Funding was also provided to them for a summer of research experience with Cornell faculty members. For applicants that had financial need, grant aid was increased (and correspondingly, self-help decreased) by $3,500 a year. The research apprenticeships were paid positions, and hence applicants could satisfy the work requirement in their financial aid package through this job. Cornell is not unique in establishing such a program; Stanford, for example, developed a similar program earlier, and the University of Pennsylvania, with which Cornell often directly competes for students, quickly established its own Trustee Scholar program the year after Cornell established its program.

Cornell's Presidential Research Scholar program is a wonderful program because it enables some freshman students at a large research university to have the same type of intimate intellectual engagement with faculty members that many students at selective small liberal arts colleges regularly have. This program is but one of a series of special programs that Cornell established to attract admitted applicants to the university and to strengthen their commitment to the institution both while they are undergraduates and after they graduate. A second is the Cornell National Scholar program, which is directed at selected students who have demonstrated leadership abilities prior to entering Cornell. A third is the Cornell Tradition Fellowship, which is awarded to selected students who have demonstrated a willingness to devote substantial time each week to volunteer activities or to paid work to help support their education. Together these programs cover about 10 percent of the student body. Each provides special activities for the students and up to $3,500 a year in increased grant aid in place of loans for students with financial need. Each is thus a form of preferential packaging.

Michael McPherson and Morton Shapiro have very appropriately pointed out that there is something incongruous about selective private institutions saying that they do not award merit aid, but then proceeding to practice preferential packaging, which is merit aid within a need class.[9] Why preferential packaging is acceptable for students with need but not for students without need is unclear. If schools like Cornell increasingly lose top students to institutions that offer pure merit aid, it will be difficult for these institutions to resist starting to offer grant aid to top students who do not have any demonstrated financial need. A number of selective private institutions, including Duke, Washington University, Rochester, and Cal Tech, already offer some merit aid. With a fixed financial aid budget, dollars for still further increases in merit aid will come at the expense of dollars for need-based aid. We thus may be nearing the death of need-based financial aid at all but the richest institutions in the country.

Early Decisions

As the competition for top students has heated up, selective institutions have increasingly filled a substantial share of their first-year classes through an early-decision process.[10] To provide a sense of how prevalent the use of the early-decision process has become, Table 5.5 displays information for ten selective private colleges and universities on the percentage of the first-year class for the fall of 1996 that was enrolled in this manner. Harvard enrolled over half of its class that year via early decisions and Princeton was close behind at 49 percent. Each of the ten institutions enrolled at least a quarter of its class through early decisions. Cornell informs potential applicants that it enrolls about a quarter of its class this way, but by the fall of 1999 Cornell's number had crept up to about 30 percent.

Why do students and institutions like using the early-decision process? Students who are sure which school is their first choice like it because it allows them to avoid the tensions associated with having to wait until the spring of their senior year to learn whether they have been admitted to that school. Institutions like it because it provides them with students who have decided that that institution is their first choice and thus will be very happy to attend the institution. Some students who are admitted and enroll via the regular admission process were rejected by a preferred alternative and are not as happy about attending the institution.

As I said earlier, another reason the institutions like early decisions is that the larger the fraction of the class enrolled via the early-decision process, the higher the institution's accepted applicant yield rate will tend to be. High yields are viewed positively by raters, such as *USNWR*. In addition, although institutions rarely admit this publicly, students who apply for early decisions are more likely to be students who do not require financial aid. The reason is

Table 5.5   Early and regular decisions at ten selective private colleges and universities for the class entering in the fall of 1996.

| Institutions | Acceptance rate | | Percentage of class enrolled via early decision |
	Regular pool	Early-decision pool	
Universities			
Harvard	7	25	53
MIT	20	29	32
Princeton	8	38	49
Stanford	15	19	35
Yale	16	38	29
Colleges			
Amherst	18	25	39
Bowdoin	27	35	38
Haverford	33	55	25
Swarthmore	29	64	26
Williams	22	43	34

Source: 1997 America's Best Colleges (Washington, D.C.: *USNWR,* 1996), p. 33.
Copyright © 1996, *U.S. News & World Report.*

that students who have financial need are more likely to want to shop around to learn how much grant aid they will be offered at a number of schools before deciding which one to attend. Students applying for early decisions have committed themselves to attending the one institution to which they have applied.

By admitting more students via the early-decision process, institutions can limit their financial aid costs while claiming that they are remaining true to their stated policy of need-blind admissions and need-based financial aid. An important study by Christopher Avery, Andrew Fairbanks, and Richard Zeckhauser, using data from a set of selective private institutions, confirms that early-decision applicants are less likely to be students with financial need.[11]

Data displayed in Table 5.5 indicate that at each of the ten institutions the acceptance rate for early-decision applicants was higher than the acceptance rate for applicants who applied through the regular applicant process. Of course, this is like comparing apples to oranges. Early-decision applicants often are the students who believe that they have the best chance of being admitted. Although many institutions claim that an applicant's chance of admission actually does not depend upon whether the applicant applies via the early-decision or the regular admission route, some now do acknowledge that they give preference to early-decision applicants. By doing so, of course, they encourage more students to apply for early decisions.

Underrepresented minority students tend to come from families with lower incomes than do white and Asian American students. Hence, it is not surprising that at many institutions underrepresented minority students are not heavily represented in early-decision application pools. To the extent that students admitted via early applications tend to be white or Asian American, institutions that are committed to enrolling a student body that is racially and ethnically diverse will have put more emphasis on attracting underrepresented minority students through their regular admission process. But as they do this, white and Asian American applicants' chances of being admitted through regular admission pools will decrease. Astute high school students, parents, and guidance counselors will realize this is occurring and there will be more pressure on white and Asian American students to apply for early decisions. So a reasonable conjecture is that in the future selective colleges and universities will increasingly enroll their student body through the early-decision process.

Although this may be in these institutions' best interest, it is not clear that it is in students' best interest. High school students will be forced to make early decisions on where they want to apply and to enroll, and these decisions may not be as informed by as much information on the characteristics of different institutions as the students should have. They will be forced to think about higher education options early on in their high school careers, and this will put unnecessary pressure on them. If they enroll at institutions that prove not to be the best place for them, it is likely that in the future we will see more students transferring from one institution to another after their first or second semester.

It is reasonable to suggest that we would be better off as a society if institutions limited the number of students that they enroll through the early-decision process. It is not in any single institution's best interest to do so on its own. But if all selective institutions voluntarily agreed to place limits on the fraction of the class that they admit via early decisions, no institution would be placed at a competitive disadvantage and students as a group would probably be better off. Sadly, the consent decree also prevents the Ivy League institutions from collaborating to reduce early-decision admissions. So, again, a government policy has an adverse effect on the higher education system.

PART III

THE PRIMACY OF SCIENCE
OVER ECONOMICS

CHAPTER 6

Why Relative Prices
Don't Matter

One of the most fundamental propositions in economics is that relative prices matter. Consumers are sensitive to prices and when the price of one thing increases relative to the price of other things, they tend to buy less of the first and more of the other. For example, when the price of apples goes up relative to the price of bananas, typically people will buy more bananas and fewer apples. By purchasing fewer of the now relatively more expensive item, consumers reduce the impact of the price increase on their well-being.

Does the same type of phenomenon occur when the relative cost of doing research in the different disciplines changes at a university? The answer appears to be no if the fields in which research costs are rising rapidly are ones from which the university's reputation is largely derived.

Cornell's Strengths in the Physical Sciences and Engineering

Cornell has long been known for its strengths in the physical sciences and engineering. Indeed, four Cornell physics professors were awarded Nobel Prizes while they were members of the Cornell faculty. Several other winners in physics were faculty members at Cornell during parts of their careers or received undergraduate or graduate degrees at the university. The university currently also has a Nobel Prize–winning chemist on its faculty.

To take another example, during the 1997–98 academic year Cornell was host to six major national, federally funded physical science and engineering research centers: the Cornell High Energy Synchrotron Source, the Cornell Nanofabrication Facility, the National Science and Technology Center for Computer Graphics and Scientific Visualization, the Cornell Electronic Storage Ring/Newman Laboratory of Nuclear Studies, the Cornell Theory Center, and the National Astronomy and Ionosphere Center. The last is located in Arecibo, Puerto Rico. When federal officials schedule major reviews of the Arecibo facility during winter months, when the temperature is well below freezing and a foot or more of snow is on the ground in Ithaca, high-level Cornell administrators never complain about having to attend the meetings.

Finally, Cornell is always among the leading institutions in the nation in the levels of federal research funding it receives. A major source of funding for research in the physical sciences and engineering is the National Science Foundation. In recent years Cornell has often ranked first in the nation in terms of total National Science Foundation funding received by a university.

The Increasing Costs of Research

Over time, the cost to Cornell of doing research in these fields has increased substantially for a number of reasons. In the past, much research conducted by physical scientists and engineers was theoretical in nature. These mathematical modelers worked at their desks, and the only tools they needed were their minds and paper and pencils. But increasingly, scientists now rely on sophisticated laboratory facilities that are expensive to build and operate.

The federal government funds most of the research by Cornell's scientists and engineers. Through what is usually a competitive process, federal agencies, including the National Science Foundation, make grants to university faculty members to help support their research. These research grants have budgets for both the direct and the indirect costs of a project. Direct costs are those budget items that can be uniquely attributed to a research project. This category includes, but is not limited to, money to pay for faculty members' time during the academic year and in the summer, graduate research assistants, post-doctoral fellows, lab technicians, computers and other durable equipment, expendable equipment (such as chemicals), travel, communications, and clerical assistance.

Indirect costs are those research costs that the university incurs because it is a research university, but that cannot be easily assigned to any specific project. Included in indirect costs are expenses such as the cost of administering research incurred by the central university, the colleges, and the departments; depreciation on research equipment and the space in buildings used for research; the costs of maintenance and utilities for space used for sponsored research; and the portion of library costs that can be attributed to sponsored research on campus.

Each year Cornell, like other universities, estimates what its indirect costs are likely to be in the forthcoming year. It next estimates how much of its direct costs of research is likely to be funded by external grants and contracts. Following government directives, it subtracts from this latter figure estimates of the portion of the direct costs that are assumed to be unrelated to any indirect costs to obtain an estimate of its expected "modified total direct costs" in the year. These deductions include equipment costing more than $500, subcontracts that cost more than $25,000, and graduate student tuition payments. It then divides its estimated indirect costs by its estimated modified total direct costs to obtain a proposed indirect cost rate for the year.

For example, if a university estimated that it would have a modified total direct cost volume of $10 million and would incur $3 million in indirect cost expenses, it would divide 3 by 10 to arrive at an indirect cost rate for the year of .30, or 30 percent. This is the rate that it would need to "mark up" its modified total direct costs on each grant application to allow it to recover all of its indirect costs if its projections of its modified total direct cost volume and indirect cost expenses both proved accurate.

The university then makes a request to the federal government that this indirect cost rate be established for it for the year ahead. This is only a request and auditors from the government agency that is responsible for setting the rate for the institution and the institution itself pore over the data and eventually come to a negotiated agreement on what the actual rate will be. If the rate chosen turns out to generate more indirect cost recoveries during the year than expected, because the university had a higher volume of modified total direct costs than it anticipated, the excess amount that the university received in indirect cost recoveries will be deducted from its permissible recovery in following years until the excess is paid back. Thus the university's indirect cost rate during these subsequent years will be lower than the data for those years alone would justify. Many faculty members erroneously believe that a university is permitted to overrecover its indirect costs. Thus they argue that their grants impose no extra indirect costs on the university but generate extra indirect cost revenue for it and that they should be given a share of the indirect cost revenue to reward them for having received external grant funding.

Conversely, if the university underrecovers its indirect costs in a year, because its volume of modified total direct cost funding proved lower than expected, sometimes, but not usually, the university gets permission to carry forward the amount that it underrecovered to the next year. If this occurs, its indirect cost rate will temporarily be higher.

In a well-documented case during the early 1990s that involved Stanford University, government auditors alleged that items were being charged as indirect costs that were not legitimately related to research.[1] Much media attention was focused on this case because of allegations that Stanford had overcharged the federal government for its indirect cost recoveries by as much as $200 to 400 million over a ten-year period. The two parties ultimately settled the dispute by Stanford's agreeing to return to the government $1.5 million for the inappropriate recoveries it had been alleged to have received over the period. But since the university averaged over $200 million in federal research funding each year during those ten years, this repayment was not of any real consequence.

What was of consequence was that government auditors began to take a much harder look at what universities had been including as indirect cost expenditures. The auditors increasingly either disallowed items that previously had been allowed or simply "capped" the rates that they were willing to pay for some categories of indirect cost expenses, regardless of the actual expenditures that universities had incurred. The reduction in indirect cost rates that resulted was a second reason that the cost to Cornell of doing research in the sciences has increased.

The pressure to reduce indirect cost rates was felt primarily at private universities, such as the endowed portion of Cornell, where indirect cost rates tend to be higher than the indirect cost rates at public universities. The difference in rates between these two groups exists because the private institutions always have tried to document as much of the indirect costs that they are incurring, while the public institutions have tended to be less thorough in their documentation efforts. The public institutions have behaved this way because funding for their indirect cost items (administrative personnel, maintenance, building costs, libraries) often comes from state governments, which do not always require public universities to repay all of these expenses back to them if externally funded research is obtained by the universities. Since many faculty members believe that high indirect cost rates reduce their chances of winning grant competitions and the size of the direct costs they are awarded if they do win a competition, the public institutions believe that they have an incentive to hold their indirect cost rates down.[2]

The net result of this pressure is seen in Figure 6.1. After reaching a peak of 62 percent on July 1, 1990, the average indirect cost rate that was in effect at 39 major private research universities fell to 56 percent on July 1, 1997.

In contrast, the average indirect cost rate at 85 major public research universities remained roughly constant at 47 percent during this period. For every $10 million in modified total direct cost funding that a private university received from the federal government, the average indirect cost recoveries that the university received fell from $6.2 million in 1990 to $5.6 million in 1997. If a private university received modified total direct cost federal research funding of $100 million each year and had the average indirect cost rate in the group, it would find itself with $6 million a year less in indirect cost recoveries in 1997 than it received in 1990.

What would a university faced with such a reduction in indirect cost recoveries do? On the one hand, it might try to reduce its expenditure on research infrastructure to match the reduction in indirect cost funding that it was receiving. But such a strategy would alienate its faculty, who would see their support services for research declining. In addition, if the reductions that the university made were not in areas in which the university was already spending more than the federal government permitted it to charge, the federal auditors would respond by reducing allowable indirect cost recoveries even more in the next year. Hence, the university would get a dou-

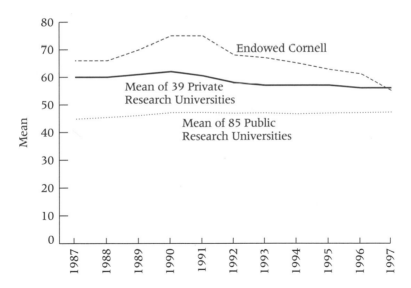

Figure 6.1. Indirect cost rates in effect on July 1, 1987–1997. (Source: Author's calculations from unpublished data provided by the National Science Foundation.)

ble whammy: irate faculty and still lower indirect cost revenue the next year.

On the other hand, the university might continue its expenditures on re-search infrastructure and seek other ways to find budget savings. Inevitably, this strategy would mean that some other activities at the university would have to "pay" for the decline in indirect cost recoveries through reductions in levels or rates of growth of expenditures. In practice, most private universities probably opted to pursue both strategies, leaving no one on the campus very happy. To the extent that undergraduate education was one of these other activities, the popular belief that undergraduates are increasingly bearing some of the costs of the research conducted at research universities has some validity.

At Cornell, the decline in the indirect cost rate was even more precipitous than the decline at the average private research institution. As Figure 6.1 indicates, between July 1, 1991, and July 1, 1997, the indirect cost rate in the endowed part of the university fell from 75 to 55.01 percent, a decline of almost 20 percentage points. Almost 3 percentage points of this decline occurred because during several years in the early 1990s the university achieved a higher level of federal grant funding than it had expected and thus it overrecovered its indirect costs.

For a number of years thereafter, the indirect cost rate that the university was allowed to charge was reduced so that the federal government could recover its overpayment of indirect costs during those earlier years. To the extent that the university had treated the extra indirect cost funds that it had received in the earlier years as a windfall and used them to help balance its budget in those years rather than sequestering them to protect against a probable mandated reduction in indirect cost recoveries in future years, the university probably behaved in a short-sighted manner and added financial stress to its budgets in the later years.

Most of the decline occurred, however, because of pressures put on the university by the federal agency that established Cornell's indirect cost rate. Allowable administrative costs at all levels of the university were capped at 26 percent by federal directive, and the university was initially spending more than that. The university had done special studies of space use to justify the fraction of depreciation, utilities, and maintenance costs that were charged as indirect costs to research grants. The federal auditors challenged the results of these studies and ultimately the fraction was reduced, which in turn reduced the university's indirect costs and its indirect cost rate.

It is customary in some universities, and especially at medical colleges, for faculty conducting research to fund at least part of their own salaries during the academic year from external grants and contracts. Cornell has never required this for faculty on its Ithaca campus because it views the research that faculty members conduct as part of their normal job responsibilities. Faculty in the physical sciences and engineering at Cornell are on nine-month contracts, and typically faculty members submitting grant applications do request funding for summer salaries for themselves.

The federal auditors pointed out that a university's total direct costs must include all of the time that its faculty members spend working on sponsored research projects, even if the university did not receive government funding for all of that time. In cases where faculty members did not report how much time they spent on sponsored research during the academic year, Cornell had assumed in its calculations that the appropriate percentage was about 5 percent of the faculty member's time. The auditors challenged this assumption, and to avoid having to do a formal study of how much time each faculty member actually spent during the academic year on sponsored research, the university agreed to increase its modified total direct cost base by about $7 million.

Since the endowed university's modified total direct costs were about $58.5 million at the time, adding $7 million more dollars to modified total direct costs reduced Cornell's indirect cost rate substantially. And since the actual modified total direct cost funding that the university received from the federal government had not changed, its total indirect cost recoveries fell. This occurred because some of the indirect cost expenses that it incurred now were assumed to be charged to the extra $7 million of time that the university agreed that the faculty had "contributed" to sponsored research. Hence the federal government's share of the university's indirect cost expenses fell.

The university thus found that, because it had generously shared the cost of research with the federal government by not including a portion of its faculty members' academic year salaries in their research grant applications, the federal government had reduced the university's indirect cost recoveries. The university did not consider this an appropriate response, and discussions were held about whether Cornell should ask faculty members to put requests for recovery of part of their academic year salaries in their grant applications. These discussions never got very far because faculty members were concerned that adding to the cost of their grants would make their grant applications less competitive with grant applications from the faculty at other universities.

Indirect cost recoveries in the endowed Ithaca budget in fiscal year 1997–98 were roughly $30 million. If the indirect cost rate in effect in 1997–98 had been the rate that was in effect in 1991–92, the endowed part of the university would have received 36 percent more indirect cost revenue (computed by dividing 75 by 55), or $40.9 million. Hence the reduction in Cornell's indirect cost rate "cost" the endowed budget $10.9 million dollars in 1997–98. Of course, some of this reduction was due to Cornell's over-recovery of indirect costs in earlier years.

Although part of the reduction in indirect cost recoveries was made up by reductions in the administration of research throughout the university, most was made up by not doing other things. For example, faculty salaries were not raised as much as they otherwise would have been, fewer new faculty members were hired, and tuition was increased at a higher rate than otherwise would have been the case.

In addition to reducing indirect cost rates, federal funding agencies, faced with tight federal budgets, began putting more pressure on Cornell and other universities to provide more "matching" funds as part of their research proposals. To be competitive for research grants, universities had to provide more of the direct costs for the projects themselves. This was a third factor that increased the universities' costs of doing research in the physical sciences and engineering.

At Cornell, this additional provision of direct costs often took the form of funding a portion of the tuition revenue for graduate students working as research assistants on external grants. When the university does this, it receives less external tuition revenue to fund its operations, and the impact of this reduction in revenue is felt throughout the university. In the case of grants to large national centers, bearing a share of the cost of the tuition revenue often was not sufficient for the federal agencies, and the university had to make increased commitments of funds to national centers, usually in the form of paying for staff or equipment. Several large national centers won renewal competitions for direct cost funding levels equal to or lower than the funding levels they had received in the previous funding round only after the university committed increased matching funds to the project. Anteing up an additional $500,000 in matching funds per center became almost automatic, and these were funds that could have been used for a host of other purposes by the university.

Finally, as scientists' equipment became more expensive and the competition for top-quality young scientists intensified, the "start-up" funds that the university needed to attract new physical scientists and engineers increased. By the late 1990s, it was not unusual to find the university providing $500,000 to $1,000,000 of funding to help young scientists set up their laboratories. The costs of attracting distinguished senior scientists were often even larger.

Costs Don't Matter

When I joined the Cornell administration, I suggested that if the increase in the costs of doing research in the physical sciences and engineering was expected to continue, then Cornell should seriously consider reducing its investments in engineering and the physical sciences and redirecting these saved resources to other areas. Only if the marginal importance to the university of being preeminent in these fields had also risen relative to the marginal importance of being strong in other areas should the university not consider doing this. Of course a university's reputation derives from the strength of its top departments, and it is often much harder to build a weak department than it is to maintain the strength of a top department. Hence any such reductions in Cornell's support of these fields should be applied only very gradually, with an eye kept on what other top universities were doing in the same area.

Even to suggest this in the presence of faculty from the physical science and engineering disciplines would have marked me as a very dangerous person in the administrative hierarchy. The notion of the university's backing away from the areas in which it had been traditionally strong was not something that any Cornell physical scientist or engineer would rationally be willing to entertain. After all, they could point out that all of Cornell's six Nobel Prize–winning faculty during the last thirty years had come from the fields of physics and chemistry.

Cornell's president, provost, and graduate school dean were all humanists, and neither I nor the other academic vice president came from the core physical sciences or engineering disciplines. Given the complaints by Cornell's physical scientists and engineers that they were not represented at the highest levels of the university's central administration, I suspect that neither the president nor the provost wanted to bear the heat of suggesting that Cornell should contemplate whether maintaining its relative investments in these areas made sense. Just as it took a Republican, Richard Nixon, to move the United States toward diplomatic relations with China and a Democrat, Bill Clinton, to end welfare as we knew it, Cornell will, I think, have to await a president who comes from the physical sciences or engineering before serious thoughts are given to reducing the university's emphasis on these areas.[3]

When I left my administrative position at Cornell, the vice president for research, an agricultural engineer, also stepped down. He was replaced by a triad of vice provosts for research. A Nobel Prize–winning physicist headed this group. It included a professor of applied and engineering physics, who also was head of one of Cornell's major research centers, and a biological scientist. The physical scientists and engineers finally had their desired representation at the highest levels of Cornell's central administration. One does not convince a Nobel Prize winner to become a senior central administrator by promising to deemphasize the areas in which he is interested.

An observant reader might note that I have said nothing so far above about the implications of the similarly rapidly rising costs of biological research. Perceptions of the relative benefits of being strong in biology have also increased because of the growing importance of biomedical research and the intellectual excitement caused by recent advances in microbiology and cell biology. If perceived relative benefits increase by more than perceived relative costs, an economist would predict that more, rather than fewer, resources should flow to biology. That is exactly what is occurring at many universities.

In the fall of 1998 Cornell's chemistry department emulated Harvard's chemistry department and changed its name to the Department of Chemistry and Chemical Biology. In part, this name change reflected the interests of several key faculty members in the Cornell department. In part, it reflected the perceptions of other faculty members that by aligning themselves with the biologists, they would have a stronger claim on future university resources.

I jokingly told friends at the time that I wished that there was a natural intersection between biology and economics so that economists could also attach themselves to the discipline that was likely to get increasing funding in the future. I then went to a professional association meeting in early 1999 and learned, much to my surprise, that sometimes wishes do come true. A new journal, the *Journal of Bioeconomics,* was founded in 1999. Its goal is to encourage dialogue between biologists and economists and to transfer concepts and tools between the two disciplines.

The publisher of this new journal has set the subscription price that it charges academic libraries at $200 a year. I think that I will recommend to Cornell's library system that Cornell acquire the journal so that our economists and biologists will be able to keep abreast of the latest research in the new field of bioeconomics. Of course the proliferation of new academic specialties and their literally thousands of new expensive academic journals increases the costs of research universities' libraries and puts further pressure on the institutions to increase tuition. I will discuss library costs in much more detail later.

CHAPTER 7

Staying on the Cutting Edge in Science

Deciding to Build a New Research Facility

To remain preeminent in the physical sciences and engineering requires state of the art facilities. In the spring of 1995, Cornell's engineering dean informed the central administration that to be at the cutting edge in research relating to electronic and photonic devices, biotechnology, and advanced materials processing, the university required a major new research facility. He added that unless a commitment was made to the facility in the near future and assurances were provided that it would be constructed by the year 2000, Cornell ran the risks of losing some of its top faculty and of finding it very difficult to recruit new faculty in these areas.

State of the art facilities are very expensive to construct, operate, and maintain. Hence when this issue was first raised, the administration stressed to scientists and engineers around the university that it probably could afford to build only one new science research facility during the next decade, and that they had better be sure that this was the one that would be most useful to them. Discussions were held with chairs of major science departments, with directors of all of Cornell's research centers, and with a group of faculty that provided advice to the vice president for research and advanced studies. No other competing proposal came forth and the conclusion was reached that if a building was to be built, this was the investment in science infrastructure that Cornell should undertake.

A very preliminary estimate of the cost of the project was in the $40 million range. Funding for a project of this magnitude must be obtained from external sources. So Cornell's development office conducted a feasibility study to determine if funding of that magnitude could be raised from individual, foundation, and corporate donors, as well as from state and federal government sources. The conclusion was reached that $40 million was possible, although by no means certain, that it would require considerable efforts to raise that sum, and that most of the funding would come from private donors, not from government. With this assurance that it would be feasible to raise the funds, the university administration committed the university to the project.

Of course, feasibility had to be converted into reality: the university had to actually raise the money to construct the building. Moreover, the Cornell trustees had long known that the presence of a new building adds to the operating and maintenance costs of the university. A rough estimate was that the funds needed annually to cover utility, custodial, and routine and planned maintenance costs of the building over its useful life would be around $1.6 million, or roughly 4 percent of the total cost of erecting the building. As was explained earlier, 4 percent also is roughly what Cornell and many other universities target as their annual payouts, after investment and administrative expenses, on endowment funds. Thus if no other sources of funds were found to meet these expenses, Cornell would have to raise an additional $40 million to establish an endowment to meet these expenses. Cornell's development staff was not happy when asked if it was also feasible to raise such an endowment.

The building was going to be used to conduct research that it was hoped that the federal government would fund through research grants, and such grants include indirect cost recoveries to pay for those very expenses. Hence there was hope that a large proportion of these necessary funds would come from indirect cost recoveries on research grants. However, the university's best estimate was that the indirect cost recoveries would cover at most one third of the necessary operating and maintenance funds for the proposed building. This estimate was an optimistic projection based on the university's then current indirect cost rate, the assumption that all the research space in the building would always be used to conduct research funded by the government, and the assumption that none of this research would otherwise have been conducted in existing facilities. As indicated earlier, the indirect cost rate in the endowed sector of Cornell, where the building would be "located," had fallen steadily between 1991 and 1995 (when discussions about whether to undertake the project were taking place). Hence assuming that the rate would remain constant was quite optimistic. In fact, as shown in Figure 6.1, between July 1995 and July 1997, the rate fell further from 62.75 percent to only slightly more than 55 percent.

As detailed planning for the content, design, and location of the building began, so did the fund-raising efforts. A major breakthrough occurred in

January of 1997 when it was announced that David A. Duffield, the founder and chief executive officer of PeopleSoft, Inc., a leading developer of software, had agreed to provide a $20 million gift to the university to aid in constructing the building. In gratitude, the university announced that the building would be named after Duffield, who had received both an under-graduate engineering degree and a master in business administration degree from Cornell.

Cornell's trustees have long required that a plan for meeting operating and maintenance costs be in place before construction of a new building can begin. But once a major donor has committed to funding half of the predicted costs of the building and it has been publicly announced that the building will be named after him, holding up construction on the building because an endowment for maintenance has not yet been raised is not an option. Cornell hoped that Duffield's gift would stimulate further giving by others, and it did, but there was no guarantee that the university would be able to raise the money to defray additional expected construction costs, let alone any extra costs that accrued because of cost overruns or changes in the project. So although the university hoped to raise at least some money to help endow a maintenance fund for the building, it instead planned to pay for much of the needed operating and maintenance that could not be funded by indirect cost recoveries by taking money out of its annual operating budgets.

Inevitably then, this new building will compete for funds with new faculty positions, additional supports for graduate students, and higher faculty salaries. Faculty members who vehemently argued that the institution needed the new facilities to remain preeminent in the physical sciences and engineering are likely to turn around and chastise the administration for spending too much on buildings and not enough on faculty salaries, new faculty positions, and graduate student support. Proposals for a moratorium on new construction on campus, which are suggested regularly by faculty groups, will reemerge. Many faculty members *do* understand the tradeoffs that exist between the costs of constructing buildings and other costs. But sometimes they articulate their understanding only after their unit's new building has been approved.

Deciding Where to Build the Facility

Once the decision had been made to build the new research facility, the next decision was where to locate it. Research in the building will often involve chemicals and other hazardous materials and substantial safety precautions must be included in the design of the facility. Although one might think that these facts would argue for an off-campus location that is safely far away from most faculty, students, and staff, the disadvantage of an off-campus location is that it separates faculty and graduate students conducting the research in the building from their colleagues. Indeed, since virtually all faculty conducting research at Cornell are also teaching undergraduates and graduates, an off-campus location, coupled with constraints on parking at Cornell (to be discussed later) simply would not be feasible. There was an available site that was approximately a one-quarter-mile walk from the main campus, but even that site was judged to be too far away by the likely users of the facility.

The discussion then shifted to whether the facility should be built on the main engineering college quadrangle or on the university's varsity baseball field, Hoy Field, which is directly across the street from the engineering college. Hoy Field was favored by many people associated with the project because it would "claim" extra space for the engineering college. This would provide room for expansion of the facility at a later date. Proponents of this location ignored that the field was one of the few "green spaces" remaining in that area of the campus (although only varsity baseball players could use it). Moreover, if the building were constructed there, the university would have to find a site for a new baseball field. The only available sites were off campus, and using one of them would have required construction not only of a field, but also of dressing facilities, seating for spectators, and lights. Thus locating the building on the field would create what economists call a negative externality—it would impose additional costs on the rest of the university.

Some opponents of the baseball field location also worried that the university would have trouble affording even the proposed building and that leaving open the possibility of future expansion also left open the possibility of further increases in the university's operating costs. At a time when concern was being expressed about limiting the rates of tuition increases, it seemed prudent to take steps to decrease costs rather than increase them. If the building were located on the engineering quadrangle itself, there would be little room for expansion.

Ultimately concern over taking green space and the historical significance of the baseball field to some important alumni carried the day. (The fact that Cornell's president was a former college baseball player—who had been offered a contract by the Baltimore Orioles' organization but had turned the offer down to pursue an academic career—had no impact on the decision.) The engineering college was told to plan for the building's being located on its quadrangle.

A team was assembled that consisted of a faculty representative, staff from Cornell's Planning and Construction group, financial officers of the college, and members of the Campus Planning Committee. External consultants were hired, various locations were considered, preliminary designs were developed for each location, and in the spring of 1998 a single location was chosen and recommended to the university. The college's faculty members were told of the decision and then all hell broke loose.

The faculty had been invited to participate more fully in selecting the building site. But by and large they had declined because of the demands of their teaching and research. Now many faculty members, primarily those in the departments that would not use the new facility, began to worry about their own interests and claimed that they had not been fully consulted. Some opposed the location on rather petty grounds, for example, what the erection of the building would do to their views. Others worried about having a facility in which hazardous materials were to be used located at the center of a college that contained a large number of faculty, staff, and students. Still others worried that the increased physical density of buildings on the engineering quadrangle would have an adverse impact on students' perceptions of the college. Faculty unrest prevented the project from going forward as planned.

The first five-year term of the engineering dean had ended, and he was reappointed with specific instructions to find a site that was agreeable to the college's faculty as a "whole." So the process continued. In the fall of 1998 discussions about where to site the building resumed, and by late November 1998 agreement was reached to locate the building on the engineering quadrangle, as had been originally proposed by the building's planning committee. But to achieve the support of enough of the college's faculty to approve the site, an atrium has been added to the facility and plans have been made to renovate more classrooms for departments that will not directly benefit from the new facility. As a result, the project budget has been increased from $40 million to $58.5 million.[1]

Does a system of shared governance between faculty and administration mean that the faculty members in the engineering college should have veto power over the location of a facility? If the faculty of the college had chosen the baseball field location and persuaded the administration that that location was preferable, should faculty from other colleges at the university have had the right to veto the decision because they would be losing a green space? More generally, is the decision of where to locate a building on campus one in which the faculty, either of the college involved or of the university as a whole, has more than an advisory role? Under the bylaws of the university, it is the trustees who have legal responsibility for deciding where to situate buildings and they take this authority very seriously.

As one key faculty member involved in the discussions at the college level remarked to me, the faculty does much of the important work of the university. If faculty members are upset about their working conditions, and the siting of the new building very much influenced the work environment of faculty in the engineering college, they may well focus on their own careers rather than on the well-being of the institution. Key faculty members in these fields are in demand elsewhere, and it is incumbent upon department, college, and university administrators to keep these faculty members involved and happy. So shared governance on these issues is essential at major research universities, regardless of which party has the formal legal responsibility to situate buildings on the campus.

Shared governance means a slow process. In November 1999, it was announced that construction was not slated to begin on Duffield Hall until early in 2001. Hence the chances that the new building would be constructed and open by the year 2000 were zero. The discussions that took place to win the support of the college's faculty for the building site delayed the progress of the project by at least six to nine months and substantially increased its costs. All of these additional costs are for things that will benefit students, but they will at least partly be financed by higher tuitions. The alternative of treating the original project budget as a binding constraint and requiring that additions to the project be offset by cutbacks in the original project was not judged possible.

The delay in the project's completion did not prevent a Cornell-based consortium of institutions from being awarded a five-year grant for $19 million in July 1999 by the National Science Foundation to establish a National Center for Nanobiotechnology.[2] Knowledge that Duffield Hall was in the works clearly was a major factor in the university's being awarded the grant. Cornell will contribute $7.3 million to purchase new equipment, to provide start-up funds, to pay for graduate students' tuition, fees, and fellowships, and to defray administrative expenses. Some of the "matching funds" that Cornell has committed are monies that the university would have spent for the same purposes anyway. But some are undoubtedly new expenditures. So getting the grant still further increased the university's costs.

PART IV

THE FACULTY

CHAPTER **8**

Salaries

Each year colleges and universities determine the average percentage increase in salaries that they will provide for their faculty members in the subsequent year. In many public institutions, the increase is determined by the state legislature or through a collective bargaining process. But collective bargaining for faculty is not permitted at most private colleges and universities as a result of the U.S. Supreme Court's decision in the Yeshiva University case, which essentially said that faculty members were managerial and thus not eligible for collective bargaining.[1] Consequently, in private institutions it is typically the central administration that makes the determination after consultation, often extensive, with the faculty.

The higher faculty salaries are, the easier it is for an institution to attract and retain high-quality faculty. So, other things being equal, central administrators want their faculty to be paid generously. Unfortunately, however, other things are not always equal. In particular, the number of faculty and staff and their salary levels are among the few items in the budget over which administrators have real discretion. At most private institutions, tuition revenue is the major source of funds for faculty salary increases that the institution controls. Hence in the absence of a willingness to cut the numbers of faculty and staff at an institution, there is an inevitable tradeoff between the administrators' efforts to moderate the rate of tuition increases faced by students and their efforts to provide generous salary increases for the faculty. Given their fiduciary responsibilities, administrators often swallow hard and, to maintain a balanced budget, recommend to the institution's trustees that they raise tuition by more and faculty salaries by less than students and faculty, respectively, want.

I describe below how Cornell determines what a reasonable level of faculty salaries is for its endowed faculty. Although faculty members in Cornell's state-assisted statutory colleges are not covered by a collective bargaining agreement, the university has little control over their salary increase pool. In most years, New York state provides Cornell with a salary increase

113

pool for these faculty members that is equivalent in percentage terms to what the state and the union representing all faculty members employed at the campuses operated by the State University of New York (SUNY) have negotiated. In contrast, the Cornell central administration unilaterally has the authority (after approval by the Cornell trustees) to determine faculty salaries for endowed faculty members.

The process of determining the endowed faculty salary increase pool involves, as on most private campuses, extensive discussions between the faculty and the administration. This often becomes an adversarial process and much administrative time is spent on these discussions. Inasmuch as academic administrators can be effective only if they have the support of the faculty, administrators make every effort to explain to faculty how and why they came to their decision. Put another way, good administrators know that it is important that faculty understand the motivation for the final administrative faculty salary recommendation, even if the faculty members are not entirely satisfied with what that recommendation means for their pocketbooks.

I take it to be a fundamental proposition of faculty life that at every university, faculty members believe their salaries are too low. I certainly believe that about my own salary now that I have returned to the faculty. While I was a member of the Cornell administration, my fellow administrators and I also believed that faculty salaries in both our endowed and statutory colleges were too low and made a determined effort to improve them.

Funding for our statutory faculty members' salaries comes from New York state and Cornell has little control over the size of the salary increase pool that the state provides. We were able, however, to generate about $500,000 in permanent utility cost savings one year through statutory college energy-conservation efforts at the statutory colleges. New York state permitted Cornell to use these funds to supplement statutory faculty salaries.

Even with this increment of funds, the salary funds provided to Cornell by New York state during the 1990s were not sufficient to maintain the level of statutory faculty members' salaries relative either to other institutions' faculty salaries or to faculty salaries in the endowed part of Cornell. In 1988–89, the average nine-month equivalent salary for Cornell statutory college full professors was about 91 percent of the average salary for Cornell's endowed college full professors. A decade later, this figure had fallen to only about 80 percent.

It is in the endowed part of Cornell that the central administration actually recommends the size of the faculty salary increase pool to the trustees. For a number of years, Cornell's central administration attempted to increase endowed faculty members' salaries, both relative to inflation and relative to competitor institutions' faculty salaries. In spite of the tremendous pressure that the university was under to limit tuition increases, the administration thought this was necessary because it had tracked faculty members' average salaries for a number of years and found that they had declined substantially relative to faculty salaries at other universities.

Table 8.1 presents data on the average nine-month salary for faculty at thirty-three major research universities during the 1997–98 academic year. These data are collected by the American Association of University Professors from almost all colleges and universities in the United States and are published every year in the association's journal. They are typically the focal point for the salary discussions conducted by faculty and administrative groups at institutions around the country. The institution's faculty and administration usually reach agreement on the institutions that are its competitors for faculty. They also often reach agreement on how the institution should rank, vis-à-vis these competitors, on faculty salaries. For example, a goal might be to keep the institution's average faculty salaries at the median of the group. The faculty and administration then track the institution's relative position over time and, on the basis of how that is changing, the faculty presents recommendations for salary improvement programs.[2]

Cornell is a heterogeneous university and it competes with a wide range of institutions for faculty. Over time the faculty and administration came to the conclusion that the thirty-two other institutions listed in the table are Cornell's most common competitors. Hence for a number of years Cornell has traced how its average faculty salaries compare to these institutions' average faculty salaries.

The data in Table 8.1 indicate that Cornell's endowed average faculty salaries ranked twentieth at the full professor level, fourteenth at the associate professor level, and ninth at the assistant professor level in 1997–98. At first glance, the rankings at the full and associate professor levels appear to be too low for a university that tied for sixth place in *USNWR* 1999 rankings of undergraduate programs and that has many Ph.D. programs that rank in the top ten in the nation. Some faculty also expressed concern that such low relative salaries left Cornell in danger of losing its best senior faculty.

This concern was magnified by the extent to which Cornell's average endowed faculty salaries had declined relative to the average salaries paid to

Table 8.1   Average salaries at selected research universities in 1997–98, by rank.

	Full professor		Associate professor		Assistant professor	
	Institution	Average salary	Institution	Average salary	Institution	Average salary
1	Harvard	116,800	Stanford	75,300	Pennsylvania	62,000
2	Stanford	111,000	MIT	70,300	Chicago	61,400
3	Princeton	110,300	Pennsylvania	69,700	MIT	61,000
4	Yale	108,400	NYU	68,400	Harvard	60,900
5	NYU	106,400	Chicago	68,000	Stanford	60,100
6	Chicago	106,000	Northwestern	67,400	Northwestern	58,500
7	Pennsylvania	104,600	Carnegie-Mellon	66,100	NYU	57,200
8	MIT	104,200	Michigan	65,900	Carnegie-Mellon	56,200
9	Columbia	103,600	Duke	65,800	Cornell (endowed)	56,200
10	Northwestern	101,400	Princeton	65,400	USC	55,900
11	Duke	100,900	Columbia	65,200	Duke	54,300
12	Georgetown	99,000	Rutgers	64,600	Michigan	53,000
13	Carnegie-Mellon	93,900	Harvard	64,300	Columbia	52,500
14	UC-Berkeley	92,700	Cornell (endowed)	64,200	UC-Berkeley	52,000
15	UCLA	92,600	USC	63,500	UCLA	52,000
16	Michigan	91,900	Georgetown	61,900	Dartmouth	51,800
17	USC	91,800	North Carolina	61,800	Johns Hopkins	51,300
18	Johns Hopkins	91,100	Virginia	61,300	Illinois	51,200
19	Virginia	90,900	Johns Hopkins	61,200	Princeton	51,000
20	Cornell (endowed)	89,900	UC-Berkeley	61,100	Wisconsin	50,600

faculty at the five highest-paying research universities in the country. Figure 8.1 displays how Cornell's average salary at each rank compared to the five highest-paying institutions' average salary at the rank during the 1987–88 to 1997–98 period. I had joined a new Cornell administration during the spring of 1995. Between 1987–88 and 1995–96, Cornell's average salary as a percentage of the average salary at the five highest-paying institutions had fallen from 86.1 to 80.7 at the full professor level, from 90 to 89.6 at the associate professor level, and from 93.1 to 87.6 at the assistant professor level. Hence it was clear to the new administration that corrective action was necessary. As Figure 8.1 indicates, by 1997–98 some improvement had occurred at each rank.

Table 8.1 (continued)

	Full professor		Associate professor		Assistant professor	
	Institution	Average salary	Institution	Average salary	Institution	Average salary
21	Rutgers	89,600	Dartmouth	60,700	Brown	49,700
22	Dartmouth	88,700	UCLA	60,700	Texas	49,700
23	North Carolina	86,000	Yale	60,500	Yale	49,700
24	Brown	85,900	Illinois	58,400	Maryland	49,300
25	Illinois	83,600	Brown	58,200	North Carolina	49,200
26	Penn State	83,100	Minnesota	57,500	Virginia	48,900
27	Texas	82,400	UC-Davis	57,000	Minnesota	48,600
28	UC-Davis	81,300	Maryland	56,100	UC-Davis	48,500
29	Maryland	81,000	Penn State	56,000	Georgetown	48,000
30	Minnesota	81,000	Wisconsin	55,500	Rutgers	47,800
31	Purdue	80,800	Purdue	55,200	U Washington	47,600
32	Wisconsin	73,900	Texas	53,700	Purdue	46,800
33	U Washington	73,000	U Washington	52,900	Penn State	45,800
	Cornell rank	20		14		8
	Cornell average relative to the average of the top five paying universities	.81		.91		.92

Source: American Association of University Professors, "The Annual Report on the Economic Status of the Profession, 1997–98, *Academe* 84 (March/April, 1998): appendix I.

One should be cautious, however, about drawing conclusions about the status of a university's faculty salaries from simple comparisons of average salaries by rank. These averages are for all faculty at the university (except those in medical school and health-related fields who are not included in the salary surveys). To the extent that salaries vary within an institution by discipline and the disciplinary composition of the faculty varies across institutions, these comparisons of broad average salaries may be misleading.

Table 8.2 presents average salary data for full professors and new assistant professors during the 1997–98 academic year for a set of land grant and state universities. These institutions are primarily large public institutions, but several private land grant universities (MIT and Cornell) are included in the set. This table suggests that faculty salaries vary widely across fields. In fields in which there are high-paying nonacademic employment opportunities, such as business and law, higher salaries must be paid to faculty to attract and retain them. Indeed, full professors in these two fields were paid between 23 and 39 percent more and assistant professors paid between 46 and 47 percent more than their average counterparts in all disciplines. Conversely, in fields in which high-paying nonacademic employment opportunities do not exist for Ph.D.'s, such as the humanities, faculty salaries are lower. Thus the data also show that in English, foreign language, philosophy, and history, average salaries of full professors were 11 to 12 percent below the averages across all disciplines, and at the new assistant professor level they were 19 to 21 percent less.

As a result of this variation in faculty salaries across fields, institutions that employ relatively large fractions of their faculty in high-paying fields appear to have higher average faculty salaries than institutions that employ relatively small fractions of their faculty in these fields. To see this, consider the following simple example. Suppose institution A has 100 faculty, consisting

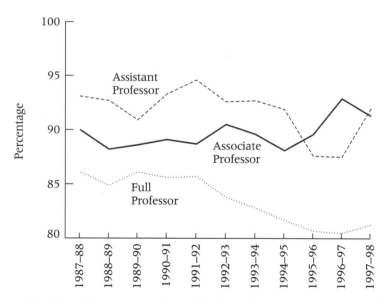

Figure 8.1. Cornell's average endowed faculty salaries as a percentage of the average salaries paid at the five highest-paying research universities, by rank, 1987–88 to 1997–98.

Table 8.2 Average salary for selected disciplines in state universities and
land grant colleges, 1997–98.

Discipline	Average salary[a]	
	Professors	New assistant professors
All disciplines	$76,309 (1.00)	$46,042 (1.00)
Agricultural sciences	64,510 (.85)	42,862 (.93)
Architecture	69,295 (.91)	40,595 (.88)
Business management	93,610 (1.23)	67,478 (1.47)
Computer and information sciences	87,600 (1.15)	57,480 (1.25)
Economics	85,498 (1.12)	53,100 (1.15)
Education	66,653 (.87)	39,168 (.85)
Engineering	86,249 (1.13)	52,024 (1.13)
English	67,216 (.88)	36,962 (.80)
Foreign language and literature	67,129 (.88)	37,148 (.81)
Law and legal studies	105,279 (1.39)	67,027 (1.46)
History	68,128 (.89)	37,228 (.81)
Life sciences	71,704 (.94)	43,874 (.95)
Mathematics	73,992 (.97)	42,543 (.92)
Philosophy	66,949 (.88)	36,442 (.79)
Physical sciences	77,429 (1.01)	42,794 (.93)
Political science	72,931 (.96)	41,283 (.90)
Psychology	73,783 (.97)	40,899 (.89)
Sociology	68,920 (.90)	39,924 (.87)

Source: Author's calculations from the Office of Planning, Budgeting, and
Institutional Research, Oklahoma State University, *1997–98 Faculty Salary Survey by
Discipline* (Stillwater, 1998).

a. The average salary of a discipline relative to the average salary across all
disciplines is in parentheses.

of 90 humanists and 10 lawyers, and that it pays these two types of faculty
average salaries of $40,000 and $70,000, respectively (which are close to the
actual national average salaries for new faculty in these disciplines in 1997–
98). The reported average salary for all new assistant professors at institution
A is 0.9 times $40,000 plus 0.1 times $70,000, or $43,000.

Now suppose institution B employs 100 faculty consisting of 70 humanists
and 30 lawyers, and pays faculty members in each discipline the same average salary that institution A does. Institution B's reported average salary
across disciplines would be 0.7 times $40,000 plus 0.3 times $70,000 or

$49,000. Institution B's average salary would exceed institution A's average salary by $6,000, or almost 14 percent—in spite of the fact that humanists were paid exactly the same average salary at the two institutions, and lawyers were also paid the same (higher) average salary at the two institutions.

Cornell's management and law schools are small, both in absolute size and in terms of their proportion of the total university faculty (excluding the medical college and other health sciences faculty), when compared to the sizes of these schools at many (but not all) of the institutions that have reported higher average salaries. In 1997–98, only 78 of Cornell's full-time endowed Ithaca campus 951 professorial faculty members were employed at Cornell's management and law schools. This means that only 8.7 percent of Cornell's faculty came from these two highest-paying disciplines. In contrast, using data obtained from their Web pages, I calculated that 24.3 percent of the University of Pennsylvania's, 13.3 percent of Stanford's, 25.6 percent of Harvard's, and 17.3 percent of Columbia's full-time professorial faculty were employed in these two fields that year (the Columbia data were for 1996–97). Hence one reason that Cornell's average faculty salaries may appear to be lower than its competitors is that the university hires relatively fewer faculty in high-paying fields than do many of its competitors.[3]

Perhaps a much more important reason is that the cost of living, especially housing prices, is lower in Ithaca, New York, than it is in many of the areas in which the institutions that pay higher salaries than Cornell are located. Table 8.3 lists the locations of the nineteen institutions from Table 8.1 that had higher average salaries for full professors in 1997–98. Most of them are located in, or are near, some of our nation's largest cities, where the cost of living is likely to be considerably higher than in Ithaca. In judging the appropriate level for Cornell faculty salaries, the Cornell administration needs to understand how the cost of living varies across areas.

To ascertain this, Cornell periodically hires a firm to compute comparative cost-of-living estimates for Cornell and its competitors. This firm has a division that computes how executive salaries should be changed when firms relocate their executives to different parts of the country, to make sure the executives do not suffer economic losses from the moves. Although there are problems with their methodology, I think it is about as good as anyone can expect. Indeed, as I indicated earlier, *USNWR* uses average faculty salaries as one of its measures of the resources that an institution devotes to educating students in their ranking system of colleges and universities, and it now similarly adjusts average faculty salaries for cost-of-living differences.

Table 8.3   Locations of the nineteen universities whose average salaries for full professors were higher than Cornell's in 1997–98.

Rank	University	Location
1	Harvard	Cambridge, MA (Boston area)
2	Stanford	Palo Alto, CA (San Francisco area)
3	Princeton	Princeton, NJ
4	Yale	New Haven, CT
5	NYU	New York, NY
6	Chicago	Chicago, IL
7	Pennsylvania	Philadelphia, PA
8	MIT	Cambridge, MA (Boston area)
9	Columbia	New York, NY
10	Northwestern	Evanston, IL (Chicago area)
11	Duke	Durham, NC
12	Georgetown	Washington, DC
13	Carnegie-Mellon	Pittsburgh, PA
14	UC-Berkeley	Berkeley, CA (San Francisco area)
15	UCLA	Los Angeles, CA
16	Michigan	Ann Arbor, MI
17	USC	Los Angeles, CA
18	Johns Hopkins	Baltimore, MD
19	Virginia	Charlottesville, VA

USNWR uses the same firm to compute comparative cost-of-living estimates that Cornell does.[4]

The cost-of-living indices that are computed for individual institutions are proprietary—after all, the firm producing them makes money selling the exact same information over and over again to different institutions. Hence I am not at liberty to disclose the relative cost-of-living levels in specific areas. I can, however, provide a summary of how the cost of living in Ithaca, New York, compared in 1996 (the last year that Cornell purchased such data while I was a vice president at Cornell) with the cost of living in the areas in which the other institutions were located.

Only three of the nineteen institutions were located in areas in which the estimated cost of living was either less than, or no greater than 5 percent more than, that in Ithaca. Another eight were in areas in which the cost of living was estimated to be 5 to 15 percent higher than in Ithaca. Still another eight were in areas in which the cost of living was estimated to be between 15 and 43 percent higher than in Ithaca. Not surprisingly, my fellow administrators and I concluded that although our faculty salaries needed to be improved, a large fraction of the difference between our faculty members' salaries and those at competitor institutions could be explained by Ithaca's lower cost of living.

Faculty members on the faculty budget committee that meets with the Cornell administration tend not to be economists. They viewed our attempts to correct for the cost of living as an administrative ploy to avoid raising their salaries more rapidly. One faculty leader also insisted that we should compare the salaries of Cornell's endowed faculty only to the salaries of faculty at other private universities; in short, he wanted us to remove from consideration all of the public institutions listed in Table 8.1.

Four public institutions paid higher average salaries at the full professor level than Cornell did in 1997–98 (Berkeley, UCLA, Michigan, and Virginia). But only two of the thirteen institutions that paid lower average full professor salaries that year were private (Dartmouth and Brown). The net effect of dropping public institutions from the comparison group would be to change Cornell's rank in terms of average full professor salaries from 20 out of 33 to 16 out of 18. This change would make Cornell's endowed faculty salaries look even poorer in relative terms and in need of even greater improvement. The faculty leader argued that restricting the comparison group to private universities was appropriate because the endowed colleges at Cornell face economic pressures that are more similar to the economic pressures that other private institutions face than they are to the economic pressures faced by public institutions. Put simply, he argued that Cornell's "ability to pay" endowed faculty salaries should be judged relative only to other private universities' ability to pay.

I explained to him, as I discussed earlier, that it is well known that over the last twenty years the salaries of faculty at public research universities have fallen relative to the salaries of faculty at private research universities. But I also showed him that in virtually all disciplinary fields in which Cornell hires faculty in its endowed units, 40 to 60 percent of the leading departments with which it competes are in public institutions. I also presented him with data showing that when faculty members leave the endowed part of Cornell, they often move to public institutions, and that prospective faculty members who turn down offers from our endowed colleges often do so to accept appointments at public universities.

Taking all these facts together, I argued that using only the other private universities as a comparison group made Cornell's competitive position look worse than it actually was because the public universities also compete with Cornell's endowed colleges for faculty. Indeed, the very fact that the endowed part of Cornell competes with public universities for faculty was the reason why a previous faculty budget committee and the Cornell administration had agreed that the broader set of thirty-two private and public universities was the relevant comparison group.

"Institutional memory" often proves elusive when it does not support the position of one of the parties in a discussion. All of my arguments fell on deaf ears. Perhaps they did so because I was wrong. Perhaps they did so because as a faculty member who temporarily held an administrative position, I was perceived as being the enemy. Perhaps they did so because the faculty member in the faculty leadership position was up for reelection to his leadership position and was trying to appear to be a militant leader to enhance his chances for reelection.[5] Sadly for him, his faculty colleagues later decided that new leadership was in order.

The faculty and the administration both observed, from looking at the data, that Cornell's faculty salaries were most competitive at the assistant and associate professor ranks and lag behind the competition the most at the full professor rank. Part of the reason for this is that a much greater percentage of Cornell's assistant professors were employed in Cornell's high-paying management and law disciplines than were the faculty more generally. Only 8.7 percent of all endowed Cornell faculty members were employed in these two high-paying fields in 1997–98, but 18 of the 137 assistant professors, or 13.1 percent, came from them.

Even if we ignore this discrepancy, it is not surprising that Cornell's assistant and associate professors are paid relatively more vis-à-vis their counterparts at competitor institutions than their full professor colleagues. It is at the former two ranks that Cornell competes most strenuously to attract new faculty and retain existing faculty, and to do so it has to "meet the market." I dared not show the faculty committee my own research of a decade earlier, which indicated that the sensitivity of faculty turnover to relative salaries is higher for assistant professors than it is for associate professors and higher for associate professors than for full professors.[6] This occurs because as faculty members age and move into higher ranks, they often become "tied" to their communities. As a result, the cost to them and their families of moving to another university increases substantially, and their salaries must decline more, in relative terms, before they seriously consider moving to another institution.

Thus Cornell's deans, who allocate salary increases to the faculty, are behaving perfectly rationally when they pay their assistant and associate professors relatively more than they pay their full professors vis-à-vis faculty at other universities. In effect, they are exploiting the reduced willingness of senior faculty to incur the monetary and psychological costs of moving to other institutions.

Several of the competitor institutions that pay considerably more than Cornell at the full professor level compete vigorously for senior faculty with high-quality competitor research institutions located nearby. For example, MIT and Harvard are both located in Cambridge, Massachusetts, Northwestern and Chicago in the Chicago area, Berkeley and Stanford in the San Francisco area, UCLA and USC (University of Southern California) in Los Angeles, and Columbia and NYU (New York University) in New York City. Within each pair, each institution risks losing senior faculty to the other if it does not maintain sufficiently high senior faculty salaries, because a faculty member can shift from one institution to the other without having to physically relocate his or her family. The presence of a nearby competitor reduces, but does not eliminate, the ability of an institution to hold down senior faculty members' salaries because a senior faculty member from one institution in an area will not always find a suitable position at the other institution in the area. Moving to more distant institutions would impose considerable costs on the faculty member.

Cornell is "centrally isolated" in Ithaca, New York, and thus its deans encounter much less competition for faculty from nearby institutions. When they face the possibility of losing a desired senior faculty member who they believe is willing to move away, they have the flexibility to respond with a salary adjustment for that specific faculty member.[7] As a result, the university's overall turnover rate for tenured faculty members (excluding retirements) has been less than 1.5 percent a year for over a decade. Any corporation would be delighted to have such a low turnover rate for its skilled employees. The deans also have the flexibility to pay salaries that are high enough to attract senior faculty that departments are trying to recruit from other institutions.

The vast majority of Cornell's endowed faculty members are full professors. The vast majority of faculty members on Cornell's faculty budget committee are also full professors. It is not surprising that the faculty committee recommended that the salary increase pool that the university delivered to them should be heavily weighted toward full professors. Not surprisingly they wanted the average percentage increase granted to full professors to be larger than the average percentage increase granted to associate and assistant professors.

When I was in the administration, I did not have the heart to tell them that such a policy probably was not in the university's best interests. The federal law that eliminated mandatory retirement for tenured faculty, which took effect in January 1994, means that tenured senior professors are likely to remain employed for longer periods of time at the university. Hence higher salary increases granted to senior professors will remain part of the university's total faculty salary obligations for longer periods of time. To generate funds to pay competitive salaries for younger faculty and to provide funds for the hiring of new faculty may require the university to look much more closely at the salaries that it pays to its full professors.

CHAPTER 9

Tenure and the End of
Mandatory Retirement

Sometimes changes in laws confer benefits on employees. One such change was the 1987 amendments to the Age Discrimination in Employment Act. Effective January 1, 1994, the act prevents academic institutions from requiring that tenured faculty members retire. The award of tenure, which previously provided a faculty member with a form of job security until the institution's mandatory retirement age, effectively became a lifetime benefit.

Legislation that benefits employees does not always benefit employers. Consequently, employers often take actions to try to mitigate the costs that the legislation imposes on them. For example, in the face of minimum wage increases, employers may respond by reducing the number of employees they hire or by trying to limit their new hires to higher-quality workers. When the employer is a university and the employees are tenured faculty, the ability of the employer to take actions to reduce the cost-increasing effects of the legislative change are limited by the system of sharing governance among the faculty, the administration, and the trustees that exists at universities.

Although the 1987 amendments to the Age Discrimination in Employment Act had eliminated mandatory retirement for most American employees in 1987, higher education was exempted from the legislation for seven years to give academic institutions an opportunity to frame policies to deal with the end of mandatory retirement. The higher educational community had convinced Congress that it faced unique problems in adjusting to the end of mandatory retirement because of the large number of American professors who have tenure. Very few higher educational institutions actually used the seven years to set new policies. Cornell, for example, did not seriously confront the issue until I joined its administration in 1995.

Typically, a faculty member at an institution of higher education is evaluated for tenure during his or her sixth year as an assistant professor. The assistant professor's research, teaching, and service to the university, the profession, and the public are evaluated first by tenured faculty colleagues in their department, next by the college, and finally by the central administration. The weights in the evaluation process that are given to each faculty role depend upon the nature of the institution and the faculty member's appointment. A positive recommendation from the central administration then goes to the board of trustees of the institution, which at most institutions has the legal authority to confer tenure.

Once a faculty member is awarded tenure, he or she may be dismissed only for "just cause" and only after a process that assures that the faculty member receives "due process" and that judgments about the faculty member's performance are made by the faculty member's tenured faculty peers. Tenured faculty members may also be dismissed if economic conditions warrant the closure of their school, department, or program, but only as a last resort and only after all other responsible means for dealing with the problem have been exhausted.[1]

The basic goal of a tenure system is to protect faculty members' academic freedom and to allow scholarship on controversial subjects of inquiry to flourish. The importance of the tenure system was brought home to me personally during the late 1970s. When I was being considered for promotion to full professor, three Cornell trustees who were prominent members of the organized labor movement tried to block my promotion. They did so because they thought that testimony that I had given in a state regulatory proceeding had negatively influenced the economic well-being of a group of unionized workers in New York state. By contesting my promotion, they were hoping to discourage me, as well as other academics, from taking similar positions in the future.

Fortunately, Cornell is a truly great university, and its president at the time, Frank H. T. Rhodes, pointed out to the trustees as a group that although they have the ultimate authority in tenure and promotion cases, they should not challenge the academic judgments of experts in the field. After a brief discussion, my promotion went through. This experience left me with a profound appreciation of the meaning of academic freedom and the importance of the tenure system.[2]

The elimination of mandatory retirement for faculty has led to concerns about the continued viability of the tenure system. Some observers envision an aged, nonproductive set of faculty members protected by tenure adversely affecting the quality of teaching and research that goes on at colleges and universities. Others worry that if faculty members are exempt from mandatory retirement, they will fail to retire at "reasonable" ages, and that this will restrict the flow of new faculty members into academia. This, in turn, will discourage the next generation of scholars from entering Ph.D. programs. It will also limit the ability of academic institutions to diversify their faculty along ethnic, gender, and racial lines, to hire faculty with new ideas and new approaches, and to reallocate resources to new or exciting areas of inquiry and to fields that students want to see expanded.

This elimination of mandatory retirement for faculty also came at a time of diminished federal and state support for higher education, along with corporate downsizing, increased layoffs, and a general decline in job security for American workers. Is it any wonder, then, that the public and state legislatures in a number of states have called for a reexamination of the tenure system and the development of formal post-tenure review systems? Properly defined systems of post-tenure review are fully consistent with the tenure system and a committee of the American Association of University Professors recently issued a statement on post-tenure review which emphasizes that tenure does not imply a lack of accountability for one's performance.[3] One well-publicized attempt by the trustees at the University of Minnesota to unilaterally impose limitations on faculty tenure resulted in a effort to form a faculty union, which very nearly succeeded, even after the trustees had withdrawn their proposal.

Concerns about the abolition of mandatory retirement are probably unfounded at most institutions. Many academic institutions make heavy use of part-time and other non–tenure-track faculty, and for these institutions mandatory retirement is simply not an issue. In 1993, the percentage of part-time faculty at U.S. institutions of higher education was over 40, and this percentage had been steadily increasing for more than twenty-five years. The use of part-time and other non–tenure-track faculty is highest at two-year colleges and at four-year institutions that do not grant doctoral degrees.[4]

At many academic institutions, those faculty members who do have tenure also behave in a manner that is similar to other American workers when it comes to retirement: They look forward to retirement, and hence the abolition of mandatory retirement is unlikely to affect the ages at which most faculty retire. Several studies undertaken in the early 1990s before the abolition of mandatory retirement concluded that its abolition would probably affect only major research universities, where faculty members (including me) are often so tied to their work that they cannot conceive of leaving their positions unless compelled to do so.

Cornell is an example of such an institution. In the endowed part of Cornell, before the abolition of mandatory retirement, two thirds of the faculty retired before reaching the age of seventy, and the other one third retired when compelled to do so at the age of seventy. Since January 1, 1994, it appears that the behavior of the former group has not changed, but the behavior of the latter group has. Many members of the latter group have tended to stay on well past the age of seventy.

Many of the faculty members staying on beyond age seventy are among Cornell's best and brightest faculty and the university is delighted to have them continually associated with it. When they continue to draw a salary, however, the flow of new faculty into the university is slowed down, and there is less money available to increase the salaries of other continuing faculty members each year. When a senior faculty member retires and is replaced by a lower-paid younger faculty member, the difference between the two salaries can be redistributed to other faculty in the form of salary increases, but when the senior faculty member does not retire that money is not available for redistribution.

Calculations done by my staff and me when I was a vice president indicated that before the end of mandatory retirement Cornell was generating the equivalent of about a 1.4 percent salary increase for continuing full professors in its endowed colleges each year owing to retirements. If, on average, retirements were postponed five years, the size of this salary increase would fall to about 1.1 percent. A reduction in the annual salary increase of this magnitude may not seem to be very significant. But by the end of a thirty-year career, a faculty member's salary would be almost 10 percent lower with these reduced annual increases than it would have been with the slightly higher annual increases.

Similarly, our calculations indicated that a five-year delay in the ages at which faculty members retire would reduce the rate at which the university could hire new faculty by about 10 percent. Because the administration judged that both of these changes would not be in the university's best interests, a joint faculty-administration committee was appointed with me as chair in the fall of 1995 to decide what Cornell's response to the abolition of mandatory retirement should be.

Responses to the abolition of mandatory retirement are conditioned by the nature of a university's retirement program for faculty. Many of Cornell's statutory college faculty members historically had been covered by a *defined benefit* pension plan provided by New York state. Under such a plan, faculty members are promised an annual pension benefit that depends on their age at retirement, years of service, and salary level. It is straightforward to show (this is done in the Appendix) that defined benefit plans can be structured in such a way as to encourage retirement and that early-retirement programs can be developed that provide further incentives for retirement. Evidence suggests that early-retirement programs for University of California faculty, who have a defined benefit plan, did prove effective during the early 1990s.[5]

In contrast, Cornell's endowed college faculty and most of its recently hired statutory faculty are covered by a *defined contribution* pension plan. Under such a plan, the employer contributes a specified percentage of the faculty member's salary to a retirement fund for the faculty member. Over time, the fund generates nontaxable earnings that, along with each year's new contributions, are reinvested in the fund. When the faculty member retires, the assets in the fund provide retirement benefits for him or her.

Unlike defined benefit pension plans, defined contribution pension plans cannot be structured in a way to provide financial incentives for a faculty member to retire. In addition, it is more difficult to build effective early-retirement incentives into them. Readers interested in learning why these statements are true can refer to the Appendix.

The preliminary report of the joint faculty-administration committee on the transition of faculty to emeritus status (henceforth the "transition committee") was circulated to the Cornell community in April of 1997. The committee had been instructed to rule out the option of expensive buyout plans because evidence from a number of campuses suggested that such plans are not cost effective when faculty are covered by a defined contribution retirement system. Because the majority of Cornell faculty are currently retiring before their seventieth birthdays, any plan that paid people to retire before the age of seventy would be paying the vast majority of faculty for doing what they would have done without extra compensation anyway.

The committee's first set of recommendations dealt with financial planning over the life cycle. The committee wanted financial resources not to be a constraint for those faculty members who wished to contemplate retirement at the age of seventy or earlier. In the absence of additional resources to increase the university's contribution to faculty retirement plans, a cost-efficient strategy is to provide financial planning assistance to faculty over their life cycles to assure that they make informed investment decisions with respect to the assets in their retirement accounts. The committee was also concerned that only about half of Cornell's faculty participated in tax-deferred supplementary retirement accounts (SRAs) and that only 2 percent of those who did contributed the maximum amount permitted by law to such accounts.

Hence the transition committee recommended that faculty members be given information on the importance of taking advantage of tax-deferred savings opportunities. The committee also recommended that faculty members be regularly informed that, owing to the power of compound interest, savings early in the career would have a greater impact on wealth at retirement than savings later in the career.

A second set of recommendations viewed retirement planning from the perspective of the academic unit and urged faculty to discuss with chairs or college officials what their plans are as they approach what typically are the latter years of the faculty life cycle. The ability of an academic unit to plan for its future depends upon its having a sense of when its faculty members plan to retire, especially since the recruitment of replacement faculty is often a multiyear process. These discussions should take place, of course, in full recognition that the individual's decision to retire is a voluntary one, protected by federal and state law.

Still viewing things from the perspective of academic units, the committee thought that the abolition of mandatory retirement increased the importance of making sure that tenure does not imply a lack of accountability. Hence it recommended that steps be taken to assure that faculty workloads are equitably distributed across all departmental faculty and that annual salary increases are awarded judiciously throughout a faculty member's life cycle to match the individual's productivity.

A third set of recommendations dealt with allowing faculty to "phase" into retirement. The university had a long-established phased retirement program that allowed faculty in the endowed part of the university to move to half-time appointments, typically for five years, during which time they would receive half salary but full health benefits and full retirement system contributions. Upon signing an agreement to enter into such a program, the faculty member voluntarily agrees to give up tenure and retire at the end of the period. This plan dated back to the time when sixty-five was the mandatory retirement age, and it needed to be revised to conform to the new federal law. It also needed to be extended to faculty in the statutory part of the university.

The transition committee recommended extension of the program with a five-year maximum term for the half-time appointments. In addition, it specified that after an initial period in which all faculty would be eligible to participate in such agreements if they were at least fifty-five and had at least ten years of service at the institution, eligibility for the plan should be restricted to faculty who were below the age of seventy. The reason for such a restriction is that it provides an incentive for faculty to begin the retirement process before the age of seventy.

A final, and probably the most important, set of committee recommendations was to greatly enhance the status of emeritus professors so that becoming an emeritus professor would be seen as a natural and desirable stage of one's career rather than as being "put out to pasture." These recommendations included providing small research stipends ($2,000 per year) for five years to emeritus faculty, guaranteeing them at least shared office space, allowing them to maintain virtually all of the privileges of active faculty members, increasing their involvement in part-time post-retirement teaching, enhancing the status of the emeritus professors' association, and encouraging emeritus faculty to become involved in volunteer activities on the campus and in the local community.[6]

At the time, the university was facing tight financial circumstances and the issue arose of where to find the funds for the small research stipends. The committee suggested capping university contributions into the defined contribution retirement plan after some point in a faculty member's career as a way of helping to free up the funds. One proposal was to cap university contributions after thirty-seven years. This is the maximum number of years of service credit for retirement purposes that faculty members could accrue under the statutory college defined benefit plan. The typical assistant professor at Cornell began his or her career between the ages of thirty and thirty-five, and the mean age of retirement in the university for faculty has been in the range of sixty-five to sixty-eight. Thus the only faculty who would see the university's contributions stopped if Cornell capped contributions to its defined contribution retirement plan after thirty-seven years would be those who started careers early at the university and postponed retirement until older ages.

Cornell's endowed retirement plan was established in July of 1976 and it provides for the university to contribute 10 percent of the faculty member's salary each year into the faculty member's retirement account. At the time the plan was adopted, faculty members were compelled to retire at the age of sixty-five, which was also the age at which full social security benefits could be received. The existence of mandatory retirement meant that there was a de facto cap on the total number of years of contributions that the university would make.

The increase in the mandatory retirement age to seventy in 1978, and then its abolition effective on January 1, 1994, meant that Cornell was contributing to its faculty retirement plan for a larger number of years than framers of the retirement plan had originally intended. To the extent that faculty members retire at later ages, retirement benefits will be higher as a percentage of the retiree's final salary than had been anticipated. Of course, the age at which full social security benefits can be received is gradually being increased and will reach age sixty-seven within twenty years. Hence some increase in the number of years of Cornell's contributions would be required to maintain the same level of expected retirement income for faculty who retire before the age at which full social security benefits can be received. However, to achieve this does not require contributions to be made indefinitely by the university.

The faculty response to the transition committee report was one of indignation. The report's mention of matching productivity and salary increases over the life cycle was assumed to be a statement disparaging senior faculty and to smack of ageism. The committee quickly dropped this recommendation from its final report.

The faculty also thought that the "carrots" that had been proposed were too small; Congress had made tenure truly indefinite and, from their perspective, the university had to "buy out" their property rights if it wanted them to retire. Although they were correct that Congress had given them an enhanced "property right," the notion that the university in its role as an employer could take actions to try to offset the effects of the change in the law was foreign to many of them. Economists who evaluate the effects of changes in federal policies such as the minimum wage often argue about what the magnitudes of employer responses actually are; but no economist questions the right of employers to respond. In general, faculty members do not think like economists, and some faculty even asserted that if the university tried to pursue policies to encourage voluntary retirement it would be violating the intent of the federal law.

Indeed, faculty response to the one remaining "stick" in the interim report, limitations on retirement contributions, is instructive. Many saw these limitations as an attempt to cut total faculty compensation, even though it was explicit that any money saved would be used to provide benefits for emeritus faculty. Most did not comprehend that the contribution rates chosen by universities for their faculty members' retirement accounts are based on a number assumptions, including the expected age of retirement. If faculty members were retiring at later ages, a smaller contribution rate would fund any desired annual annuity, both because the annuity would be paid out over a smaller number of years and because the savings in the account would experience tax-free compound returns over a longer number of years. But the faculty saw the contribution rate, rather than the implied annual pension benefit, as something that was due to them. Ultimately, given faculty perceptions that their salaries were too low, the committee, with the agreement of the Cornell administration, did not include this proposal in its final report.[7]

The administration had promised that the faculty senate would also get a chance to comment on the committee's final report and it did. Members of the senate argued that rather than a phased retirement program in which one had to agree to voluntarily relinquish tenure at the end of the period, they preferred the option of going to part-time tenured appointments indefinitely. Members of the committee explained to them that such appointments, while possible at any time if the deans agreed, were not retirement programs. The committee stressed that it believed such an option would prolong active faculty careers rather than shortening them, and would not aid departments in planning for replacements. The provost also made it clear that he did not support such an option.

The faculty senate then urged the provost to eliminate the upper age limit for eligibility for the phased retirement program, arguing that it discriminated against older faculty and would discourage, rather than encourage, the use of phased retirement. The committee did not believe that voluntary retirement incentive programs that have age restrictions of the type proposed above are in violation of the law. Many institutions already had retirement incentive programs in which the magnitude of the "retirement bonus" that a faculty member receives varies inversely with the age at retirement and falls to zero at a specified upper age.

It was somewhat unclear at the time whether age-based incentives to encourage retirement were legal. Because of this, the college and university community had sought legislation since 1994 that would explicitly recognize the legality of such incentive plans for tenured faculty. A provision to accomplish this was included in the 1998 bill that extended the Higher Education Act. The legislation was later passed by both Houses of Congress and signed by the President in October 1998.

The compromise language in this bill made clear that the legality of age-based incentives to encourage retirement would apply only to tenured college professors. Typically the age of seventy is specified as the maximum age of eligibility under such incentive programs, and the bill also requires that all professors over seventy at the time of the bill's enactment would have six months to decide if they wanted to take advantage of such an incentive. Finally, it required that any professor who turned seventy and was ineligible to take advantage of such an incentive before that date because he or she had not met the minimum service requirement must become eligible for a six-month period as soon as the minimum service requirement was met.

Cornell's provost issued his "Provost's Policy Statement on the Transition of Faculty to Emeritus Status" on May 8, 1998. The university policy that was spelled out in this statement closely followed the recommendations of the committee. In particular, it included the phased retirement policy recommended by the committee because this policy already met all of the conditions required in the bill before Congress.

The astute reader will quickly realize that the policies ultimately adopted by the university contained all "carrots" and no "sticks." This should not come as a surprise to anyone other than a naive observer. The system of shared governance that is in place at most major academic institutions makes it highly unlikely that academic administrators will take actions to which the faculty as a whole, as represented at Cornell by the faculty senate, violently objects. The faculty members on the committee that drew up the proposed policies were all appointed by the faculty senate. Thus the faculty senate both shaped the initial proposals and then weakened them.

To achieve a stronger policy that included language that explicitly indicated that faculty were accountable for their performance over the life cycle would have required an additional party to participate in the deliberations, namely Cornell's trustees. Involving trustees in campus decisions that relate to academic matters is a risky business. To paraphrase a former Cornell president, "Trustees should keep their noses in but their fingers out." Cornell's president and provost had decided, wisely in my view, that the issue of how the administration would confront the end of mandatory retirement was not crucial enough to the university to warrant intense involvement of the trustees. The trustees were kept informed of the discussions, and the committee's preliminary and final reports were given to them for their comments. But they were not asked to approve the administration's decisions.

PART V

SPACE

CHAPTER 10

Deferred Maintenance, Space Planning, and Imperfect Information

Deferred Maintenance

America's colleges and universities face staggering deferred maintenance needs. By one estimate, over $26 billion in building repair needs existed in the mid-1990s.[1] How did such a backlog of facilities needs arise? How does an academic institution finance such repairs? Where does it put people and programs "evicted" from buildings when facilities must be emptied before repairs or renovations can be undertaken? And how does it mediate all of the tensions caused when units are asked to move around the university?

As any owner of a home knows, houses and all of the systems within them must constantly be maintained. My wife and I bought our house almost twenty years ago. Since the purchase date, the outside of the house has been painted numerous times, the inside has been painted twice, one roof has been torn off and a new roof installed, a stone patio and retaining wall have been repaired and then completely replaced, virtually all major appliances have been replaced (refrigerator, oven, dishwasher, washer, dryer, garbage disposal), the electrical system has been upgraded to handle increased loads, a furnace has been replaced, and central air conditioning has been installed. Some of these changes, for example the installation of the air conditioning, have changed the way that we use our home (we no longer have to rush out to restaurants that have air conditioning when the temperature reaches 90 degrees). Most, however, simply allowed us to keep our home operating the way it did when we purchased it. We also, of course, periodically have plumbers, electricians, and major appliance repair people visit our home when something "fails" and needs to be repaired rather than replaced.

Academic institutions face the same problems with their buildings. Routine maintenance includes quickly repairing broken windows, leaks, or problems with heating systems. Preventive activities are also undertaken, for example replacing filters in heating devices and oiling mechanical parts to try to prevent serious problems from arising. Finally, planned maintenance also includes replacing systems when their useful life is judged to be near an end and before they fail and can no longer be repaired.

Table 10.1 provides estimates made for Stanford University during the late 1980s of the useful life of various systems that are included in an academic building. A building's roof was estimated to have a useful life of fifteen to forty years, if it received normal maintenance. The interior finishes, including floor coverings and the painting of walls, were estimated to last only between five and fifteen years. The moving parts in HVAC (heating, ventilation, and air conditioning) systems, such as blowers and fans, were estimated to have useful lives of ten to twenty-five years, while the static parts of the HVAC systems, such as duct work, were estimated to last much longer. Finally, the moving parts of electrical systems, such as switches, circuit breakers, and relays, were estimated to have useful lives of twenty to fifty years.

In principle, an academic institution can establish a formal system for scheduling the replacement of all the systems in each building on a regular basis. However, the leaders of an institution always face the temptation

Table 10.1 Estimated average useful life of selected facilities systems at Stanford University.

Building subsystem	Average useful life		
	Pessimistic	Likely	Optimistic
Roofing	15	30	40
Interior finishes	5	10	15
Elevators	20	40	75
Plumbing	30	50	80
HVAC, moving	10	15	25
HVAC, static	30	50	75
Electrical moving	20	35	50

Source: Adapted from Robert E. Hutson and Frederick M. Biedenweg, "Before the Roof Caves In: A Predictive Model for Physical Plant Renewal," in *Critical Issues in Facilities Management: Capital Renewal and Deferred Maintenance* (Alexandria, Va.: Association of Physical Plant Administrators of Universities and Colleges, 1987), p. 19.

to skimp on making planned maintenance expenditures. After all, faculty members want higher salaries, more colleagues, and better support for their graduate students. Undergraduate students want lower tuition increases and better financial aid packages. Since donors tend to want to fund exciting new facilities, not planned maintenance such as the replacement of a heating system, funds for maintenance expenditures invariably come from the operating budgets of universities, and there is fierce competition for budget funds from advocates of allocating the available money to pay for things that faculty members and students want done.

Consequently, administrators find it easy to defer planned maintenance expenditures. Will anyone really notice if the painting of the interior of a building is put off for one more year? Or if the air conditioning system is working, why not cross your fingers and hope that it will continue to work for another year? Reasoning like this leads to deferral of planned maintenance expenditures and eventually a backlog of deferred maintenance. Over time, this backlog had grown at many academic institutions until it reached epic proportions.

Deferring planned maintenance is risky because failing to take action at an appropriate time may cause the costs of keeping the facility in good operating condition to increase dramatically. A personal example illustrates this point. I noted above that I had to replace the roof on our home. What I did not say is that I waited until it "failed" to replace it. Being an absent-minded professor, too preoccupied with my work to keep track of how old the roof over my head was, I realized it was time to replace it only when water stains started appearing at all over my living room ceiling. Those water stains meant that much of the wood underneath the shingles on the roof had been warped by water leaking through. The cost of replacing the roof was much higher than if I had replaced it a year earlier because I also had to replace all the warped wood and have my living room ceiling repainted.

I was fortunate that the failure of my roof was minimal. You can easily envision household furnishings being severely damaged if substantial leaks occurred. Indeed, during a severe storm our local county library's roof sustained many leaks that led to the destruction of hundreds of books. The county had been debating moving the library to a new facility and, rather than invest in a new roof, it tried to keep the old roof patched until a decision was reached on whether the library would remain where it was. Deferring planned maintenance (the new roof) proved very costly.

During the late 1980s attention began to be directed at the national level to the problem of deferred maintenance at American colleges and universities.[2] Cornell's trustees became aware of the deferred maintenance problems on its campus and instructed the university administration in the early 1990s to increase substantially the university's funding of planned maintenance. The additional funds that have been added to the endowed budget now total about $3 million a year above and beyond what the university administration had otherwise intended to spend on planned maintenance. As a result, the endowed Ithaca campus has now reached the point that its deferred maintenance inventory appears to be stabilized. But although all on campus applaud the improved physical conditions of the buildings and the way the campus looks, these funds could have been used to increase faculty salaries or to lower the rate of tuition increases. Improved maintenance of Cornell's physical facilities has come at the expense either of expenditures that the university might have undertaken or of lower tuition increases.

The university now prioritizes planned maintenance, ranking different needs, as indicated in Table 10.2. Life safety or legal compliance require-

Table 10.2 Priority categories for planned maintenance at Cornell University

Priority	Category	Time frame
1 (high)	Life safety or legal compliance requirement	Immediately
2	Avoidance of loss of a significant building system	0–1 year
3	Prevention of accelerated deterioration	0–1 year
4	Maintenance of building utilization or provision of more economical operation	3–5 years
5	Maintenance that can be postponed	5+ years
6	Correction of building design deficiencies	When possible
7 (low)	Items to be addressed with major renovations, updating to comply with current codes	With renovation

Source: Cornell University Facilities and Campus Services Division, April 1994.

ments, such as removing asbestos that is exposed or repairing leaking underground petroleum storage tanks, are taken care of right away. Building systems, such as heating, ventilating, and air conditioning, that are considered close to permanent failure are replaced within a year. Action is also taken within a year to stabilize systems that are in danger of rapidly depreciating.

Actions needed to provide more economic operation of buildings, such as improving insulation, installing double-pane windows, or installing more energy-efficient lighting systems, are undertaken within three to five years. Maintenance that can be postponed without any substantial cost to the university, such as upgrading public spaces by painting their walls and installing new floor finishes, is postponed, but these systems are closely tracked to make sure that they do not shift into a higher-priority category. Finally, corrections of building design deficiencies that make buildings less than optimal for current use, updates to comply with building codes that have changed since the original dates of construction of facilities, or maintenance that can be postponed, are delayed until they can be addressed in major renovations of buildings. The trustees, understanding the natural inclination of academic administrators to stress academics, revisit the issue of deferred maintenance periodically to make sure that the administration still has it under control.

Space Planning and Imperfect Information

Early on in my term as an administrator, I inherited "Sage Shuffle." Sage Hall is a historic building on the Cornell campus that then housed the Cornell graduate school, which administers doctoral programs at Cornell, and a number of other administrative units. It unfortunately needed about $3.5 million in deferred maintenance expenditures to maintain it in usable, though outdated, condition. As noted above, such funds are not easily found in university annual operating budgets, and at Cornell administrators have tended to fund major deferred maintenance expenditures, such as the replacement of mechanical systems, as part of major renovations that modernize and improve the space within a building. Given the historic nature of Sage Hall, historic preservation organizations had made sure that Cornell did not have the option of tearing the building down and replacing it with a new building.

Cornell's Johnson Graduate School of Management, which had outgrown its space, was the only college on campus thought to have the donor base needed to fund a major renovation of the building. Ultimately, a project that cost $38 million was undertaken. To renovate the building, Cornell first had to move all its inhabitants out of the building and into other locations. A series of moves was begun that became known as the Sage Shuffle because other offices had to be vacated in turn to make room for those displaced from Sage Hall. When finished, these moves involved 26 different units and over 390 faculty and staff members, as well as an equivalent number of graduate students.

This series of moves cost Cornell's current operating budget almost $5.7 million, which far exceeded what the cost would have been of directly doing the deferred maintenance. Of course, if Cornell had opted to undertake the deferred maintenance directly, rather than renovating the building, the university would have incurred some additional costs associated with temporarily housing residents of the building in other locations. It also would not have benefited from the new, renovated facility.

Near the end of the series of moves, one important scheduled move was canceled. At the last minute the biometrics department, one of the units to be displaced by the move of units out of Sage Hall, realized that it was not in the department's best interest for it to move far away from the sight of the dean of the College of Agriculture and Life Sciences, who provides it with its budget. This cancellation caused my staff and me to scramble for other solutions. One option that was attractive to us was to move a second research center into a building that had been promised to one research center. There was excess space in the building and the second center could have been accommodated with some squeezing.

The director of the first research center came to my office and, pounding his fist on my table, informed me that if he did not get all the space that he had been promised he would resign. Because the provost had told me that one of my roles was to solve problems for him, not to create problems, I swallowed hard, told the director that he could have the whole building, and moved the second research center elsewhere. Doing so generated much controversy, and in the process I had to "dump" on a nonacademic support unit that reported to me by moving it to a building far away from the center of the campus. This unplanned move further increased the cost of the Sage Shuffle.

Two months later, the vice president for research and advanced studies informed the director of the first research center that he was not going to be reappointed to his position when his term expired. This decision had been made well in advance of the director's discussion with me, although neither he nor I had been informed of it at that time. If I had known that he was a lame duck, I would have housed the two research centers in the one building as had been planned and saved the cost and aggravation associated with the extra move of the support unit.

The vice president for research and advanced studies and I were friends and never intentionally withheld information from each other. But information does not always flow smoothly between high-level university administrators at the same institution because there are too many things going on for them to be continually filling each other in on everything that each is doing. They should be filling each other in on important matters, and this was done while I was an administrator in a series of biweekly executive staff meetings. But the reappointment of the director and my need to find space for different units were not important enough issues to discuss at these meetings. The imperfect information that resulted led to a less than optimal decision and increased the university's costs.

In contrast, information flows very quickly around the university whenever an administrator says anything, even in confidence, to any faculty member or other administrator. This phenomenon leads prudent administrators to "tell the same story" to everyone. But since information flows are often imperfect, multiple versions of what the administrator said often proliferate even when the administrator said the same thing to everyone. No matter how hard I tried to be perfectly consistent in what I told different faculty members, deans, and central university administrators about my position on an issue, I often found that multiple views of my position were circulating in the university. This led me to do something many administrators do: spend too much of their time writing memos to try to assure that no one misinterprets anything that they have said. At least in today's world these memos often are transmitted by e-mail and trees are conserved.

Alternatively, some administrators adapt the attitude that the less they say, the less they can be misinterpreted. Often they conclude that the optimal policy for them is to say nothing, even though they have no desire to withhold information from their faculty and administrative colleagues. When faculty members regularly complained to me about their inability to get one of my administrative colleagues to articulate positions on issues, I smiled and tried to explain to them why he was behaving that way.

CHAPTER 11

The Costs of Space

Universities' Physical Plants

The public is well aware that major private research universities have large endowments of financial assets. Table 11.1 provides information on the value of the endowments that were held at twenty major private research universities as of June 30, 1995. More recent data on endowment levels were presented in Table 3.1. The 1995 data are presented here because 1995 is the most recent year for which data were also available on the physical plant assets of universities. In 1995, the endowments of these institutions ranged from about $250 million to over $7 billion. Financial endowments are important to universities because they provide income to help support the current and future operations of the institutions.

What the public is less aware of is that these institutions also have large physical plants that rival their endowments in value. Column 2 of the table provides information on the replacement value of the physical plants at these same institutions in 1995. These numbers are estimates, by the institutions, of what it would have cost them to build facilities comparable to the ones that they currently had standing. The estimated replacement value of the physical plant at these institutions ranged from about $235 million to over $4 billion. The physical plant at a university contributes directly to the educational mission of the institution through the classrooms and research laboratories that it houses, and to student life through its dormitories, dining facilities, student unions, medical facilities, and athletic facilities. The physical plant also provides the infrastructure for the institution's support and administrative services.

Many observers of Cornell's financial situation have pointed to the annual cost of operating and maintaining all Cornell's buildings as limiting the university's ability to hold down its tuition costs and increase its faculty salaries. In short, they believe that Cornell has too many buildings. One way to begin to examine this claim is to look at a set of universities and contrast the ratio of the value of the endowment to the value of the physical plant at each. Universities that have low ratios have chosen to put more of their wealth

Table 11.1   Market value of endowments and replacement value of buildings at selected private research universities on June 30, 1995.

University	(1) Endowment (millions of $)	(2) Replacement value (millions of $)	(3) Ratio of endowment to replacement value
Boston	378.6	1034.4	.366
Brown	676.0	1016.2	.665
Cal Tech	695.9	604.9	1.150
Carnegie-Mellon	453.5	234.9	1.931
Cornell	1244.5	1958.7	.635
Duke	790.6	1053.2	.750
Emory	2025.7	944.1	2.145
Georgetown	415.7	864.1	.481
Harvard	7045.9	4098.3	1.719
MIT	2093.2	1400.0	1.495
Northwestern	1367.1	1650.0	.829
Princeton	2872.9	1126.2	2.551
Stanford	3295.6	1855.5	1.776
Tufts	247.2	429.7	.575
Pennsylvania	1675.7	2300.0	.729
Rochester	733.8	772.7	.950
USC	883.8	961.3	.919
Vanderbilt	967.0	1203.0	.803
Washington (St. Louis)	2014.2	885.3	2.275
Yale	3967.8	1781.8	2.227

Source: Institutional data on 1995 current replacement value of physical plant assets and on the end of 1995 fiscal year value of endowment from the National Center for Education Statistics, Integrated Postsecondary Education Data System (IPEDS). Most of the major private research universities that fail to appear in the table did not include replacement value data in their IPEDS submission that year.

into the physical plant and less into financial assets that can help support current operations.

Column 3 of the table presents such comparisons. Cornell's endowment value was roughly 63.5 percent of the value of its physical plant in 1995. This was the fifth lowest ratio among the twenty institutions. The richest institutions in terms of the absolute size of their endowments—Emory, Harvard, MIT, Princeton, Stanford, Washington University of St. Louis, and Yale—all have more financial assets than they do physical plant assets. So at first glance Cornell does appear to be among the institutions that have put too much of their "wealth" into buildings.

First impressions, however, may not be accurate because it is difficult to control for all of the relevant factors that need to be considered. One factor that is unique to Cornell is that part of the university is supported by New York state. As a result, many of the buildings on campus were funded by the state, and the university never had the option of converting those funds into endowment.

Other factors apply more generally. The cost of construction varies widely across geographic areas of the country, and institutions in areas where construction costs are high will tend to have larger estimated replacement values for their physical plants than institutions in areas where construction costs are low. Some universities house all of their undergraduate students in university-owned buildings while others house few in such buildings, and the former tend to have larger physical plants than the latter. The mix of undergraduate and graduate teaching and research varies across universities, as does the intensity of the science program, and these factors all influence the amount of space that an institution has. Institutions with large volumes of federal research funding may fund some of the operations and maintenance costs of their buildings out of indirect cost recoveries, and thus at least part of their space may not add that much to the operating costs of the university. Finally, some universities are located in urban areas, where land for construction of new facilities is expensive to acquire, while others, such as Cornell, are located in more rural surroundings, where land for new construction is relatively cheap. Thus one might expect a rural university to have more space than a comparable (in terms of student body) urban university.

For all of these reasons, it is hard to make judgments about whether Cornell actually has too much space. If it does, part of the reason is undoubtedly that many users of space are totally unaware of the costs of the space that they are occupying, and bear none of the costs of the space directly.[1] If the price of space is zero (to the users), it is natural for the faculty always to want more of it. All the pressure at Cornell is to add space; no one ever voluntarily gives up space that is no longer needed.

Can a Price System for Space Be Established at a University?

No faculty or staff member, or academic or nonacademic department, ever has enough space. Back in the early nineteenth century, a French economist named Jean Baptiste Say, coined Say's Law, which asserts that supply creates its own demand.[2] Say's Law has been shown to be false as a general economic proposition, but it certainly applies to academia. A department may shrink and have fewer faculty members, staff, or students than it did before, but somehow it always finds a use for the space that it has. Moreover, my experience is that there are always unmet space needs at the university and that these increase if more space becomes available.

The size and number of offices that a faculty member has are often taken to be a measure of the faculty member's prestige at universities. When I first came to Cornell in 1975 with a primary appointment in the School of Industrial and Labor Relations, I negotiated a second office in the Department of Economics, where I also had an appointment. Having two offices, even though I could only use one at a time, conferred extra status on me.

Space is so important to departments that sometimes a faculty member can't give space back even if he wants to. After a number of years, I realized that it made more sense for me to keep all of my books in one office and to stay close to my talented administrative assistant in Industrial and Labor Relations than it did for me to have two offices. So I offered to give my office back to the Department of Economics. The department was petrified. The dean of the college knew that the office was assigned to me and the department worried that he would try to reclaim it for other uses if I moved out. We compromised. I agreed to keep the office in my name but never to use it. Instead, the department uses the office to house visiting faculty members from other universities who come to Cornell several times a week to present seminars. This arrangement has now persisted for almost twenty years.

Understanding such behavior, I found it quite reasonable when I became a vice president at Cornell that my fellow administrators and I should develop a system that allowed us to understand what the actual operating costs were of the space each unit occupied. These costs would include the costs for routine and preventive maintenance, utilities, and custodial services. Our building and grounds people tell us that to properly maintain buildings and all of their systems, approximately 1.5 percent of the replacement value of the buildings should be set aside each year for planned maintenance, and this too would be included in the costs.[3] Certain overhead costs of buildings, including insurance and police and fire protection, would also have to be included.

Preliminary estimates made by my staff indicated that the operating and maintenance costs of space varied widely across buildings on the campus.

For example, the average annual operating and maintenance cost for assignable (usable) space in a social science office and classroom building was estimated to be $12.50 per square foot. The comparable average cost in a biology building that housed both laboratories and offices was estimated to be $27.00 per square foot. To give you a sense of the magnitude of these numbers, my office in a social science building contains approximately 180 square feet of space, so the university is incurring a cost of about $2,250 a year to house me. The comparable number for a biological scientist who had both a 180-square-foot office and a 360-square-foot laboratory would be $14,580 (540 times $27).

Similarly, preliminary estimates indicated that the annual operating and maintenance costs for the space occupied by our College of Art, Architecture, and Planning, which is housed in four buildings on campus, were in the range of $1.135 million a year. The annual operating budget of the college, which excludes space costs, was roughly $10 million at that time.

Estimates such as these have a number of potential uses. At the college level, such information would allow deans to identify the space costs associated with each of their departments just as they identify the costs of faculty, teaching assistants, support personnel, and so forth. Deans, at least implicitly, base their allocation of faculty and other operating resources on the activity levels of their departments, such as numbers of students taught and the amount of external research funding, and having this information would allow them to do the same things with space.

To take another example, when I was negotiating the move of our mathematics department into a building that had far more space than the department was currently occupying, the department was not very anxious to share the building with a newly formed university-wide statistics department. To encourage the people in the mathematics department to accept a sharing arrangement, I told them that I was thinking of computing the cost of the space that I wanted the statistics department to occupy and reducing the operating budget of the College of Arts and Sciences, in which the mathematics department was located, by an equivalent amount. In short, I was contemplating "billing" the College of Arts and Sciences for the space that the mathematics department was refusing to give up in the new location. If I did so, I would leave it to the college to decide whether the reduction in its budget would affect only the mathematics department.

I had no authority to make such a budget reduction. But faculty sometimes believe that administrators have more power than they actually do, and my "threat" provided a strong incentive for the mathematics department to negotiate a compromise with the statistics department, which it did. Having the ability to think systematically about trading off operating and space budgets in this manner can be very important to universities.

At the provost's and deans' levels, such estimates are also important in helping the university understand the extent to which cross-subsidies are occurring. Resource allocation decisions at universities should always be based on the academic values of the different activities, but the monetary benefits and costs of the activities provide the context in which such decisions should be made. Systematic failure to include space costs in the calculations will cause a university to spend too much on activities that are space intensive and that have high operating and maintenance costs per unit of space.

Knowledge of space costs can be used to help ration space and curb people's appetites for space. Placing "prices" on space and permitting units to trade off spaces for operating budgets is likely to be an efficient way of carving space out and minimizing the need for new space. The argument is often made that freeing up only one or two contiguous offices does not always do an institution much good. But in a world in which universities continually worry about where they will find office space for emeritus faculty, which is needed to encourage faculty to retire, even small contractions of space use would be very valuable to universities.

Finally, allowing market prices to determine the allocation of space sometimes can improve the way that space is allocated at universities. An example from Arizona State University is instructive.[4] When the economics department moved into a new building in 1983, decisions had to be made as to which faculty members would get which offices in the new building. All offices were roughly the same size, but half were interior ones and had no windows. The other half had windows, but the view differed depending upon the side of the building on which they were located.

Traditionally, departments often allocate space based upon the seniority (in the department) of faculty members. Such a system, however, gives no weight to the needs of different faculty members for space or to how important different offices actually would be to each.

The economics department at ASU hit upon the idea of allowing faculty members to bid for offices in a sealed bid auction. Each faculty member was given three weeks to submit in a sealed envelope the amount that he or she was willing to pay for an office. The highest bidder would be the first to pick an office, the second highest would choose second, and so on until everyone was housed in offices. All of the proceeds from the "sale" of offices would go to a student scholarship fund and thus would be tax deductible.

When the envelopes were opened, it turned out that the twenty-four faculty members had bid a total of $3,200, for an average of $133 per office. The highest bidder paid $500 and the second highest $250. A bid of about $75 was sufficient to get an office with a window—apparently many of these economists did not feel that windows and a view were worth even $75 a year. The only one disappointed with the results was the faculty member who got his first choice. After the fact he realized that he had paid $249 more than he needed to win the auction. His disappointment is symptomatic of what is often called the winner's curse—winners of sealed bid auctions often pay more than was actually necessary.

Once an office was assigned to a faculty member, the office "permanently" became his or hers. When new people arrive, they can take a vacant office or offer to "buy" an existing faculty member's office. Within five years, the "price" for an office with a window had risen to $350. All faculty members in the department seemed happy with the system. Using a price system to allocate space clearly worked in this situation.

Despite my concern that Cornell had no effective way to ration space, after two years of effort I gave up trying to implement a space cost model for the university. Too many objections were raised to the details of the calculations that my staff and I were proposing to assure that the approach would have enough support around the campus to be adopted. One major set of objections involved our inability to distinguish whether "high-cost" space was expensive because it was "high quality" or because it was inefficiently designed. This concern could be addressed in theory, but was difficult to handle in practice.[5]

I met with the business officers for each college and they encouraged me to write a statement for the weekly faculty newspaper that would educate faculty about the costs of space. They indicated, however, that they would not use space cost estimates on a regular basis, preferring instead to negotiate with departments, using a set of space standards that the university had developed long ago. So, for example, as a full professor I am "entitled" to an office of a certain size and as a vice president to an office of another size. If departments have more space than the standards indicate they deserve, the college business officers can then negotiate with the departments for reductions. That they would rather do this than let the price system work should not have been surprising to me. Setting up a price mechanism to help allocate space would reduce the authority of these administrators.

I took pride during my term as a central administrator that my office was 40 percent smaller than the space standards indicated my position was entitled to have. One of my responsibilities was to supervise Cornell's office of space planning. Whenever people came to me complaining that they did not have enough space, I simply shrugged my shoulders and complained to them about my own allocation of space.

I never told the business officers that imposing fixed space/faculty ratios that do not change as relative costs change, or as the budget constraints facing the university shift, does not make sense from the perspective of an economist. Instead, I followed the dictum of the provost, who although a musicologist often thought more like an economist than I did, that if information is not going to be used, don't bother to incur the costs of collecting it. The additional cost of developing space cost information for Cornell far exceeded the additional benefits the institution would get from collecting the information while I was an administrator.

A postscript: I accumulated many new books on higher education and numerous files of materials (from which much of this book has been written) as an administrator. When I left my vice president's position, I asked the dean of my college for a second office to store most of my old books and files. Not wanting to be faced with a flood of requests from colleagues for similar treatment, he agreed to give me the office only if I succeeded in receiving external funding for a research institute that had been established for me. In that way, he could claim the office was for the institute, not for me in my faculty role, and avoid creating pressures to give more space to all my colleagues.

I did receive the external funding and most of my books and files now reside in the second office. I put one of my graduate assistants in the office to further the fiction that the office was for the institute. The dean also did not charge me any "rent" for this office and I never suggested to him that I should pay any.

If the person at the university who best understood the need to try to ration space (namely me) behaved in this manner once he returned to the faculty, is there any hope that the university will be able to limit future construction of new space?

PART VI

ACADEMIC AND ADMINISTRATIVE ISSUES

CHAPTER 12

Internal Transfer Prices

Any university with multiple units has to devise methods to take account of the fact that its units trade services back and forth with each other and with the central offices of the institution. For example, students enrolled in one college may take courses in other colleges. To take another example, the central university provides administrative and support services to the individual colleges, but tuition revenue that is needed to pay for these services may come directly to the colleges. Often institutions set up internal pricing systems to take account of such transactions, and the prices that result are called internal transfer prices. Unfortunately, the presence of internal transfer prices may distort educational outcomes and prevent universities from behaving in an efficient manner.

As discussed earlier, seven of the ten colleges at Cornell's Ithaca campus operate as responsibility centers, or "tubs," either by statute (the New York State Colleges of Agriculture and Life Sciences, Human Ecology, and Veterinary Medicine, as well as the New York State School of Industrial and Labor Relations) or by trustee designation (the Johnson Graduate School of Management, the School of Law, and the School of Hotel Administration). Each tub keeps all of the revenue that it generates and is responsible for its own costs. Each pays the central university for courses that its students take in the colleges whose budgets the central university controls directly, the "general-purpose" colleges (Arts and Sciences, Engineering, and Art, Architecture, and Planning). Each receives payments from the center for courses that students enrolled in the general-purpose colleges take in it. The designated colleges also transfer resources between each other based upon the net credit flows between their colleges. This system of payments is referred to as accessory instruction. Similarly, each tub pays the center for central administrative costs that are attributed to it: these are computed through a complicated resource allocation model.

Accessory Instruction

Under the New York State Education Law, all transactions between Cornell's endowed colleges and statutory colleges take place on an average full-cost basis. Historically, Cornell received an allocation from New York state for the net accessory instruction cost deficit that the statutory colleges incurred. This deficit resulted from the undergraduate statutory colleges' requiring their students to take a large number of arts and science courses. The endowed colleges had no requirement that their students take statutory college courses.

Table 12.1 displays data on the number of credit hours taught by Cornell's general-purpose, designated, and statutory colleges during the 1995–96 academic year. Of the 313,029 credit hours generated by the general-purpose colleges, about 81 percent were from teaching their own students, 1 percent from teaching students from the designated colleges, and 18 percent from teaching students from the statutory colleges. Similarly, the statutory colleges generated 86 percent of their credit hours from teaching their own students, 1 percent from teaching designated college students, and 13 percent from teaching general-purpose college students.

As Table 12.2 indicates, when these numbers are netted out, the general-purpose colleges "bought" 1,604 more credit hours of instruction from the

Table 12.1   Distribution of credit hours taught by and taken in Cornell colleges in 1995–96.

| | | Credit hours taken by students from | | |
	Credit hours taught by	General-purpose colleges	Designated colleges	Statutory colleges
General-purpose colleges	313,029	252,307 (.81)	4,192 (.01)	56,530 (.18)
Designated colleges	65,434	5,796 (.09)	54,887 (.84)	4,681 (.07)
Statutory colleges	153,997	20,510 (.13)	1,764 (.01)	131,723 (.86)

Note: Numbers in parentheses indicate the proportion of courses taught by the category of colleges to students from each category of colleges.

designated colleges than they sold to them. Similarly, the statutory colleges "bought" 2,917 more credit hours of instruction from the designated colleges than they sold to them. Finally, the statutory colleges "bought" 36,020 more credit hours of instruction from the general-purpose colleges than they sold to them. The net result is that the statutory college credit hour deficit to the two endowed parts of Cornell represented over 25 percent of the total credit hours taught by the statutory colleges.

Although in principle New York state was fully committed to funding net accessory instruction costs, over time, as more and more liberal arts requirements were introduced into the statutory college curriculum, the state's payments proved to be insufficient. The statutory colleges were billed directly for the excess. Not surprisingly, the deans of these colleges became interested in reducing the flow of their students to the endowed colleges. This interest had nothing to do with what was best educationally for the students; it was purely a response to economic forces.

So, for example, all undergraduate colleges at Cornell, except the School of Hotel Administration, require that their first-year students take two semesters of a freshman writing seminar. Most of the instructors in this program are faculty, lecturers, or graduate students from Cornell's College of Arts and Sciences' humanities departments. Many of these departments have graduate programs that are ranked in the top ten in the nation, and the freshman writing seminar provides a major source of financial support for their Ph.D. students.

Cornell's College of Agriculture and Life Sciences has a communications department, which is widely thought to not be among the university's strongest departments. The dean of the college realized quite quickly that if faculty and graduate students from this department taught in the freshman writing program, this would reduce the college's accessory instruction pay-

Table 12.2 Distribution of net credit hour flows between Cornell colleges in 1995–96.

College Pair	Number
General-purpose colleges to designated colleges	1,604
Statutory colleges to general-purpose colleges	36,020
Statutory colleges to designated colleges	2,917

ments. Of course, this would also reduce the revenue available to support the College of Arts and Sciences and its highly ranked graduate programs. But that wasn't his problem.

The provost was not willing, or able, to limit participation in the freshman writing program to faculty and graduate students from the College of Arts and Sciences (although he did require that anyone wishing to be an instructor in the program had to go through serious training provided by the program). As faculty and graduate students from the communications department began to teach in the writing program, the resource flow from Agriculture and Life Sciences to Arts and Sciences was reduced. The university as a whole never had judged that, or even discussed whether, this was desirable.

The School of Hotel Administration is one of Cornell's designated colleges. For many years, two of the most popular elective courses in the university were both taught by this school: Introduction to Wines (popularly called Wine Tasting) and Principles of Investment Management (popularly called Personal Investments). The former was open only to students over the age of twenty-one, who could legally consume alcohol in New York state. Each of these courses generated substantial accessory instruction revenue for the school.

The dean of the College of Agriculture and Life Sciences, reasoning that his college studies the production of grapes and that wine is produced from grapes, decided that his college had as much right to teach a wine-tasting course as the hotel school did. At his urging, his food science department introduced Understanding Wines, a course that included wine tasting. Similarly, since this dean's college also included the Department of Agricultural, Resource, and Managerial Economics, which teaches courses on small business, and small business owners should have knowledge of how to invest their money, the college developed its own advanced course on personal investments, Futures and Options Trading. Under the tub system, whenever a college can teach a course at a lower cost than what it is charged when its students take the course in another college, an incentive is created for the college to establish its own "duplicate," or at least similar, course. Such duplication is not an efficient use of resources from the perspective of the university as a whole.

The hotel school lost revenue when both of these Agriculture and Life Sciences courses were established. But lest the reader feel sorry for the hotel school, I should note that it has been absolutely the worst offender of the colleges in the university in terms of the development and teaching of "in-house" courses that are already taught by other colleges at Cornell. Over the years, the hotel school developed its own one-semester freshman writing course, its own communications courses, its own French course, its own elementary macroeconomics course, and its own courses in organizational behavior, human resources, and employment discrimination law. Variants of the first four courses had long been taught in Cornell's Colleges of Arts and Sciences and Agriculture and Life Sciences. Variants of the last three courses were long taught in the building next to the hotel school by the School of Industrial and Labor Relations.

Frustrated by the hotel school's "isolationism," one Cornell provost finally took the step of limiting the amount that the hotel school could earn through the accessory instruction system and set an upper limit on the amount he was willing to pay them. This move eliminated the school's incentive to further separate its students from the rest of the university. But by then the school had become so insular that one senior central administrator (best unnamed) suggested that if it moved to New York City (where many people thought it should have been located), no one in Ithaca would ever notice. That administrator obviously had forgotten about the undergraduates from around the university who take the school's wine-tasting and personal investment courses.

All units have an incentive to use the accessory instruction system to their own financial benefit. Currently, the flow of money is based on the average cost of producing a credit hour of instruction in each unit. You do not have to be a space scientist to realize that the marginal (additional) cost of creating a new 10-student seminar class (the cost of the share of a professor's time that the new class will represent) is larger than the cost of adding 10 more students to an existing 200-student lecture class (the creation of a discussion section taught by a graduate student that will meet once a week), which in turn is larger than the cost of adding 10 more students to an existing 40-student lecture class (and perhaps providing a little more grading help for the professor).

A very popular and talented psychology professor annually teaches a freshman class of about 2,000 students in Cornell's largest auditorium. Students love his multimedia presentations. I have attended some and can attest to how interesting and substantive they are. This class was required for the roughly 150 first-year students in the School of Industrial and Labor Relations. If we assume an average cost of $350 per credit hour (actually it was higher), this three-credit course was costing the school over $150,000 a year in accessory instruction costs.

The dean quickly realized that if a comparable course was taught in house by a faculty member from the school's Department of Organizational Behavior, he could save the school a considerable sum of money. Teaching the course would involve no more than half of one faculty member's teaching time per year plus the time of several teaching assistants. Given the level of faculty salaries and benefits in the school, he could use the saved funds to hire two new assistant professors. So the course is now taught in house. Students in the School of Industrial and Labor Relations are deprived of attending a course taught by one of Cornell's most superb instructors, unless they use one of their free electives to take it. If they do, they will be taking a course that is similar in content to the newly required course.

Cornell's senior administration was long aware of the problems caused by the accessory instruction system. In the early 1990s a committee of deans and other administrators was formed by the Provost and asked to formulate recommendations for improvement. The committee issued its final set of recommendations on April 1, 1994. Among them was that the accessory instruction calculations should be modified to take account of the differences in the marginal costs that exist of adding students to classes of different sizes. The committee acknowledged, as my example above illustrates, that when students from one college enroll in other colleges, the size distribution of the classes in which they enroll influences the costs of providing education for them.

Six years after this recommendation was made, it had yet to be implemented. Its issuance on April Fools' Day was not responsible for the lack of progress. Rather, the lack of progress reflects a combination of the pragmatic and political factors that slow down change in universities.

In order to implement the recommendation, the university needed to know the size of each class in which its students enroll. Although it may be hard for the reader to believe, the Cornell information systems that existed during the late 1990s could not provide this information for cross-listed courses. So, for example, when I teach my popular course on the economics of the university it has both Arts and Science and Industrial and Labor Relations course numbers because I have a joint appointment in both colleges. Cornell's student information systems did not have the capacity to aggregate the two course numbers to create the total enrollment in the course. Hence the university could not assign the correct marginal cost per student number to it. One can readily understand why Cornell is in the process of investing many millions of dollars in a new student information system.

It would, of course, simplify things if each Cornell course were taught under only one course number. But often a Cornell college requires that students take a specified number of courses within it to graduate. For example, all students enrolled in Arts and Sciences must take at least 100 credit hours within the college. Cross-listing of a course increases the accessibility of the course to students in other colleges. By cross-listing my economics of the university course and giving it an Arts and Sciences course number, I made it easier for economics majors in Arts and Sciences to take it.

Another factor that has prevented the implementation of this change is that any deviation from the strict average cost rule will need to be negotiated with New York state for those transactions that involve the statutory colleges. Cornell cannot begin to discuss this issue with the state until it has information systems in place that can compute what the cost implications of the change would be for the state. Still another factor is that any change in the "rules of the game" always creates losers as well as winners. The losers quickly figured out, making their own rough calculations, who they will be, and have resisted the change. The dean of one large college, who initially approved the committee's recommendation (indeed, he served on the committee), quickly turned against it when he realized what it would probably mean in dollar terms for his college.

Cornell's medical college not being on the Ithaca campus, Cornell's highest faculty salaries in Ithaca are paid to professors in the Johnson Graduate School of Management (JGSM). Not surprisingly, JGSM's average cost of producing a credit hour of instruction is far higher than that of most of Cornell's colleges. Many JGSM faculty members are not very interested in teaching undergraduates or professional masters students from other colleges, such as engineering, who would find finance, accounting, and management courses of great use to them. They would rather focus on improving the ratings of their MBA program.

Over the years, the deans of JGSM realized that staffing a few such courses for out-of-college students, using lecturers or JGSM graduate students as instructors, had the potential to provide a large financial windfall to the school. Put in simple terms, they could charge their "average cost" of instruction for these courses, but their actual cost of providing them would be much lower. JGSM became a net winner in the accessory instruction game. One Cornell provost finally caught on to what the school was doing and decreed that he would pay accessory instruction charges for the JGSM courses only at the average per credit hour rate in the university. Not surprisingly, JGSM moaned and groaned about this "arbitrary decision."

During my years as a Cornell vice president, the failure of New York state to fully fund the accessory instruction bill of the statutory colleges allowed us to make considerable progress in integrating Cornell's disparate undergraduate economics programs. By way of background, Cornell has over 120 economists on its faculty whose main undergraduate departmental homes are economics (Arts and Sciences), labor economics (Industrial and Labor Relations), policy analysis and management (Human Ecology), and agriculture, resource, and management economics (Agriculture and Life Sciences). Each of these departments had its own undergraduate curriculum. While many students from the statutory colleges took freshman economics in Arts and Sciences, very few economics majors from Arts and Sciences took any courses in the other economics departments, partly because the College of Arts and Sciences required all majors in the college to take at least 100 of the 120 credit hours required for graduation within the college.

In the mid-1990s, the accessory instruction deficit of the statutory colleges, the difference between the funds that New York state provided to Cornell for accessory instruction payments and what the administration calculated these colleges owed the endowed colleges, reached over $3.5 million a year. The provost realized that the statutory colleges did not have the financial resources to make such a payment. So he agreed to "cap" their obligations at $1.2 million a year, provided that they took steps to reduce the deficit and participated in cooperative university endeavors.

Within a short period of time, the first-year economics course, which had been taught solely by economists from the College of Arts and Sciences, became a university-wide course with many of the instructors coming from other colleges. Knowledge of economists in the other colleges, gained by having some as instructors in first-year economics courses, encouraged students in the College of Arts and Sciences who had completed freshman economics to take economics courses in the other colleges. To facilitate this, many statutory college economics courses were cross-listed and given Arts and Science numbers. The statutory colleges were willing to do this because the capping of their accessory instruction obligations meant they would not incur any additional costs if students signed up for their courses under Arts and Science course numbers. In one fell swoop the administration drastically increased the number of courses that Arts and Science students could take toward their major.

Once the economists from across the campus started talking to each other, they realized that there were some courses that were similar that were taught in more than one department. In some cases, a department eliminated a course, because of the availability of another department's course. This freed up faculty resources that could be used to teach other courses. In other cases, colleges gave students the option of taking either their own college's course or another college's course to satisfy a requirement. Often these alternative courses were taught at different times or on different days of the week. This variety greatly enhanced undergraduate students' ability to take the courses they wanted without running into scheduling conflicts. Undergraduate students were the big winners from these changes.

These educational benefits came about because of the "breakdown" of Cornell's internal transfer pricing system. Because the provost placed a cap on the statutory college payments, a whole set of desirable changes occurred.

It should be clear from this discussion that internal transfer pricing systems set up economic incentives that do not always square with educational objectives. If such systems exist, central administrators should pay constant attention to them and exert strong academic controls to ensure that the actions taken by the units are in the best interest of the institution as a whole, not just of the individual units. But given central administrators' time constraints, this is not always possible. Hence inefficiencies invariably result from internal transfer price systems.

Administrative Charges

In 1997–98, the budget of the Ithaca campus of Cornell totaled over $1 billion. More than $100 million were for central "administrative charges" that were allocated across all the university's budgetary units. "Administrative charges" actually is a misnomer because included in these charges are components that cover a wide range of the activities of the university. Table 12.3 summarizes the broad categories of expenditures that are allocated across units; they include the costs of academic administration, the costs of general institutional administrative activity, the costs of student services, physical plant costs, and central library costs. Examples of the types of costs in each category also appear in the table.

A complicated accounting algorithm is used to apportion these costs among the university's colleges; instructional, research, and public service centers; and enterprise units. In some cases, for example, financial adminis-

Table 12.3   Cornell University administrative cost allocation system in the late 1990s.
Key: A = colleges; B = instructional, research, and public service centers;
C = enterprise and service departments; MTDC = modified total direct
costs (expense measure).

Expenses	Allocated to	Method of allocation
I. *Academic Administration*		
1. Central Administration (Provost's Office)	A,B	MTDC
2. Faculty Administration (Dean of the Faculty)	A	Number of faculty
3. Research Administration (Office of Sponsored Programs)	A,B	Research expenses
II. *General Institutional*		
1. Business Administration (VP for Finance and Business)	A,B,C	MTDC
2. University Administration (Treasurer, Attorneys)	A,B,C	MTDC
3. Financial Administration (Budget, Audit, Purchasing)	A,B,C	MTDC
4. Human Resource Costs (Human Resources, EEO)	A,B,C	Number of employees
5. Population Costs (Parking, Traffic)	A,B,C	No. students & employees
6. Alumni Costs (Alumni Affairs and Development)	A	Number of Alumni
III. *Student Services*		
1. Undergraduate Student Services (Admissions, Financial Aid, Learning Skill Center)	A	No. undergraduate students
2. Graduate Student Services (Graduate School Office, TA Training)	A	No. graduate students
3. All Student Services (Registrar, Bursar, Health Services)	A	No. graduate and undergraduate students
IV. *Physical Plant Costs* (Public Safety, Environmental Health, Maintenance, Utilities)	A,B,C	Square feet occupied
V. *Library*	A	Volumes, volumes added, expenses, user surveys
VI. *Program Costs* (Athletics and Physical Education, Art Museum)	A	No. graduate and undergraduate students

Note: Examples of members of each category are given in parentheses.

trative costs, the costs are allocated across units in proportion to their share of the university's total expenditures (formally modified totally direct costs). In other cases, they are based on "counts" of bodies. So, for example, alumni costs are allocated across colleges on the basis of each college's share of living alumni, and parking costs are allocated on the basis of each unit's shares of faculty, staff, and students. Still other costs, for example utility and maintenance costs, are allocated based on the share of the university's physical space that a unit occupies.

Although a system that tries to apportion costs in such a manner may seem fair—after all, each item is allocated on the basis of a measure that is thought to be close to the unit's share of usage of the item—it actually leads to many problems. For example, for many years Cornell's athletics department ran a deficit and this deficit had to be "covered" by the central university. Since athletic costs are allocated across units based on their share of the student body, this meant that the statutory colleges, which enrolled roughly 40 percent of Cornell's students, had to cover the same percentage of the athletics department's deficit. One year these colleges faced a cutback of over $1 million in their state appropriations and their deans had to drastically slash expenditures and lay off staff. You can imagine their reactions when they learned that the athletics department deficit was over $500,000 that year, and that they had to cut their budgets still further to pay the central administration for their share of this deficit.

As I will discuss later, athletics is a special case because many Cornell trustees and key alumni strongly believe in the importance of having winning varsity athletic teams. They attribute the relatively poor performance of Cornell's varsity teams in Ivy League sports competitions and the athletics department's persistent deficits at least partly to the department's being underfunded. Hence they put pressure on the central administration to increase the funding of athletics. They would not look kindly upon the university's "punishing" the athletic director for spending more than his budget.

Most units of the university are forced to live within their budgets. Somewhat perversely, however, the system does not put a lot of pressure on the central administration to hold down "administrative costs." If, for example, student health services were to claim that they needed another $1 million to operate, the central administration understands that it will only bear a fraction of these costs. The rest will be distributed around the university to the designated and statutory colleges. And since the central administration does not bear the full cost of the increase in health center costs, it does not have an incentive to be as "tough" on the health services' budget as it would have been if it bore the full costs. This is true for all central administrative expenditures, whether they are for information technology, athletics, or true administrative functions.

This system also perversely causes units' shares of costs to change independently of actions they take. So, for example, the decline in statutory colleges' expenditures caused by New York state's decreasing their funding led to a decline in their share of total university expenditures. This in turn led to a decline in their share of administrative costs, and thus other units' shares necessarily had to rise. In at least one year, the Johnson Graduate School of Management's allocated share of total administrative costs rose from 5 percent to 6 percent because of a decline in other units' expenditures. An increase of this magnitude seems small until one realizes that it meant a 20 percent (!) increase in the school's administrative cost bill, above and beyond whatever administrative cost increases actually occurred during the year. You can be certain that the dean and the school's advisory council complained bitterly about this increase. This problem arose because when one or more units' expenditures decline, the central administration does not automatically take action under this costing system to reduce central administrative costs.

As I said earlier, salaries of Cornell faculty and staff are determined separately in the statutory and endowed parts of the university. The salary increase pool in the endowed units is determined by the university and has kept pace with, or slightly exceeded, the rate of inflation in recent years. But during a recent six-year period, statutory faculty and staff received salary increases in only two years owing to the financial difficulties that New York state faced.

As a result, the following frequently occurred during the period: Budgets in the statutory colleges were very tight and statutory faculty and staff received no salary increases. Endowed employees received increases that at least kept up with the rate of inflation. These increases caused central administrative costs to go up, and the statutory colleges then received increased administrative cost bills from the central administration. The statutory deans vociferously complained that at the same time they were cutting their administrative costs in an effort to protect their academic programs, the central administration was increasing its costs, which would require further reductions in their budgets. Administrators explained to them that although they were certainly correct, denying endowed employees salary increases because of tight state budgets did not seem to be the best way to attract and retain high-quality endowed faculty and staff.

Many academic institutions get around the problems that such an administrative costing approach causes either by specifying in advance the share of each tub's revenue that the central administration will take to cover central administrative costs, or by having the central administration agree to fund all administrative costs out of its own revenue. Either system provides a stronger incentive for the central administration to take actions to hold down its rate of administrative cost increases.

Unfortunately, Cornell cannot pursue the second strategy because very little unrestricted revenue flows directly to the central administration. Most endowments are "owned" by the colleges, and less than $4 million a year of the annual giving that the university gets comes to the central administration for its unrestricted budget. Having the central administration finance all the central administrative and support activities at Cornell would mean that most of these costs would have to come out of the tuition revenue the university receives for the endowed general-purpose colleges. This would diminish the resources available to support the academic activities of these colleges.

Cornell is tentatively moving toward the first strategy: a system in which the central administration takes a specified proportion of each unit's revenue to cover central administrative and support costs. This movement is tentative because although most units are in favor of such a system, they are only in favor if the new share of the administrative cost bill that they will pay is less than or equal to the current share. Put differently, what makes sense to a unit in principle makes sense in practice only if that unit will not lose by the change. Units also try to structure the evolving system to their advantage.

While I was a central administrator, the Johnson Graduate School of Management offered to pay the provost a fixed percentage of its on-campus MBA tuition revenue in lieu of the current administrative cost charge. It also agreed to set the percentage at a level that would generate the same amount of revenue that it was then providing to the central administration under the administrative charge scheme. Such an offer seemed quite reasonable until one realized that JGSM was in the process of expanding its executive education programs and also was likely to increasingly generate revenue through synchronous and Web-based distance learning programs. All of these activities will undoubtedly add to the university's central administrative costs. Yet the school has in return offered the central administration a fixed share of what is likely to become a decreasing share of the school's total revenue.

CHAPTER 13

Enrollment Management

Undergraduate Enrollment

Undergraduate enrollment management encompasses several issues. The university wants to enroll a certain number of new undergraduate students and to have these students be the best students it can get. It tries to enroll these students in a way that does not require it to devote an excessive share of the university's resources to financial aid. Many of the issues related to freshmen admissions and financial aid were discussed earlier.

The university is also concerned about maintaining control over the total number of enrolled undergraduate students each year, as well as over the distribution of these students across the different colleges in the university. The total number of enrolled students determines the tuition revenue available to help fund the university's operations. In a university in which all tuition revenue does not flow to the central administration, the distribution of students across colleges determines which colleges will have revenue to expand and which will have to tighten their belts.

For many years, Cornell's trustees have set 3,000 as the target number of freshmen they wanted to enroll. This number was not arbitrarily chosen, but was based on the university's capacity to house freshman students on campus and the academic resources available to teach a set of first-year courses that are either required of or taken by most freshmen. The latter include freshman writing seminars and introductory calculus.

Table 13.1 presents the size of Cornell's freshman class as of the third week of the fall, for each year between 1987 and 1997. These numbers are about 100 students higher than the average number of freshmen in residence throughout the academic year because some students leave the university, either for personal or for academic reasons, before the end of the academic year. The early leavers represent less than 3 percent of the students who initially enroll at Cornell, a figure that ranks Cornell among the best universities in the nation in terms of its freshman retention rate.[1] Given the numbers in the table, the average freshman enrollment during the period was thus usually about, or slightly above, the target level of 3,000.

Table 13.1   Freshman and total undergraduate enrollments at Cornell University, fall 1987 through fall 1997.

Fall	Freshman	Total Registration
1987	3,138	12,958
1988	3,047	12,943
1989	3,004	13,026
1990	2,959	12,801
1991	3,100	12,915
1992	3,022	12,861
1993	3,308	13,097
1994	3,125	13,262
1995	3,245	13,372
1996	3,205	13,512
1997	3,164	13,294

Source: Cornell University *Fact Book* (electronic version, available at <http://www.ipr.cornell.edu>). Data are as of the third week of classes.

Missing a freshman enrollment target by enrolling 50 fewer students than the university had planned would mean that the university was within 1.67 percent of its target. Such a small percentage difference might be thought to be insignificant. However, with annual endowed tuition levels that have exceeded $20,000 a year ever since 1993–94, if the enrollment shortfall was all in the endowed colleges, it would represent a loss of over $1 million relative to what had been planned in the budget. Although this sum is only a small share of the total budget, it does represent the funding necessary to support the salaries and benefits of about ten faculty members.

In some years freshman enrollments exceeded 3,000 because more accepted applicants enrolled than the university expected. But in other years freshman enrollment levels above 3,000 resulted from a conscious administrative strategy in a tight budget year to take a "few more" students to provide extra revenue. Such a strategy is likely to prove self-defeating in the long run if the budget is out of balance because of factors expected to persist over time. The extra tuition revenue provides the university with an "excuse" not to take corrective actions that are necessary. Put another way, it is easy for administrators to get "hooked" on the extra revenue provided by a few added students and for enrollments to continue to creep up over time.

Indeed, if we consider total undergraduate enrollments, which are also displayed in the table, it is clear that this is exactly what occurred at Cornell during the 1987 to 1997 period. During the first seven years of the period, fall enrollments averaged slightly under 13,000 undergraduate students. During the next four years, they averaged over 13,300. The temptation to increase enrollment levels in the sophomore, junior, and senior years to generate revenues always exists if administrators believe there is excess capacity in those academic classes. The temptation is enhanced if they also know that they do not have to worry about providing on-campus housing for additional upper-class students. During this time period, Cornell guaranteed housing on campus only for freshmen, and many students moved to off-campus apartments after their first year.[2]

How can an institution have a freshman class of around 3,000 but a total on-campus undergraduate enrollment of about 13,000 if it takes four years of course work to complete college? The answers are what make enrollment management such a complex subject and the job of the administrator in charge of enrollment management so difficult. One set of factors causes overall on-campus enrollments to be *less* than four times the size of freshman class enrollments, in the absence of offsetting actions taken by the university. Some students leave the university voluntarily or involuntarily before receiving their degrees. Most of those who do so leave during or at the end of their freshman year. Some students take advantage of advanced placement credits, summer school courses at Cornell or elsewhere, or course overloads and graduate in fewer than four years. Other students enroll in off-campus programs that Cornell offers in the United States and abroad. In most cases, tuition paid by students in these programs goes toward the operation of the programs and does not help to cover the salaries of faculty and staff, or other operating costs, at the Ithaca campus.

If the university can predict, on average, how many students will leave without graduating, will graduate early, or will be involved in off-campus programs each semester, it can attempt to "replace" these students to maintain the desired on-campus enrollment level. One way is to admit some freshmen starting in the spring rather than the fall. Typically, these students come from the waiting list for fall admission and are offered the opportunity instead to start in the spring. If Cornell is a student's first choice, the student will often choose to postpone college entry for a semester to have the opportunity to attend Cornell. A second way is to admit transfer students at the start of their sophomore and junior years. These tend to be students who attended two-year colleges or other four-year colleges and have demonstrated by their performance at these institutions that they are can do well at Cornell if given the opportunity.

A second set of factors causes Cornell's total on-campus undergraduate enrollment to be more than four times the size of its freshman class. Cornell's undergraduate architecture program is a five-year program, so it will always have five years of students, rather than four, enrolled. Some other students take five years to graduate rather than four. Indeed, students from disadvantaged backgrounds are often encouraged by the university to take an extra year, with a lighter course load each semester, to increase their likelihood of succeeding. The university even gives them financial aid, if needed, for the fifth year of study.

A third reason is that, by agreement with New York state, about 55 percent of the undergraduate students enrolled in Cornell's statutory colleges are juniors and seniors. This is so because New York state wants to provide opportunities for graduates of its two-year colleges to attend Cornell's statutory colleges. Consequently, the statutory colleges enroll more transfer students each year than are needed to "replace" students not in attendance for the reasons noted above. Several of the statutory colleges have formal "articulation agreements" with two-year colleges in the state that provide that any graduate of those colleges who attains a specified grade point average and completes a specified set of required courses will be admitted to the statutory college. Finally, one of Cornell's endowed undergraduate colleges, the hotel school, which is not included in the general-purpose budget envelope, has moved to aggressively recruit transfer students to increase its revenues.

The net result of all these forces is that while 3,164 freshmen newly enrolled at Cornell in the fall of 1997, 506 transfer students also enrolled. Put another way, almost 14 percent of the new students enrolling at Cornell in the fall of 1997 transferred to Cornell from other institutions. The percentage varied widely across the undergraduate budgetary units of the university, ranging from a low of 5.7 in the endowed general-purpose colleges, to 13.9 in the statutory colleges, to a high of 19.8 in the School of Hotel Administration.

Table 13.2 shows how the percentages of undergraduate students enrolled in these three budget units changed during the 1987–1997 period. Cornell's endowed general-purpose colleges (Arts and Sciences, Engineering, and Art, Architecture, and Planning) averaged between 55 and 56 percent of undergraduate enrollments throughout most of the period, before falling to 54.4 percent in the fall of 1997. The three undergraduate statutory colleges' enrollments fluctuated between 38.3 and 39.2 percent, before jumping to 39.5 percent in the last year. Finally, the School of Hotel Administration ranged between 5.2 and 5.3 percent of the total through the fall of 1992 and then rose steadily to 6.1 percent in the fall of 1997.

Table 13.2   Percentage of undergraduate students enrolled in different budgetary units at Cornell University, fall 1987 through fall 1997.

Year	General-purpose colleges	Statutory colleges	Hotel school
1987	55.9	38.9	5.2
1988	55.5	39.2	5.3
1989	55.7	38.9	5.3
1990	56.0	38.8	5.2
1991	56.2	38.7	5.2
1992	55.8	38.9	5.3
1993	56.2	38.3	5.5
1994	55.2	39.2	5.5
1995	55.0	39.1	5.9
1996	55.0	39.0	6.0
1997	54.4	39.5	6.1

Source: Cornell University *Fact Book* (electronic version, available at <http://www.ipr.cornell.edu>). Data are as of the third week of classes.

The increase in the statutory colleges' share of students in the last year was partly due to a decision to allow them to expand enrollments to help offset a budget reduction that had been imposed upon them by New York state and the SUNY system. As a share of the total enrollment, the hotel school's increase over the entire period from 5.2 to 6.1 percent was small. However, this increase represents more than a 17 percent increase in its share of total undergraduate enrollments. If total undergraduate enrollment had remained constant, this would have led to more than a 17 percent increase in its tuition revenue. The hotel school accomplished the growth in its enrollment share both by aggressively increasing the number of transfer students that it enrolled and by enrolling more freshmen.

The drop in the endowed general-purpose colleges' enrollment share from 55.0 to 54.4 in the fall of 1997 represented only about a 1 percent drop in these colleges' share. But this translates into several million dollars of revenue for them. No central administrator made the decision that the implicit transfer of revenue from the general-purpose colleges to the hotel school that occurred in the year was in the best interest of the university as a whole. Given the budgetary arrangements in place at the university, the administration could not "tax" the hotel school's revenue gain to provide some budget relief for general-purpose colleges.

If we focus on numbers of undergraduate students rather than percentage shares, this point is even clearer. Between the fall of 1987 and the fall of 1996, undergraduate enrollments in the hotel school increased from 679 to 817, or a total of 20 percent. During the same period of time undergraduate enrollments in the general-purpose colleges, by far the two largest being the Colleges of Arts and Sciences and Engineering, increased from 7,238 to 7,427, or 2.6 percent. It would be nice if I could tell you that the university valued the hotel school's academic programs more than it valued the academic programs in Arts and Sciences and Engineering and thus chose to increase the hotel school's enrollment by more than it did enrollment in the other two colleges. But I doubt that that judgment was ever made.

Rather, the central administration could not, or did not choose to, allocate firm "quotas" for enrollment to the hotel school. Since that school was a tub, any "mistakes" that it made that led its enrollments to be higher than expected generated tuition revenue that accrued primarily to itself. I say primarily because the share of the university-wide administrative costs that the hotel school pays is related to its share of the student body. But all of the tuition income that came from these extra students, net of these administrative costs and financial aid costs, went to the school and not to the university as a whole. Hence while the dean of the College of Arts and Sciences had to make a small cut in the size of his college's faculty between the fall of 1992 and the fall of 1997, the hotel school increased its faculty size by 20 percent during the period.

As Table 13.1 indicates, total undergraduate enrollment at Cornell fell by slightly over 200 students between the fall of 1997 and the fall of 1998. Virtually the entire drop occurred in the three general-purpose colleges. As a result, the provost, who controls the budgets of these colleges, collected about $4.2 million less in undergraduate tuition revenue than had been planned that year. This shortfall resulted from the inability of the university to perfectly predict how many students will graduate early, how many will go to off-campus programs, how many will transfer to other universities, how many will take medical and other leaves, and how many admitted freshmen and transfer students will actually enroll.

Most universities are aware that they will experience annual fluctuations in the number of enrolled students, so they establish "enrollment reserves," or "rainy day" accounts. In good years, when more students enroll than are expected, the extra revenue that is received is sequestered in a reserve account. In bad years, when fewer students enroll, the loss in tuition revenue is made up from the reserve account. Unfortunately, in years when budgets are tight for reasons other than enrollment shortfalls, administrators face pressures to use any unexpected tuition revenue or to draw from the reserve account to help balance the current year budget.

As federal and state funds to support higher education have dried up, universities have increasingly become dependent on the undergraduate tuition revenue that they generate. An institution can expand tuition revenue either by increasing tuition levels or by expanding enrollment. Given external pressures to limit tuition increases, expanding enrollments becomes a subject of hot discussion. One way to expand enrollments is to increase freshman enrollments. But given the capacity constraints that exist in freshman housing and classes at Cornell, to do so would be an expensive proposition. Moreover, if Cornell did expand freshman year enrollments, it would have to "dig deeper" into its applicant pool to admit more students. This would, at least marginally, reduce its selectivity, which would reduce its ratings as an undergraduate institution.

Another strategy is to admit more transfer students. Both the statutory colleges and the hotel school already admit a substantial fraction of their students via the transfer student route. Many of these are students who almost qualified for admission when they initially applied to be admitted as freshmen and who were asked to defer their admission for a semester or a year. Others are graduates of two-year colleges. In the main the academic credentials of Cornell's transfer students are not as strong as the credentials of those students the university accepts as freshmen. However, this does not "cost" the university anything in the ratings game because the ratings of undergraduate student quality are typically based only on the test scores and class rank of entering freshman students.

Of course, employers recruit at Cornell both because of the quality of the education the university provides and because of the quality of the students that it enrolls. To date, the university has not observed that students who first enrolled at the university via the transfer student route fare poorer in the post-college job market than students who spent their entire undergraduate career at Cornell. If the university did substantially increase the recruitment of transfer students, it is possible that recruiters might begin to worry about whether transfer students were as high in quality as Cornell's other students.

During my term as a Cornell vice president, my fellow administrators and I suggested to the Colleges of Arts and Sciences and Engineering several times that they seriously consider increasing their enrollment of transfer students to generate revenue that could be used to help support their colleges. These suggestions were never warmly received. The College of Engineering worried that its curriculum, with its emphasis on required courses, would put transfer students at a serious disadvantage. Little thought was given by the college to admitting a substantial number of freshmen in the spring and offering some sections of required sequences starting in the spring and finishing in the fall, so that these students could catch up.

The admissions staff and some faculty in the College of Arts and Sciences were also hostile to these proposals. To them, the essence of a Cornell Arts and Science student's education was to enroll at Cornell for four years and take the majority of courses within that college. They worried that an Arts and Science diploma would mean less if students received a larger share of their education elsewhere. Interestingly, the college allows its own students who begin as freshmen to receive academic credit for advance placement courses and summer courses taken at other academic institutions. It also allows its own students to receive up to a year's credit for study at a foreign university and in the Cornell-in-Washington program. Hence the college already allows students to receive credit for more than a year's study elsewhere. Faculty and staff opposed to increasing the number of transfer students appear not to understand (at least to judge from their public statements), the logical inconsistency in their position.

Both of my sons were admitted to Cornell's College of Arts and Sciences. My younger son started his college career elsewhere. When he decided to transfer to Cornell, he spoke to a staff member in the college's admission office. Even though he had already been admitted and had done well at the college he was attending, that staff member was very negative about the college's desire for transfer students. So my son quickly visited one of the statutory colleges, where the admissions staff arranged almost instantaneously for him to transfer to Cornell. Cornell's statutory colleges understand the importance to the university of talented transfer students. My son graduated from Cornell with a strong academic record and went on to graduate from one of our nation's top law schools.

Graduate Enrollment

Graduate education at Cornell encompasses both research and professional degree programs. Determining the mix of graduate students between these two types of programs is an important enrollment management issue. So too is monitoring the mix of research-oriented doctoral students, between those for whom the university pays tuition and those for whom tuition payments are made by external payers or the students themselves. When the university pays the students' tuition itself, enrollment of the students generates no net revenue for the institution.

The primary research-oriented degree is the Doctor of Philosophy degree (Ph.D.), and about 2,700 students were pursuing this degree in the fall of 1997. About another 300 students were enrolled in research-oriented master's degree programs. Some of these students will end their studies once they receive their degree, while others will enroll in Ph.D. study at the university or elsewhere.

Three units on Cornell's Ithaca campus do not offer undergraduate degrees. The primary teaching responsibility of these schools—the Johnson Graduate School of Management, the Law School, and the College of Veterinary Medicine—is professional education for graduate students. They offer in turn the Master of Business Administration (MBA), the Doctor of Jurisprudence (JD), and the Doctor of Veterinary Medicine (DVM) degrees. Slightly more than 1,400 students were enrolled in these programs in the fall of 1997. There are several other professional master's programs at the university, offered by the faculty of other colleges under the supervision of Cornell's graduate school, that prepare students for professional careers. In the fall of 1997, about 875 students were enrolled in these programs. In total, there were almost 5,300 graduate students enrolled at Cornell's Ithaca campus that fall.

Doctoral education and the production of new Ph.D. students is in many ways the lifeblood and soul of the academic profession and major research universities. Ph.D. students contribute to faculty research projects, especially in science and engineering fields, by serving as research assistants. Others make important contributions to the undergraduate teaching mission of the university by serving as teaching assistants. In this role they may conduct discussion sections for large lecture classes, hold office hours, and grade exams. Many faculty members view the production of the next generation of scholars and researchers as among their most important missions.

Table 13.3 presents information on the major source of financial support for Cornell's doctoral degree students in the falls of 1988 and 1997. "Major" means the source that provided at least half of a student's support. In 1997, 43 percent of all students received their major source of support from Cornell University, in the form of a teaching assistantship, a research assistantship, or a fellowship. Fellowships, unlike assistantships, carry no work ex-

Table 13.3   Major sources of financial support for doctoral degree students at Cornell University, 1988 and 1997 (percentage of total number of students).

Support	1988	1997	Change, 1988–1997
All Fields			
Cornell funds	1,237 (41%)	1,184 (43%)	−53
External funds	1,545 (53%)	1,222 (52%)	−323
Self/unknown	186 (6%)	107 (4%)	−79
Physical Sciences			
Cornell funds	418 (32%)	343 (38%)	−75
External funds	811 (64%)	544 (60%)	−267
Self/unknown	47 (4%)	20 (2%)	−27

Source: Cornell University, *Annual Report of the Graduate School: 1997–98* (August 1998), table E11 where Cornell funds = fellowships, teaching assistantships, and research assistants paid for by internal university funds; external funds = fellowships, research assistantships, and research traineeships financed by the federal government and other external funders; self/unknown = self-financed or major source of funding cannot be identified.

pectation. Typically, but not always, each type of support includes a stipend as well as funds to cover the cost of the student's tuition. In effect, the university is giving funds to these students so that they can give them right back to the university in the form of tuition payments. The university receives no net tuition revenue from enrolling such students.

The majority of the students, 52 percent in 1997, were supported by funds that were provided by external sources. These include fellowships from federal and state governments, private foundations, and international agencies, as well as research assistantships and research traineeships provided by government, industry, and foundations. These awards usually include funds to cover the recipient's tuition. But in recent years some external funders have placed limitations on the amount of tuition that they will pay for each student, and pay only a share of the student's tuition. When students are supported on external funding, tuition dollars do flow into the university.

Finally, there are a small number of students, only about 100 in 1997, who were paying their tuition out of their own resources or whose major source of support could not be determined by Cornell's graduate school. For simplicity, I will ignore these students in what follows.

Although doctoral education is the lifeblood of the academic profession, the number of doctoral students at Cornell fell substantially between 1988 and 1997. Doctoral program enrollments, which were around 3,100 in the fall of 1991, rose slightly during the next three years but then plummeted to around 2,700 in 1997. Although there were fluctuations in the number of doctoral students enrolled in the biological sciences, the humanities, and the social sciences during the period, the major disciplines responsible for the decline were the physical sciences and engineering. During the period enrollments in these disciplines fell almost continuously from 1,298 to 925.

One contributing factor to this precipitous decline was a decision by Cornell's physics department to reduce the size of its doctoral program. It did so because the job market for new doctorates in physics had dried up, and the department was having difficulty placing its graduates in suitable positions. This was a responsible, but difficult, decision to make for one of the most distinguished departments in the university.

Another factor was a cutback in the size of Cornell's engineering faculty. Because of tight budgets, Cornell's engineering faculty size contracted from 230 in 1990–91 to 212 in 1995–96. The engineering dean noted that the fewer faculty that he had, the fewer external research grants the college would receive and thus the fewer the graduate students that could be supported on external funds. If the amount of university funds to support graduate students remained constant (it actually decreased), the college necessarily would have had to cut back on the size of its doctoral programs.

Still a third factor was the growing difficulty Cornell faculty faced in obtaining external research funding, in particular funds to support graduate students. The share of National Science Foundation research funding, for example, that went to faculty at the twenty universities that received the largest shares of National Science Foundation research funding had declined for a number of years. Cornell had been among the top three universities in the nation in National Science Foundation research funding, and its faculty members were among the faculty that had lost by the redirection of funding to other universities. In addition, research grants had become more and more equipment intensive, and thus for any given total research budget, there was less money available to support graduate students.

Finally, the cost of including graduate students in grant applications was felt by many faculty members to be becoming prohibitive. A faculty member had to budget between $40,000 and $50,000 a year in a grant to cover the stipend and the tuition for a graduate research assistant. The assistant would work half-time (fifteen to twenty hours a week) during the academic year and full-time during the summer. The cost was this high because of the high endowed Cornell tuition.

For a similar amount of money, the faculty member could instead hire a full-time post-doctoral fellow. This person would give the faculty member more research help than the graduate research assistant would. Faculty members were faced with a conflict: was their primary obligation to produce Ph.D. students or to produce their own research? Increasingly, the faculty worried about maximizing their research output and eliminated graduate assistants from their grant applications.

The data presented in Table 13.3 suggest that the major decline in doctoral students that occurred during the 1988–1997 period came in externally funded students. Between the ten years, the number of externally funded students declined by 323. Over 80 percent of this decline, 267 students, occurred in the physical science and engineering fields. The tuition level was $21,876 for endowed doctoral students in 1997–98. If externally funded doctoral enrollments in the physical sciences and engineering had been maintained at their fall 1988 level, the endowed general-purpose budget, which receives externally paid graduate tuition for students in these fields, would have had almost $6 million more to spend in 1997–98.

Interestingly, enrollments of doctoral students supported on Cornell funds also fell by 53 during the period. One reason for this decline was that the university had to cut back on the number of teaching assistants it funded owing to budgetary reductions. This decline did not lead to any decrease in the net tuition revenue received by the university because it was paying these students' tuition revenues itself. It did lead, however, to larger discussion sections in some first year undergraduate classes.

A second reason was that the university was increasingly losing top students, particularly in science and engineering fields, to competitors that were increasing the number of fellowships they offered and their stipends. For example, Stanford University announced one major new fellowship program in May of 1996. Inasmuch as money matters, if Cornell wanted to remain among the leaders in graduate education, it had to "even out" the playing field by increasing its number of internally financed doctoral fellowships and their stipend levels.

Over a number of years the university moved aggressively to try to stem its losses in doctoral enrollments. One provost agreed to provide half the tuition for any graduate student supported by external funds. Most of the revenue that was lost to the university by this change was made up by raising the level of tuition charged to graduate students working on their dissertations. It was hoped that reducing the cost of including a graduate assistant in an external grant would encourage faculty members to include graduate assistants, rather than post-doctoral fellows, in their external grant applications. It was also hoped that this reduction in costs would make their grant applications more competitive in external grant competitions. This new policy went into effect on July 1, 1997. When I wrote this chapter, the university had yet to determine whether the policy is having its intended effect of generating more external tuition support for doctoral students.

The successor to the provost who made this policy change, along with Cornell's president and graduate dean, worked hard to improve the number and stipend size of the fellowships that Cornell offers in the physical sciences, engineering, life sciences, and applied social sciences. The number of such fellowships awarded annually to incoming first-year students was increased from 20 to 100 and the stipend levels were also increased.

The university was able to do this because, as I described earlier, the payout rate on its endowment had fallen to a low level owing to the rapid rise in stock market prices during the 1990s. The Cornell trustees responded by substantially increasing the payout rate for the academic year 1998–99. As a result, no activities had to be cut at the university to fund the larger number of more generous graduate fellowships. The university simply used some of the increased payout on the endowment to fund the fellowship program.

The increase in the number of fellowships and their stipends will eventually cost the university about $1.25 million a year.[3] But although no other activities were cut back to provide for this program, the money could have been used elsewhere, for example to increase faculty salaries or to moderate undergraduate tuition increases.

Whether Cornell's efforts to increase, or at least stem the decline in, the external funding it receives for doctoral students' tuition will succeed is an open question.[4] The university faces a difficult task because many universities are facing the same pressures. An additional strategy, which is not mutually exclusive, is to try to increase the graduate tuition revenue that the university takes in to its general-purpose budget by expanding existing professional master's programs or creating new ones.

Table 13.4 provides information on the enrollment levels in professional master's degree programs at Cornell in the fall of 1997. There were 878 students enrolled in these programs. This figure does not include the 1,400 plus students enrolled in professional programs in Cornell's Johnson Graduate School of Management, the School of Law, and the College of Veterinary

Medicine. Since these three units are tubs, the revenues they generate stay with the unit, and hence expanding their programs would not generate direct benefits for the general-purpose budget. An issue here Cornell must address is whether it should focus on expanding professional master's programs in its general-purpose colleges. As the table should make clear, existing professional master's programs are concentrated in the College of Engineering and the applied social science fields. Virtually all of the latter programs, except for Public Administration and City and Regional Planning, are not part of the general-purpose college budget.

The attraction of expanding professional master's programs is that students enroll in such programs because of the payoff in improved employ-

Table 13.4   Professional master's degree program enrollments at Cornell University, fall 1997. Key: G = general-purpose colleges; S = statutory colleges; H = the hotel school; and L = the law school.

Program	Budget envelope	Enrollment[a]
Humanities	G	49
Fine Arts		11
Creative Writing		16
Biological Sciences	S	8
Physical Sciences	G	326
Engineering		323
Social Sciences		495
Health Administration	S	30
Hospitality Management	H	112
Industrial & Labor Relations	S	53
Landscape Architecture	S	29
Law	L	54
Public Administration	G	35
City and Regional Planning	G	46
Total		878

Source: Cornell University, *Annual Report of the Graduate School, 1997–98* (August 1998), table E3, and Cornell University *Fact Book* (electronic version, available at <http://www.irp.cornell.edu>).

a. These numbers exclude enrollments in first professional degree programs in the three Cornell colleges that do not award undergraduate degrees. These are the MBA program (560), the JD program in law (528), and the DVM program in veterinary medicine (318).

ment opportunities that they expect. They typically receive much less financial assistance from university funds than do students enrolled in Ph.D. programs and also receive less financial aid, on average, than do the university's undergraduates. Hence these programs have the potential to generate revenues that can help support the core undergraduate and doctoral programs at the institution. Many urban institutions, being located amid large populations, offer part-time evening professional programs to enhance their revenue base. Some offer executive master's programs in which instruction takes place one or two weekends a month in a concentrated fashion. Still others now offer programs through distance learning methods, with occasional weekends or weeks on campus.[5]

Cornell is blessed with an idyllic rural location that is often described as being centrally isolated. Without a large urban adult population nearby to draw on, if it hopes to generate substantial additional revenue from professional master's programs, it probably must do so through distance learning technologies. (Distance learning will be discussed in the next chapter).

I "preached" the importance of expanding Cornell's professional master's programs throughout my term as an administrator. By doing so I risked being declared a heretic, especially by faculty in Cornell's College of Arts and Sciences, which currently has professional master's programs in only a handful of arts and humanities fields. After all, many Cornell faculty believe that the primary purpose of the university is to conduct research and to educate undergraduates and Ph.D. students on campus. They saw calls by the administration to get them involved in professional master's programs and distance learning as indicative that the administration had different values than they did. Some viewed such calls as evidence of a battle for the very "soul" of the university, with the administration trying to reorient the university away from what the faculty valued. They did not understand, or pretended that they did not understand, that the economic climate is no longer favorable to the university. The administration called for these efforts to generate revenue to enhance Cornell's core research and teaching programs, not to weaken them. In the absence of such revenues, Cornell will probably have to reduce its efforts in Ph.D. education.

One faculty group that did understand the change in the economic environment facing universities was the newly formed university-wide department of statistics. Working with me, members of this department proposed and received approval for the creation of a Master's Degree in Applied Statistics. This program is designed to provide liberal arts college graduates and practitioners in the field with the technical training that they will need to serve as statisticians in industries, such as the pharmaceutical industry. Thus academically the program has an important justification. Although some faculty members will need to devote part of their time to teaching courses to students enrolled in the program and to supervising their master's projects, the revenue generated by the program will come back to the department to help it expand its academic programs. The revenue will be used to hire an additional faculty member who will bring new research capabilities to the department, to provide teaching assistantships for several more Ph.D. students, and to provide computer support and equipment that will enhance the research capabilities of the department's faculty and Ph.D. students.

You need only read the pages of the Sunday *New York Times,* or any other large city newspaper, to see the extent to which major research universities are trying to expand their professional master's programs to generate revenue. Even the University of Chicago's College of Arts and Sciences, long a bastion of academic idealism and elitism, now finds faculty in a number of its fields involved with applied master's programs. For example, Chicago's mathematics department now offers a master's degree in financial mathematics in conjunction with professionals from the financial industry. The program is structured to attract part-time enrollees and taught in evenings at a downtown Chicago location. Perhaps the fact that the president of the University of Chicago when the program was instituted, Hugo Sonnenschein, is a distinguished economist helped awaken that university's faculty to the need for such programs.

Faced with the need to generate more revenue to support the annual operations of the University of Chicago and an ambitious capital construction plan, Sonnenschein also saw the need to expand undergraduate enrollments at the university. A restructuring of the undergraduate curriculum that it was thought would make the university more attractive to a wider range of students was adopted by the faculty. But constant protests by some of the university's long-time senior faculty that this would fundamentally change the institution and protests by many alumni caused Sonnenschein to conclude that the university would best be served by new leadership. Although he had strong support for his program from the university's trustees, he announced his intention to resign his position twelve months later in June of 1999, and he did resign in that month.[6] His experience shows how difficult it is even for a president to "move" a major university.

CHAPTER 14

Information Technology, Libraries, and Distance Learning

Information Technology

Changes in information technology are sweeping American campuses. As the price of computer power and memory has declined, the appetites for them have grown at an even more rapid rate. All facilities on the campus are linked to each other by fiber-optic networks and in turn to the outside world through the Internet. Things only dreams a decade ago are now taken for granted. Pity the poor college or university that makes its students stand in long lines at the beginning of each semester to register for courses. Students now expect to be able to register on line.

Each student at Cornell is given an e-mail account on the day that he or she enrolls at the university. Students can easily communicate with their professors via e-mail if they have questions. They no longer need to wait for a professor's office hours. Professors can establish electronic mailing lists for each of their classes and for their advisees and can easily communicate with each group. Students can keep in touch with friends around the world and with their parents by sending the same message to all of them simultaneously.

Professors can almost instantaneously update teaching materials and then make these easily accessible to students at any hour of the day using the World Wide Web. Some faculty members put their lecture notes on the Web, permitting their students to read them before class. This practice can enhance the value of the lectures, and if anything is unclear to students during a lecture, the students can go back to the lecture notes themselves for clarification. But the availability of lecture notes on the Web does allow students to skip early morning classes more often than they formerly did.

One of my colleagues conducts office hours both in real time and via e-mail. If any student asks a question using either method, the professor inserts a "star" at the point in the Web-formatted lecture notes that relates to the question. Any student in the class can then click on the star to see both the question and the answer. In an earlier era, if a student came to my colleague with a question, the colleague would answer it and one student would have a misunderstanding cleared up. Now if any one student asks that a point be clarified, all students can see the clarification.

In many university classes extensive reserved readings are assigned. In an earlier era, students had to go to the library to find these readings and usually were permitted to keep them only for a few hours. If one student had borrowed an article, other students had to wait until it was returned. To avoid having students do this, some professors arranged, after having received copyright clearances from the publisher of each reading, for packets of course readings to be copied and then sold through the campus store or local copy outlet. Now, with back issues of journals in some disciplines, as well as many working paper series, available on line and free of copyright restrictions (see the discussion of JSTOR in the next section), it is sometimes possible for professors to "link" the electronic version of their reading lists to journals, working papers, or data sources. Students can read these materials from their dorm rooms if they are connected to the World Wide Web.

The quantity of information that is available on the Web is almost unfathomable. At numbers of places in this book, you will find references to data I obtained from sources on the Web or from searches of the Web pages for sets of universities. The availability of such information has drastically increased my research productivity. So too has e-mail and the ease of attaching documents to e-mail messages. The latter has made conducting research with colleagues at other universities often as easy as conducting research with colleagues and students at my own university.

These are but a few examples of how changes in information technology have transformed academia. Additional examples will appear below. Clearly, changes in information technology are altering the educational and research process at universities. Increasingly, even within residential campuses such as Cornell, *distributed learning* is taking place. Both learners and the sources of learning are no longer tightly bound by either time or location. In many respects, these changes are enhancing the quality of students' educational experiences.

The quality of a product is an important concept. Take automobiles as an example. I bought my first car over thirty years ago. The quality of the cars that I buy today is very different from the quality of the ones that I purchased back in the 1960s. To name but a few changes, AM radios have been replaced by AM-FM radios with tape decks or CD players and quadraphonic sound. Rear-wheel-drive cars have given way to front-wheel-drive cars and increasingly now four-wheel-drive ones. Lap seat belts have been replaced by seat belts that constrain wearers both at the waist and across the chest, and air bags have been added for extra protection. Finally, hand-cranked windows have been replaced by power windows. Many of these features have substantial costs and add to the price of new cars.

The Bureau of Labor Statistics, the government agency that collects data to compute the consumer price index, is well aware that the quality of automobiles is changing. It attempts to take account of quality changes in automobiles and other products when it computes changes in the consumer price index. Changes in the consumer price index are intended to represent changes in the prices of a given market basket of goods and services. The bureau goes to considerable effort to ensure that increases in consumer prices that are due to increases in product quality are not reflected in measures of inflation.

Unfortunately, while public attention is often focused on how high tuition levels in selective private colleges and universities have become and how rapidly they are rising, little recognition is given to how technology changes have influenced the quality of the product the institutions are delivering to their students. Improvements in quality do not necessarily translate into improved student learning. However, they do often translate into improved student satisfaction; students like to spend less time standing in lines to register for courses and obtain reserve materials and to take advantage of information on the World Wide Web.

This is important because while changes in information technology enhance the quality of students' collegiate experiences, they often increase costs. Thus part of the reason that tuition increases at selective universities have outpaced the rate of inflation in consumer prices in recent years is that the consumer price index tries to take account of the changing quality of products being consumed while published data on changes in tuition rates do not.

If the price of computer power is falling, why are information technology costs at the university rising so rapidly? One reason is that the shift to networks, the Web, and a client/server computing system based heavily on personal computers and individual work sites has multiplied the number of staff needed to support the use of information technology at the university. When I came to Cornell in 1974, my college had one computer/statistical consultant on its staff to support all academic and administrative computing. Now, with a student body and faculty unchanged in size, the college has ten professionals and many part-time student employees in the information technology area. The functions they perform include maintaining networks, purchasing and installing computer hardware and software, maintaining and supervising networked computer labs, creating and maintaining Web pages for the college, responding to problems that individual faculty members are having with their computers or printers, helping professors prepare on-line materials for classes, and answering students' questions.

Another reason for high costs is that personal computers must now be placed on the desks of all faculty members and support staff at the university. These machines become obsolete rapidly because software and Internet browser developers keep adding features to their programs, and the minimum amount of memory that a personal computer must have to allow its user to connect to the Web and use new and revised software keeps growing. What is a large personal computer today in an academic environment may be barely adequate in three years and totally obsolete in five. Although memory can be added to existing machines, such upgrades too have a cost.

Yet another reason for high costs is the continuing and rapid growth of information flowing between users on the network. As usage of the network expands exponentially, the network becomes overburdened and can no longer meet the demands that the campus community places on it. Electric power systems sometimes sustain blackouts when they are overtaxed on extremely hot summer days because of the load that extra air conditioning usage places on them. Similarly, when the university's network is overloaded, users find it takes longer to connect to the network and periodically the system crashes from overuse. So at regular intervals the campus must be rewired at considerable expense with more modern and larger-capacity fiber-optic cables to handle the increased volume of traffic.

Cornell has roughly 1,600 faculty members and if each was provided with a $2,500 personal computer every three years, the university would have to spend $1.33 million a year for this equipment alone. To this cost would have to be added the costs of the software licenses, the fees for connecting these machines to the network (which cover the capital and debt service costs of the network), and the costs of all of the information technology support personnel employed by each of the colleges and the central information technology group. To these costs must be added similar costs for all the administrative staff at the university, the costs of computer laboratories for undergraduate and graduate students, and the costs of operating and maintaining all of the high-end research computing on the campus. It should therefore come as no surprise that in 1997 Cornell's vice president for information technology estimated that the Ithaca campus of the university was spending almost $80 million a year on information technology, broadly defined. This represented over 8 percent of the total expenditures on the Ithaca campus that year.

Finally, costs keep rising partly because it is often hard to convince those in charge of information technology in academia that their jobs are not to install what is technologically the most satisfying and most advanced system, but rather to balance what they would like to see done with the fiscal reality that their institution faces. Because most central university administrators' eyes glaze over when the technical details of networks are discussed, information technology administrators have an advantage in the internal university battle for scarce funds. Most central administrators don't have the technical know-how to figure out whether what is being proposed is really needed by the campus or whether it is simply in the professional interests of the information technology administrators.

This point was brought home to me when Cornell's central information technology networking group warned Cornell's senior administrators that its internal computer network was rapidly approaching the point where it could not handle the information flow. The members of the group proposed that Cornell could demonstrate to the world that it was a leader in the application of information technology by installing a new network that would integrate the transmission of both data and voices. That is, they proposed replacing the existing internal voice telephone network and the data transmission network with a single integrated system. This would mean the elimination of telephones as separate pieces of equipment. Stand-alone phones would be replaced by devices that plugged into desktop work stations. Although the technology they proposed to install was still being tested, they felt sure that it would be operational within the two-year period it would take to install the new system.

The costs of the networks at Cornell are born by users in the form of monthly charges for connections. In the initial plan the networking group presented to the university's senior administrators, the borrowing needed to finance the installation of all the new fiber-optic cable and system hardware was structured in such a way that, on average, users would not see any increase in their connection costs. So the group believed that its proposal was a "no-brainer" and that the university should eagerly approve it.

I almost went through the roof! Although on average users would not see any increase in their rates, there would be substantial distributional effects. In particular, those faculty and staff who previously used only a telephone and did not need a work station would see their rates rise, while individuals, such as myself, who previously had two connections—one for the telephone and one for the work station—would see their rates decline.

In addition, everyone would need to have a new, larger work station that was compatible with the proposed system. The costs users would incur to replace their personal computers were not included in the networking group's cost estimates because the group argued that personal computers are regularly replaced on campus anyway. The tremendous decline in the cost of computational power and computer memory meant, the group pointed out, that the necessary computers could be purchased at a cost no greater than that of the older models that they were replacing.

Although this was certainly true, implementing the group's recommendations would effectively mandate a more rapid replacement cycle for personal computers than the university had been able to achieve in the past. The number of work stations on campus would have to expand. Any savings that could have been achieved because the cost of computing power and computer memory had declined would be eaten up by the increase in memory that the new computers would have to have. Put another way, the group's plan would prevent the university from achieving any savings when it periodically replaced personal computers for faculty, staff, and student computer laboratories, savings that could be used for other purposes or to hold down costs. Nowhere is it etched in stone that if a university spends $2,500 to provide a faculty member with a personal computer in one year, then it must periodically replace that machine by a machine of at least equal cost.

I mentioned what our networking staff was proposing to colleagues at other universities. One was an economist who has served his institution as vice president for information technology for a number of years. He could not prevent himself from laughing when he heard my story. Although he agreed that at some time in the future data and voice transmission networks would be merged (and they may well have been by the time this book is published), he did not see any cost advantage from being one of the first institutions to attempt to achieve this. His university, which is not as dominated as Cornell is by the sciences and engineering, had made an explicit decision not to be a national leader in the provision of information technology to the campus. He and his fellow administrators seemed to understand much better than Cornell's networking staff did that what a university needs to provide for high-end users to remain at the forefront of scientific and engineering research can be very different from what it provides for most users on the campus.

Faced with budgetary pressures, Cornell's other senior administrators recognized and shared my concerns. The information technology people were told to come back with a cheaper proposal, and planning for a new unified voice and data transmission network was placed on the back burner.

Libraries

Cornell University has a truly magnificent library system. Table 14.1 summarizes information for 1996–97 on the holdings, staffing, and expenditures of the thirteen highest-rated private selective private universities by *USNWR* in its 1999 ranking of undergraduate institutions. Harvard's library was by far the largest in the group, with holdings of 13.6 million volumes, the addition of 295,000 new volumes, and the receipt of 101,000 different serials (primarily academic journals and magazines) in 1996–97. Cornell's library was ranked fifth in the group in total holdings, second in total volumes added, and fourth in the number of current serials received. About 225,000 volumes in Cornell's collection were housed at its medical college in New York City and in Geneva, New York, at the Cornell Agricultural Experiment Station. By far the bulk of its collection was housed in fifteen different library facilities on the Ithaca campus.

My bragging about the size of Cornell's collection immediately points out one of the major difficulties universities face in trying to reduce library costs. If libraries are valued by the size of their collection and their number of new acquisitions, librarians have little incentive to try to reduce either.

Cornell's fifteen different libraries include ones in the areas of Africana studies, engineering, fine arts, hotel administration, law, management, mathematics, music, physical science, industrial and labor relations, agriculture and human ecology, and veterinary medicine, as well as an undergraduate arts and sciences collection, a central graduate library, and a rare books and manuscript collection. Many of the individual libraries are situ-

Table 14.1 Holdings of selected private university libraries in the United States in 1996–97.

Institution	Volumes in library (millions)	Volumes added (thousands)	Current serials (thousands)	Permanent staff (FTE)	Total expenditures (millions)
Harvard	13.6	295.0	101.0	1008	$70.9
Yale	9.9	182.9	53.3	512	39.1
Stanford	6.9	163.0	46.0	489	43.0
Columbia	6.9	153.2	64.9	427	29.2
Cornell	6.1	195.2	61.8	412	28.4
Princeton	5.5	120.1	34.2	317	24.9
Chicago	6.1	141.3	37.0	252	19.7
Pennsylvania	4.5	117.1	33.8	288	26.3
Duke	4.6	115.8	32.0	288	23.2
Northwestern	3.9	94.1	40.1	242	18.6
Brown	2.9	121.5	13.3	181	14.8
MIT	2.5	48.9	17.4	195	12.5
Dartmouth	2.2	53.9	20.0	156	11.8

Source: "Holdings of Research Libraries in the United States and Canada, 1996–97," *Chronicle of Higher Education: 1998–99 Almanac Issue,* August 27, 1998, p. 40. The data were provided to the *Chronicle* from the *ARL Statistics, 1996–97* publication by the Association of Research Libraries (ARL).

ated in colleges whose budget the provost does not control; others developed over the years because faculty members wanted easy access to materials for themselves and their undergraduate and graduate students.

It is clear that if there were fewer physical locations within the library system there could be substantial savings in staff costs. But the university has never been able to succeed in consolidating its library system because of resistance from stake holders. During my years as a vice president the administration explored consolidating the mathematics and physical science libraries and also considered moving the fine arts library to the main graduate library building. In each case there were loud protests from the faculty of the affected departments or colleges and planning for these moves never got far along.

If one divides the roughly 195,000 new volumes that Cornell added to its collection in 1996–97 by its holdings of 6.1 million volumes that year, one obtains a collection growth rate of roughly 3.2 percent. But the university's holdings actually grew by less that year because the library system does regularly prune its collection and deacquisition some books. For example, if a textbook has been through multiple editions, often the earlier editions will be discarded. I say "often," not "always," because all seven editions of my co-authored labor economics text are still in Cornell's collection. (Apparently it is considered bad taste to get rid of early editions of books written by Cornell professors.) The university spends considerable sums each year trying to preserve old books, but some deteriorate beyond the point of repair and are in such bad shape that copies cannot even be made of them. Some books also vanish from the library each year, presumably owing to theft. On balance the growth rate of the collection is probably in the range of 3 percent a year.

Three percent a year may not seem large, but it implies that the size of the collection will double roughly every twenty-four years, and more and more space will be required to house the collection. There is, however, enormous pressure at Cornell to limit the construction of library facilities on the central campus because of the desire to preserve the scenic quality of the campus. One new library, that housing rare books and manuscripts, was built on the central campus and opened in 1992. But it was situated entirely underground for esthetic reasons.

The cost of that facility was $25 million, approximately double what it would have cost to build a conventional above-ground facility. If an above-ground facility had been built instead and the savings in costs had been placed in an endowment paying out 4 percent a year, the library system would have gained an additional $500,000 a year in revenue in 1992–93. Given the increases in the payout from the endowment that occurred from then to 1996–97, by 1996–97 this figure would have grown to about $625,000. As Table 14.1 indicates, this equals roughly 2.2 percent of the library system's budget that year. This is the cost that building the facility underground, in response to esthetic concerns, imposed on the university's budget.[1]

By the mid-1990s, many of Cornell's libraries had reached capacity. This literally meant that to add any new books to the collection, an equivalent number of existing books had to be deacquisitioned or removed from those libraries and shipped to an off-campus storage location. Having books off campus, where they were not easily accessible, defeated much of the purpose of having them in the collection. This off-campus location was also not one where the temperature and humidity could easily be regulated, and for that reason there was concern that the stored collection would deteriorate.

Given the continued growth of the collection, the university decided that it had to build a modern facility away from the central campus in which rarely used books could be densely stored in a controlled environment, but easily retrieved and delivered to users on campus within a few hours. Harvard University had been one of the first universities to build such a facility and Cornell modified a design that Harvard had used.

Ultimately, the estimated cost of this project reached $4.8 million. In addition to construction costs, this figure included the costs of going into the collections at each library, choosing the books that appear to be rarely used to move to the storage facility, physically moving these volumes, sorting them by size once they arrived at the facility (which was the way to maximize the number of volumes that could be stored in it), and then shelving them in storage bins. Each book was given a unique code that identified it and indicated the precise storage bin in the facility in which it was stored. Retrieval was then a computer-operated process.

Where were the funds to come from to cover the costs of constructing the new facility and the moving of all the materials? Donors are not anxious to provide funding for an out-of-the-way library annex, especially one that was constructed at minimal cost and looked it. Since many people thought of the annex as a form of storage facility, I suggested that the university try to identify some wealthy alumni who were in the moving and storage business and solicit support from them.

Cornell's development office did not view the building as a "naming opportunity" and never took my suggestion seriously. Instead the facility was funded by unrestricted gifts that the university had received. Some of the costs of operating the facility, including the costs of its staff and the costs of courier service to deliver books that users wanted from the facility to on-campus libraries several times a day, were borne by the library system, which reduced its staffing levels in other library units. Other costs, including those of utilities and maintenance, were borne by the general operating budget of the university. So when this new facility opened in 1998, its costs were among the factors that contributed to tuition's rising as much as it did in that year.

Could the university have avoided building this new facility? The simple fact is that for the foreseeable future any research university's library collection will keep expanding. Indeed, the facility has been built in such a way that it can be easily expanded to double or triple its current size. To remain a first-class research university, Cornell needs a library that continues to provide its faculty and students with access to important new materials in their fields.

Of course whether Cornell will be able to afford to continue to maintain its rate of library acquisitions is an open question. Over $7 million of the Cornell library system's budget of $28.4 million in 1996–97 came from the federal government in the form of indirect cost recoveries on research grants in the endowed portion of the university. Cornell has done special studies to show that these expenditures are legitimately related to research that is conducted on sponsored grants. But as the federal government puts increasing pressure on indirect cost rates, the university may no longer be able to anticipate this much federal support for its library system.

In addition, in recent years academic libraries around the nation have seen the prices of the books and periodicals that they purchase increase at rates that far exceed the rate of inflation in recent years. For example, one study of the prices of 312 biology and agricultural journals found that between 1988 and 1994 the average price rose by 35.5 percent for the biology journals and 64.7 percent for the agricultural journals.[2] During the same period, the consumer price index rose by about 25 percent. A more general study by the Association of Research Libraries, a group of 121 primarily university-based research libraries, indicated that between 1986 and 1997 the average costs of serials and monographs rose by 169 percent and 62 percent, respectively.[3] During this time period, the consumer price index rose by only 46 percent.

The decline in the value of the U.S currency that has occurred relative to the value of many foreign currencies over a number of years has also hurt libraries at the many universities that have internationalized their curriculums and that buy a substantial proportion of their books from foreign publishers. Libraries have also seen the internationalization of the publication of English-language materials. Many of the leading scientific journals in English are now published abroad. This too has made library costs very sensitive to the decline in the value of the dollar.

Since library acquisition budgets have tended to rise at rates only slightly greater than the rate of inflation at Cornell, these forces mean that the library acquisitions have declined somewhat over time. The first reductions in acquisitions that were made were in the area of duplicate copies of journals and books. With multiple libraries and colleges, many library volumes appeared in several Cornell libraries. Financial stringency has reduced the duplication of copies, and acquisitions librarians from around the university now collaborate a great deal more in their purchases.

One might think that the availability of digital information sources would reduce the need for acquisitions of print materials. But to date it has not. Many publishers price digital products so that for an additional cost a library can subscribe to them in addition to the print materials. They either do not provide libraries with the option of buying only the digital version of the material or they offer to sell it the digital version alone at a price greater than the price that they charge for the print version.

Furthermore, when institutions are granted access to digital products, it is only for a specified time period. There is no guarantee made of what the price will be in the future, or even whether the digital form of the materials will be preserved indefinitely. So institutions must maintain their print subscriptions. As a result, the availability of these digital information sources increases rather than decreases library costs.

Other periodicals, for example the *Chronicle of Higher Education,* provide access to electronic versions of the publication free to all subscribers to the print version. The electronic version includes access to an archive of articles in back issues, which reduces the need for subscribers to keep the back issues on file. Its archive, however, currently provides access only to the last ten years' issues of the publication. So although the electronic version of the *Chronicle* provides additional benefits, it too does not lead to any reduction in library costs.

The Andrew W. Mellon Foundation has been among the leaders in encouraging the development of ways to reduce library costs through technology.[4] In one series of projects, the foundation has given funding to a set of universities to allow them to make digital images of subsets of their collections that were published many years ago (and hence are no longer subject to copyright restrictions). The hope is that it will prove less costly to preserve and grant access to historic volumes in this manner than it would to try to preserve print volumes. Doing so would also free up space in libraries, since the print volumes could eventually be discarded. Moreover, if one institution has preserved digital images of historic materials and makes it available to individuals at other institutions via the World Wide Web, this reduces the need for other institutions to preserve their print copies of the materials and thus potentially may reduce costs at these institutions also.

In a similar vein, the foundation has developed an independent subsidiary

named JSTOR (for journal storage). As of January 1999, JSTOR had negotiated arrangements with publishers of 117 major journals in the humanities,
social sciences, ecology, and mathematics and statistics to digitize *all* issues of
their journals that are at least five years old.[5] JSTOR makes this collection
available on the World Wide Web to students and faculty at colleges and universities for an initial institutional membership fee and then an annual subscription charge. These charges vary with the type of institution. For example, major research universities now pay a one-time fee of $45,000 to join
the JSTOR consortium (which helps to cover the development costs of the
system) and an annual fee of $5,000 (which helps to cover the recurring cost
of updating and maintaining the system). As of January 1999, 364 American and 36 foreign institutions were members of the consortium.

The restriction to journals that are at least five years old was made so as
not to interfere with the economic interests of publishers of journals. Many
of these publishers are professional associations (such as the American Economic Association) that use the provision of journals as a way of generating
membership and revenue. As each year passes, one more year of issues of
each journal is added to JSTOR's digitized collection.

One might wonder what the economic gain of JSTOR is to academic institutions if they still must subscribe to the current issues of journals. The answer is that potentially they may achieve considerable cost savings. Journals
typically are issued in a paperbound format four to six times a year. After
several years, they are sent to a bindery to have each year's issues bound together with a hard cover to help preserve them. With JSTOR, there is no
need to incur these costs because potentially back issues of journals can be
discarded after five years.

More savings come because each time a volume of a journal is checked
out of the library and then returned, staff time must be spent checking it out
and then reshelving it. The availability of the electronic version via the Web
eliminates these costs. In addition, there are potentially substantial cost savings from not having to keep collections of back issues of the print versions
of journals that libraries have already accumulated in the library collection.
Academic libraries, such as Cornell's, have literally miles of shelving devoted
to storage of back issues of academic journals. One study cited by JSTOR on
its Web page suggests that roughly 25 percent of all university library shelves
are filled with back issues of journals and government documents. If many
of these could be discarded, the need for academic institutions to construct
and maintain new library facilities would be substantially reduced. Careful

economic analyses have shown that the potential cost savings that JSTOR offers academic institutions far exceed the membership fee and the annual maintenance fee that institutions are asked to pay to belong to it.

When I returned to my faculty position, the first task that I faced was to clean up my office and make room for all the new materials I was bringing back from my life as a vice president. Without hesitation, I got rid of (actually donated to eastern European universities) all of my back issues of the economics journals that JSTOR had digitized. I did so because I needed the space that they were taking up in my office and knew I could obtain the journals electronically through JSTOR. I also knew that there was very little risk to me if JSTOR collapsed and its digitized journal issues were no longer preserved, because the Cornell library was going to keep all of its print copies of back issues of JSTOR journals for the foreseeable future.

Therein lies the reason that I use the phrase "potential cost savings" so often above. University librarians worry about whether JSTOR will survive in the long run (even though the Andrew W. Mellon Foundation has committed to seeing it survive), and they also worry about whether the format used to digitize print materials today will be the standard used in the future. Hence although some universities may remove duplicate copies of back issues of journals that JSTOR has digitized from their shelves, very few will take the next step and eliminate the back issues completely from their collections. Until they do so, JSTOR will add marginally to university libraries' costs rather than reducing them.

In the long run, JSTOR promises to be one of the few changes in technology that will reduce universities' costs rather than increasing them. Its digitized journal collection also can deliver services that the standard print version cannot. For example, you can search articles on line looking for a particular author's name and in doing so learn which subsequent articles have cited an article by that author. Then you can retrieve those articles virtually instantaneously, if they are included in the JSTOR collection. As JSTOR grows and includes more and more professional journals, its value to students and faculty will grow. But one must caution that the 117 journals included in its collection in 1999 is a far cry from the almost 62,000 serials that Cornell receives each year. For JSTOR to have a major impact on university library costs, it must substantially expand its scope.

One final point about libraries. Faculty members, who are among the major beneficiaries of university libraries, are also unintentionally among those who contribute to increasing libraries' costs. Upon votes of the faculty, universities are constantly adding new disciplines to their curriculums. For example, a number of years ago Cornell took a very successful China-Japan program and expanded it to cover Korea, renaming the program the East Asia Program. When the teaching and research in the university are expanded to cover a new area, library collections must also be developed for the area. So in addition to having to develop a strong collection of newly published materials relating to Korea, the Cornell library system had to attempt to build a collection of previously published material relating to Korea. This required both new staff and an increase in the acquisitions budget. The costs that new programs will impose upon a university's library system should be considered, but typically are not, in faculty decisions about whether to move into a new curriculum area.

Some of the growth of the curriculum at a university does come at the expense of deemphasizing, or eliminating, other areas. If a university knew that its deemphasis of an area was permanent and that it had no plans to rebuild in that area, then a case could be made that the university should consider divesting itself of much of its library collection pertaining to that area. I know of only one case where this was done. A number of years ago the Johns Hopkins University made a decision to eliminate a certain strand of classics from its graduate curriculum. Given the expense of maintaining rare books in that area, it arranged for Yale, which intended to continue its strong interest in that area, to physically take possession of that collection of books. Johns Hopkins's largess is rarely emulated. University librarians and faculty don't like to contemplate reductions in their library collections.

Distance Learning

Distance learning, broadly defined as instruction that takes place at an off-campus site, has long been part of the portfolio of activities in which colleges and universities engage. Correspondence courses, the provision by extension staff from land grant universities of written materials and formal and informal instruction to farmers, consumers, and workers, courses given at satellite locations by regular and adjunct faculty, and courses in which lectures from a main campus are televised and beamed to other locations are but a few examples of distance learning activities in which colleges and universities have been engaged.

Changes in technology have revolutionized distance learning. E-mail and the World Wide Web permit students from around the world to view lecture notes and readings at their convenience. Problem sets or examinations can be posted on the Web, submitted electronically by students, and then returned to them by the same means. Discussions can be held in real time by using chat rooms on the Web. E-mail list servers permit professors to correspond with their students and each student to correspond with all others. Thus discussions can be generated even if students log on to their computers at different times of the day.

The development of two-way compressed video systems takes televised instruction to the next level. An instructor can lecture in one location to a class, and the images and voices of the instructor and the students at that location can be beamed to many other locations. In an analogous fashion, the images and voices of students from other locations can be beamed in real time to the host location. With practice, an instructor can treat students from different locations as if they were all in the same classroom and get conversations going between groups. With multiple large screens (one for each location) placed strategically at each location, large geographic differences cease to matter.

The possible uses of such technology in academia are almost uncountable. One colleague in my college is teaching a course on international human resource management simultaneously to students in Ithaca, New York; Shanghai, China; Caracas, Venezuela; and Ljubljana, Slovenia. Some of the students outside the United States are taking the course for credit at Cornell or at their home universities. Others are taking the course as part of executive education programs.

A Cornell law professor teaches a course on a very specialized legal topic to law students enrolled at Cornell and three other law schools. Interest in the subject is not sufficient at any one institution to warrant offering the course, and the other three institutions do not have a professor capable of teaching it. By sharing the cost of providing the course at Cornell, all four institutions are able to benefit from it. This course is taught by a combination of real-time two-way compressed video class sessions, and Web-based lectures, readings, and discussion groups.

Still another professor at Cornell jointly taught a class in fashion design with professors at two other universities to students from all three universities. Each professor had a unique specialty, and combining all three specialties in one class gave the students at each institution a much richer education than otherwise would have been the case. This course often involved a fourth site, a major clothing manufacturing facility, where student designs could be critiqued on line by professionals out in the field.

Cornell operates a semester in Washington, D.C. program for undergraduate students in a facility that the university rents. Students live in the facility, participate in internships at government and nonprofit agencies, take courses taught by Cornell and adjunct faculty, and write research papers during their semester stay.

This program reported to me when I was a Cornell vice president, and I quickly realized that the availability of two-way compressed video technology permits the university to have professors from the Ithaca campus teach Cornell students in Washington without having to travel there each week. It also permits, if class schedules can be coordinated, a professor at either location to teach students simultaneously in Ithaca and Washington. It permits the university to engage speakers for alumni events held in Washington without the speakers' having to fly to Washington. It similarly allows high-level government officials from Washington to participate in Cornell classes in Ithaca without their having to make the trek to the campus. Given all these potential uses of the technology, I quickly rounded up funds to install it in our Washington location.

Many selective private universities located in large urban areas have generated considerable revenue for their institutions by offering late afternoon and evening professional master's degree programs, as well as by providing continuing education programs for community members. Other institutions operate thriving executive education programs. Harvard, Pennsylvania, Columbia, Chicago, Duke, Stanford, and Northwestern are but a few examples of universities that are engaged in these activities. A number of institutions also operate executive master's degree programs in which degrees are obtained by intensive study one or two weekends a month for a year or two, along with a final week or several week-long periods of residency on campus.

Because Ithaca is not near a major metropolitan area and has poor airline connections, Cornell has never been able to generate much revenue from evening professional master's degree programs, continuing education programs for adults, or executive education programs. The new technologies opened up the possibility that through distance learning activities the university might be able to enter these markets much more aggressively.

Similarly, many major universities located in or near large urban areas operate large summer session programs. These programs enroll the university's own students who have obtained summer employment in the metropolitan area as well as many students from other colleges and universities who have returned to the area to live with their families during the summer. But because Cornell is not located in a major metropolitan area, few students from other institutions reside in Ithaca during the summer and only a few summer job opportunities keep Cornell students in Ithaca during the summer. Thus the market for Cornell's summer school programs has always been relatively small.

The availability of Web-based technology gives Cornell the opportunity to offer summer session courses to its own and other institutions' students throughout the world, regardless of where they are spending their summers and regardless of whether they are employed full-time during the day. With Web-based courses, students have considerable discretion as to when during the week to work on their courses.

Although summer session distance learning courses have the potential to generate considerable revenue for Cornell, two cautions are in order. First, if Cornell students can take Cornell courses on the Web, so too can they take similar courses offered by other, perhaps cheaper, institutions. Unless Cornell's courses are known to be better than competitors' courses, or there are restrictions placed on the number of courses from other institutions that can be taken during the summer and counted toward a Cornell degree, Cornell's summer session revenue may not be enhanced very much.

Second, if Cornell students take more courses during the summer, this may reduce the number of academic year semesters that they need to be enrolled at Cornell before they receive their degrees. As discussed earlier, students who graduate early present real challenges to the university, and to avoid academic year revenue shortfalls, the university needs to figure out how to "replace" these students.

The growth of distance learning at Cornell has been constrained by a number of faculty concerns. Many faculty members do not view generating revenue for the university and expanding the university's distance learning programs as their responsibility. Others worry that if these activities become part of the normal responsibilities of some faculty, other faculty will be expected to pick up the slack on campus and teach more.

Still others worry about how faculty members will be compensated for these activities. More generally, they worry about who will "own" the materials that are developed for distance learning courses and how they will be compensated for future uses of the materials. Indeed, those uses may not even involve their direct participation.

These *intellectual property rights* issues are thorny ones. The royalties that will result from sales of this book will accrue to me, not to the university. Cornell, and virtually all other academic institutions, make no claim on the royalties earned by faculty members on books they write. It is assumed that in producing these books the faculty authors do not make demands on the resources of the university, above and beyond what is normally provided to all faculty members, such as clerical support and the use of library facilities.

In contrast, if faculty members develop distance learning materials, extensive use of university resources may be involved. Thus the issue arises of who "owns" the materials and how the faculty members should be compensated for participating in preparing them. For example, one of my former graduate students who was teaching at another institution prepared several lectures that were taped and then used in a course offered through video conferencing. She subsequently left that institution.

Does that institution have the right to continue to use her taped lectures? If it does, should she receive the equivalent of royalties each time they are used? Does she have the right to take copies of the tapes with her to her new institution and use them in courses at this institution? If she does, does her former university, which invested in developing the materials, have the right to receive the equivalent of royalties from her new institution?

Intellectual property rights issues and concerns such as these exist on all campuses where the expansion of distance learning is being contemplated. Cornell faces the additional problem that its budget arrangements make it difficult for the university as a whole to approach distance learning activities in a coordinated manner. Coordination makes sense because it is certainly cost efficient to establish a central support office with facilities for synchronous (two-way compressed video) and asynchronous (Web-based) distance learning, support personnel to operate this facility, and staff to aid faculty to convert courses to distance learning formats.

Cornell began the process of establishing the centralized Office of Distance Learning in 1996–97. The colleges at Cornell that were best positioned to use distance learning methods for professional degree programs and executive education, those teaching hotel administration, management, and industrial and labor relations, were all colleges that operated as tubs. Administrators in these units were concerned that the new office was a ploy to allow the central university to share in their future revenue growth under the guise of requiring funds to cover the costs of the new office. Fortunately, the first director of the office was a former dean of the School of Industrial and Labor Relations, the school was moving into a new building that was designed while he was dean and that contained state of the art distance learning classrooms, and he was a skilled negotiator. By the third year the office was in operation, 1998–99, some progress had been made in increasing the amount of distance learning on the campus.

Cornell, like any selective institution, understands that the value of one of the core "products" that it produces, undergraduate and graduate residential degree programs, is important to maintain. The demand by students for a Cornell education depends upon the payoff that students receive from it in terms of the post-college educational and career opportunities it provides. The latter in turn depend upon the quality of the education that the university provides for students, as well as employers' and graduate schools' perceptions of the quality of the students who enroll at the university. It would be suicide for selective universities to do anything in the distance learning arena that depreciates the value of their core residential education programs.

It is therefore unlikely that Cornell will ever become a mass marketer of undergraduate degree-granting distance learning programs. The university will instead most probably focus on using distance learning to enhance its existing on-campus educational programs, to share resources with other high-quality universities to enhance the range of specialized courses available at each, and to expand offerings in the professional education, executive education, continuing education, and summer school markets.

A major target of the university's continuing education efforts will be its own alumni. With well over 100,000 living alumni, Cornell has a natural market of individuals who are attached to the university. More generally, Cornell and other institutions are rapidly moving to use the Internet as a way to keep in contact with their alumni and enhance their commitment to the university. Much of the effort that institutions put into their distance learning programs for alumni will not be expected to generate great sums of revenue directly. Indeed, these programs may even lose money. But they will be part of the development efforts of the university. It is no accident that at many universities the title of Vice President for Development is being replaced by the title Vice President for Institutional Commitment.

PART VII

THE NONACADEMIC INFRASTRUCTURE

CHAPTER 15

Parking and Transportation

Perspectives on Parking

Many faculty members believe that they have an inalienable right to park right next to their offices and to be able to leave campus and return during the day whenever they want to. Many staff members believe that parking should be provided for them free of charge. The city of Ithaca believes that Cornell should provide enough parking on campus so that faculty, staff, and students who commute to campus do not park off campus in residential neighborhoods close to the campus. The city feels so strongly about this that until an agreement was reached about such parking in the mid-1990s it held up granting major construction permits that the university needed for renovations of existing facilities and construction of new facilities. Ithaca also would like the university to provide convenient and free parking on campus for city residents so that they can take advantage of all the things the campus has to offer.

Providing parking on a campus is costly to a university and ways must be devised to cover these costs and ration demand. Invariably part of the solution leads to parking fees and restrictions on parking. As a result, it is hard to think of anyone on a campus who regularly takes more abuse than the administrator in charge of parking and transportation arrangements. Fortunately, economic incentives can sometimes be used to help solve resource allocation problems and save money in the nonacademic part of a university. I describe below how this was done when the demand for faculty and staff parking at Cornell began to exceed the available supply.

Transportation Demand Management as a Solution to Insufficient Parking

Between 1987–88 and 1990–91, the number of faculty and staff at Cornell University increased from 8,948 to 9,683. With over 700 additional employees, the available campus parking became insufficient. In addition, the construction of new buildings, many of them in the center of the campus, had created a shortage of parking on the central campus. Estimates made during 1990–91 suggested that 2,500 new parking spaces would have to be constructed by the university during the next five years. These would be needed to meet the growing demand for parking and to replace more than 1,000 parking spaces that had been lost when central campus parking lots were converted to building sites.

The cost of providing a parking spot on campus is not cheap. Cornell currently estimates that it costs about $600 to $700 per parking spot annually to provide a spot in an outdoor parking lot. These costs include the construction costs (amortized over a ten-year period), the interest on the debt used to finance the construction, the maintenance of parking lots, lighting, and snow removal. Because of the climate in Ithaca, about $50 of the cost is for snow removal alone.

An objective of the university is to preserve the natural beauty of the campus and to protect "green spaces" on the central campus. As a result, the available space for central campus parking lots is limited. Because many faculty and staff want to park close to the buildings in which they work and new outdoor parking lots would be far from these locations, a multistory central campus indoor parking garage was built during the 1980s. Although a second central campus garage could be built, the annual cost of providing a space this way was estimated in the late 1990s to be $1,200 to $1,300.

Engaging in a building program to develop 2,500 new parking spots on campus would have been prohibitively expensive. Although faculty and staff complain about having to pay for parking, the university currently subsidizes the costs of parking to the tune of over $1 million a year, or more than $50 per enrolled student. Constructing 2,500 new parking spaces either would have caused parking rates to increase at double-digit rates for a number of years or would have required the university to substantially increase its subsidy. An increased subsidy would inevitably have to come from funds that could have been used for other purposes, such as salaries and benefits for employees, or would require increases in tuition to cover the extra costs of the parking system.

The university was also concerned that building more parking would lead to an increase in the traffic flow on campus. This would create traffic problems for neighboring communities during times that employees were commuting to work. Concern was also expressed that an increased traffic flow would increase the risk of accidents to campus pedestrians (students), require more frequent maintenance and repair of campus roads, and increase the level of pollution on campus. For economic, community relations, student safety, and environmental reasons avoiding the addition of as many parking spots as possible seemed to be a good idea.

To do this, an innovative transportation management plan was developed that contained a number of parts. First, approximately 1,300 free parking spaces on or near the center of campus were converted into spaces for which an annual price was charged. More generally, a fee structure was established in which parking close to the center of campus was priced at a higher rate than parking further away. In addition, a number of lots at the edges of the campus were maintained as "free" lots and busses ran frequently to and from those lots. Any employee could reach his or her office within ten minutes from these lots.

Table 15.1 presents information on what the fee structure for faculty and staff parking looked like during the 1997–98 academic year. Tier 1 lots are the free lots. The higher the tier number, the closer the parking lot is to the center of campus. As column 1 indicates, the annual fee rises to over $500 in the highest tier, which includes the central campus indoor parking garage where I park.

Table 15.1 Annual parking fees and rebates for faculty and staff at Cornell University, 1997–1998. Tier numbers: 1 = free lots; 2 = perimeter lots; 3, 4 = near central lots; 5, 6 = central lots and parking garage.

Campus parking areas (tiers)	(1) Individual permits	(2) Two RideSharers	(3) Three RideSharers	(4) Four RideSharers
1	No fee	No fee	No fee	No fee
2	$245.89	No fee	Reserved space $130.20 rebate	Reserved space $265.35 rebate
3	$376.09	$130.20	No fee	Reserved space $135.15 rebate
4	$376.09	$130.20	No fee	Reserved space $135.15 rebate
5	$481.98	$236.09	$105.89	Reserved space no fee
6	$511.24	$265.35	$135.15	Reserved space no fee

Source: Cornell University Office of Transportation Services World Wide Web Page (<http://www.transportation.cornell.edu>), October 27, 1998.

Such a fee structure only marginally reduces the number of people who drive to campus each day. Its main purpose was to reallocate parking away from the center of the campus, where parking was scarce, to the periphery of the campus, where more parking space was available. To reduce the number of cars brought to campus, several other changes were made.

Owners of more than one car have long been able to buy a parking permit from Cornell that permitted them to bring any one of their cars to campus at a time. So, for example, if my car is in the repair shop, I can bring another family member's car to campus instead. The university did not charge an extra fee for this privilege because only one of an employee's cars could be parked on campus at a time.

Some bright administrator (not me!) hit upon the idea of allowing multiple employees to share a parking permit. If a neighbor and I share a permit, only one of us is allowed to park his car on campus at a time. To induce employees to move toward such sharing, the university sought to make it financially worthwhile. Column 2 of the table displays the discounts available for people who take advantage of this "RideSharing" plan. If two Cornell employees share a parking sticker, the parking fee for each of the pay lots is reduced by about $245. The total cost of parking for the two employees is reduced by even more because only one sticker, rather than two, is required. For example, if they share a permit and park in a Tier 3 lot, rather than each paying $376.09 a year, they each would pay $65.10, a saving of over $300.

Columns 3 and 4 indicate that to encourage RideSharing among more than two people, the cost for each level of parking is reduced even more as another person is added. Indeed, rebates, rather than fees, are paid *to* the employees when three or more people share a permit for lots near the periphery and when four or more people share a permit for a "near central campus" lot. To encourage three- and four-person RideSharing, reserved parking spots, rather than "licenses" to look for spots, are also provided for groups of these sizes. Members of RideSharing groups are also given a number of free daily parking permits, so that more than one member of a group can bring a car to campus on the few days that that is necessary. Finally, they are given free transportation by the university if an unexpected emergency arises during a workday.

The university also began what it called an OmniRide program. Under this program, free bus passes were given to all employees who were both residents of the county in which the university is located and who returned

their parking permits to the university. The university worked with local governments to improve bus service in the county. The free bus passes
could be used at any time, not just for the commute to work. As with the
RideSharing program, employees who took advantage of the OmniRide program were also given a number of daily parking passes and free transportation by the university in the event of emergencies.

Neighboring local governments loved the OmniRide program because
the usage of their transportation systems went up and automobile traffic
through them went down during the start and end of the workday. Each
neighboring locality was encouraged to establish "park and ride" locations
where employees could park their cars and then ride the bus to work. Given
the availability of space in the rural communities and the small number of
parked cars at any one location, they were all able to do this. The university
also subsidized the cost of bus transportation for those employees who lived
outside the county.

The net result of all of these actions was that 1,629 employees were enrolled in the OmniRide program in 1997–98. Another 1,331 employees (in
638 groups) were enrolled in the RideSharing program. The number of employees no longer parking on campus because of the OmniRide program
was 1,629, while the reduction in the number of parked cars due to the
RideSharing program was 693 (1,331 minus 638). Hence the two programs
have reduced the number of cars coming to campus daily by about 2,250.
Virtually all of the additional parking spots that the university projected it
would have to construct during the 1990s have been eliminated by these incentive programs.

Originally, it was thought that the cost to Cornell of the reductions in
parking fees, the rebates to RideShare groups with more than two members,
the provision of free bus passes, and administrative expenses would be in
the range of $500,000 a year. The cost has proved to be much lower because
there are very few RideShare groups with more than two members and thus
very few rebates being paid back to employees.

The estimated annual cost of constructing and maintaining outdoor parking spots and parking spots in an indoor garage are $600 to $700 and $1,200
to $1,300, respectively. If we assume that half of the spots built would have
been of each type, the university's savings each year from not having to construct 2,250 more parking spots is in the order of $2,025,000 to $2,250,000.
If the parking spots had been constructed, part of the increased costs would
have been offset by some increase in parking fee revenues. But on bal-

ance, the university, its students, and its employees all have come out ahead financially by the nonconstruction of the additional parking spots. The environment has also benefited: fewer green spaces have been converted to paved parking lots, less wear and tear is occurring on university roads, and university employees' automobiles are using less gasoline. One estimate is that because of these parking incentive programs, university employees are using 417,000 fewer gallons of gasoline each year.

To what can we attribute the adoption of these highly successful programs? Cornell has long had a transportation advisory committee that consists of two graduate or professional students, two undergraduate students, two employees, and two faculty members—each appointed by the relevant student, staff, or faculty government group—as well as five faculty members and administrators appointed by the president. Faced with an alternative that involved substantially increasing parking fees, eliminating green spaces, and increasingly damaging the environment, this group was able to work with the administrative office in charge of parking to devise a system that benefited all groups. For the most part, the parking reform was a win-win solution and it consisted primarily of carrots rather than sticks. Although it is true that there were some losers, namely those people (primarily faculty members) who parked in central campus lots and saw their parking fees increase, there was enough support from the community at large to adopt the plan. The faculty represents less than 20 percent of the employees of the university and on a nonacademic issue such as parking, they are only one of the groups participating in the decision process.

Success But Not Happiness

Cornell's Transportation Demand Management System has been an unqualified success, but, as with taxes, no one on campus is ever happy with parking and the rules associated with it. To reduce the pressure on parking, the university requires that whenever a proposed construction project forces the university to eliminate some parking spaces, the project must bear the cost of replacing the parking. This rule increases the costs of construction projects and irritates people greatly when it is the university, rather than the unit sponsoring the project, that causes the parking to be eliminated.

During the late 1990s Cornell's athletic director raised funds to construct a new outdoor track and field complex on the campus. The estimated costs of this project were in the $1 million range and he thought that he had completed his fund raising. He wanted to site the complex on an open field near a recently built athletics fieldhouse. The university agreed but added the stipulation that, for esthetic reasons, it wanted the complex sited on a particular spot on the field. Using this site would have required the elimination of a number of parking spots and, at a construction cost of $4,000 for each spot that had to be replaced, would have added costs to the project. Neither the athletic director nor his donors were happy. In the interest of maintaining good donor relations, the university agreed to a site for the project that did not eliminate any parking.

Staff members often complain that allocating access to close-in parking by price discriminates against lower-paid workers and that parking should be subsidized more for lower-paid workers. Where the funding for the subsidy would come from is never specified. The fact that an increased subsidy would increase the university's costs of hiring lower-paid workers, thereby encouraging the university to reduce its employment of them, is never considered.

Faculty members quite correctly point out that the university should be interested in maximizing their productivity and that preventing them from parking near the offices encourages them to work at home, thereby reducing their accessibility to students. Moreover, faculty members located on the center campus who need to move around during the day, either because they have laboratories in other buildings or because they have personal responsibilities (doctors' visits, picking up children from child care, and so on), think that the system is a disaster. Once they leave one parking spot they often can not find another spot when they return. These faculty members feel that the university does not take account of the value, or opportunity cost, of their time. If it did, they believe that the university would want to give them parking spots right by their office doors.

In my faculty role, I sympathize with the "faculty view" because when I first came to Cornell I could park right by my office door. Now, some twenty-five years later, the best I can do is park in a parking garage that is about a five-minute walk away. A former Cornell provost told me that when pressed for more parking for visitors on the central campus, he switched my college's parking lot to a visitors' lot because he regularly found that it wasn't filled with faculty cars by 9:00 A.M. My college's faculty had not demonstrated that they wanted to get to work early enough to "deserve" parking right by their college.

He also told me (this time joking, I believe) that when he was a college dean he partially determined faculty salary increases by the directions in which faculty members parked their cars. Those who drove in front first were obviously in a hurry to get to work and deserved large salary increases. Those who backed in were obviously in a hurry to leave at night and deserved smaller increases. Apparently administrators can make many decisions about faculty members' salaries and working conditions from knowledge of their parking habits.

Faculty members need to understand why the university is unable to provide unlimited central campus parking for them. The trustees and the administration have a responsibility to maintain the natural beauty of the campus and to retain green spaces on the central campus. They have a responsibility to raise funds to build magnificent research facilities so that Cornell can hire world-class researchers and push back the frontiers of knowledge. When buildings that house new faculty members and their research laboratories are located on the central campus in spaces that previously were used for parking, faculty members applaud because they want to keep all of their academic programs within walking distance for undergraduate students. But necessarily Cornell now has more faculty and staff competing for less parking on the central campus.

Cornell's parking system does not guarantee anyone a reserved parking spot except people with disabilities and those few people in RideShare groups containing more than two members. All it does is provide a "license" to "hunt" for a spot in a designated area. This makes sense for the university because the number of cars brought to the campus on any day is far less than the number of cars that are registered for parking. Cornell has roughly 9,200 parking spaces on its Ithaca campus. Including students' cars, there are about 10,500 cars registered for parking on campus. However, estimates made from aerial photographs suggest that on any given day there are about 1,100 empty parking spaces on the campus. This means that only about 77 percent of all cars registered for parking on campus (8,100/10,500) actually are on campus.

People who arrive early in the day almost always find a parking spot in their preferred area. But those who have to leave during the day for any reason often find returning to campus difficult. How can one square this statement with the statement above that on any given day there are about 1,100 empty parking spots? The answer is that the people who have the flexibility to leave and then return during the day tend to be faculty members and higher-paid professional staff, who buy the more expensive central campus parking permits. In the residential areas, there are about 1.1 permits sold for every parking spot, but in the central campus the ratio is more like 1.9 or 2.0 to 1. Hence people who leave the central campus during the day run the risk of finding when they return that "their" spots have been taken by late-arriving colleagues. Most of the vacant spots are found in the outer lots, away from the central campus.

One final faculty complaint about parking is that the parking permits are only "licenses" from 8:00 A.M. to 5:00 P.M. during weekdays. On evenings and weekends, most parking on campus becomes available to anyone. Faculty members complain about their inability to return to the campus in the evening and on weekends and declare that this reduces their productivity.

The administration is well aware of their concerns. However, the number of faculty members who actually do return to campus during these time periods is relatively small. To prohibit students from parking in lots that would not be heavily filled with faculty cars would not be a prudent strategy. After all, students are the ones whose tuition payments are paying faculty salaries and for whom Cornell is competing with other universities. To enforce parking regulations on evenings and weekends would also require considerable monitoring effort and additional staff. It is not clear that the parking fines that might result would more than cover the costs of the additional staff needed to monitor parking lots and issue parking tickets. It also is not clear that Cornell would want students to write home to their parents that they received parking tickets when they drove to campus on a cold winter night to use the library.

CHAPTER **16**

Cooling Systems

Parking structures are visible to faculty and students every day, but other elements of the nonacademic infrastructure are not. Nevertheless, they are important to the functioning of a university and can be quite costly. One such infrastructure element that Cornell University dealt with at the end of the twentieth century was how it should cool its campus for the next fifty years.

The reader may wonder why air conditioning is an issue at an institution that is not located in a particularly warm climate. Cornell's academic year runs from Labor Day to Memorial Day and the temperature rarely rises above 80 degrees during that period. Ithaca is not known for its mild winters, and most students, faculty, and staff worry about keeping warm, not about keeping cool.

Yet even during the coldest days of the year, universities such as Cornell require considerable air conditioning capacity. All the units of Cornell's vast library system must be kept at controlled temperatures and humidity to help preserve books. Mechanical systems in laboratories and computer rooms require environments that are cooler than the typical room on campus and must be kept at a constant humidity. As the science and engineering research on campus expanded, the demand for facilities with controlled environments also expanded, and Cornell's cooling capacity had to grow by nearly 50 percent each decade.

In Ithaca it is warm and often very humid during the summer. Although the Cornell campus is not extensively used by undergraduate students during the summer, faculty members and graduate students are there conducting research, and they require office and laboratory environments in which they will not wilt because of the heat and humidity. So too do the thousands of dedicated Cornell staff whose work continues beyond the academic year.

This point was brought home to me during the summer of 1998 when I returned to the faculty. Although my administrative office had been air-conditioned, my faculty office in an older building was not. There were many days when many of my faculty colleagues and I chose to stay in our air-conditioned homes, rather than face the humidity and temperature in our offices during that summer. Indeed, our building becomes so unbearable on hot days that my college even has an informal policy of sending support staff home when the temperature inside the building exceeds 90 degrees.

Periodically, administrators at Cornell seek ways to make more extensive summer use of Cornell's facilities to help increase the revenue generated by the university. Time and again the lack of air-conditioned housing on campus is pointed to as a factor that constrains the ability of the university to succeed in expanding summer usage of the campus. To expand summer session programs for undergraduates, executive education programs for professionals, continuing education programs for adults, or summer conference programs, more air-conditioned facilities are required on campus.

Cooling the Cornell Campus in 1995

In 1995, about 40 percent of Cornell's buildings were connected to Cornell's central cooling system, which provided these buildings with humidity control, cooling for computers and other research equipment, and air conditioning. The system was a circulating chilled-water system. At its center were seven large electricity-driven refrigeration units, or "chillers," and a large insulated storage tank for water that was chilled daily to about 45 degrees. This water circulated through underground pipes to all of the buildings to provide the cooling and humidity control required by the central campus buildings. In the process, the temperature of the circulated water rose to around 60 degrees. It was then returned through underground pipes to the center of the system, where it was again chilled and the process was repeated.

The system was rapidly approaching capacity, and given the expanded demand for cooling occasioned by the construction of new buildings and the renovation of old ones, more capacity was required. In fact, a planned addition of an eighth chiller to the system was made in 1998 at a cost of over $4 million. Many of the existing chillers were nearing the end of their useful lives and needed to be replaced. These existing chillers used chlorofluorocarbons (CFCs) as chemical refrigerants. CFCs are believed to cause ozone depletion and other environmental problems, and production of them was stopped throughout the nation in 1995. Any replacement chillers would have to use alternative refrigerants thought to be less harmful to the environment, and they would continue to use large amounts of energy to provide cooling. The newly installed eighth chiller utilized such a technology.

Looking to the future, the university was concerned that as it replaced each of its aging chillers, it would continue to add to the annual energy bill that the university faced for cooling. Indeed, as of 1995, the university was spending about $1.5 million a year on the electricity needed to power the existing chillers. The demand for cooling continued to grow on campus through the renovation of old buildings, the construction of new buildings, and the effort to increase use of the campus during the summer. As a result, the addition of a number of additional chillers, as well as those new ones needed to replace aging ones, was projected over the next fifty years. Energy usage to operate the chillers would continually increase, and because these chillers are driven by electricity produced from coal, oil, or natural gas, the university's use of fossil fuels would increase, which in turn would adversely affect the environment.

Chillers have a useful life of about thirty years, and they are installed on a staggered schedule so that replacement of only one or a few needs to take place at any one time. It was estimated that around the year 2000 the university would have to spend about $22 million to replace those chillers that had reached the end of their useful lives. The university also projected that it would need to spend another $9 million by 2010, $20 million more by 2025, and then $40 million more by 2030 on replacement chillers and new chillers to meet expansion needs. Put another way, over a thirty-five-year period, Cornell projected that it would incur capital costs totaling over $90 million to cool the campus if it continued to use a technology based on central chillers.

Lake Source Cooling

It was natural for the professional staff in Cornell's utilities division to seek alternative ways to cool the campus that were environmentally friendlier and that might also save the university money. If such a win-win alternative could be discovered, both the university and the environment would be better off. As these staff members puzzled over what such options might be, one enterprising young Cornell engineer named W. S. (Lanny) Joyce pursued the notion of using the natural cold temperature of the water in nearby Lake Cayuga to cool the campus.[1] He knew that an area in Stockholm, Sweden, was cooled during the summer months with ocean water and that consideration was being given to cooling nearly all of downtown Toronto, Canada, with cold water from Lake Ontario.

Cornell's alma mater begins with the words "Far above Cayuga's Waters" because the university is located about 450 feet above the foot of Lake Cayuga. The lake is a large one; it is over 38 miles long from north to south and, at points, over 2 miles wide. Once one moves away from the lake's shore, it is also very deep, over 400 feet in some places. Because of its depth, the sunlight that warms the top of the lake during the summer has very little impact on the temperature of the water near the bottom of the lake. The temperature of the water in the deepest portions of the lake tends to hover around 39 to 40 degrees Fahrenheit year round. Joyce thought about ways to use the natural coldness of the water near the bottom of the lake to cool the campus.

The process that was settled on became known as Lake Source Cooling and it is illustrated schematically in Figure 16.1. Lake Source Cooling makes

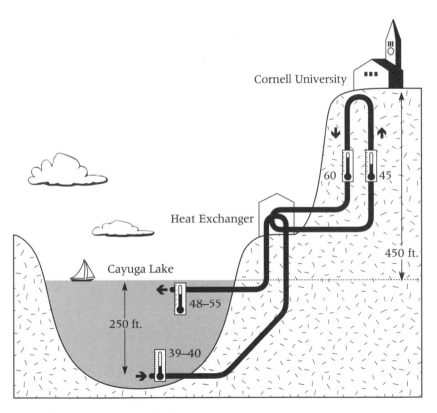

Figure 16.1. Lake Source Cooling.

use of one "open" and one "closed" loop of pipes, with large heat exchangers between them. The open loop starts at the bottom of Lake Cayuga. Water from the bottom of the lake is pumped to the shore, where it passes through the heat-exchange facility and then returns to the lake.

The closed loop starts on the Cornell campus, and water at a temperature of approximately 60 degrees comes down through an underground return pipe to the lake shore, where it passes through the heat-exchange facility. Within the facility, the two flows of water never physically come in contact with each other. But the heat-exchange technology transfers the heat removed from the campus buildings to the lake water. The lake water, now warmed to about 55 degrees, is then carried back into the top of the lake. The Cornell water, now at a temperature of about 45 degrees, is pumped through an underground supply pipe back to the campus, where it circulates to provide the cooling for the buildings on campus. After its coolness is dissipated, it goes back down the hill to the heat-exchange facility and the process is repeated.

Lake Source Cooling potentially had a number of advantages. First, the heat-exchange facility technology was well developed and used minimal electric power. Power would be required to operate the heat-exchange facility and to pump the water from the lake and back and forth to the campus. However, it was estimated that the usage of electric power to air-condition the campus would fall by about 80 percent annually if Lake Source Cooling was adopted. The university was spending about $1.5 million a year during the mid-1990s on electricity to air-condition the campus, and Lake Source Cooling had the potential to substantially reduce its annual electricity costs. In the initial years of its operation, the annual savings would be in the range of $1.2 million. Whether this sum increased or decreased over time would depend upon both the rate of growth in cooling requirements on the campus and on the future path of electricity prices.

Second, Lake Source Cooling was technologically very simple, and the system was estimated to have a useful life of over seventy-five years. If constructed with large enough pipes, it would have enough excess capacity to satisfy future campus cooling needs during its expected life. Adopting Lake Source Cooling would enable the university to avoid having to buy replacement chillers and chillers to meet new capacity needs during at least the first half of the twenty-first century. Two of the newest and largest existing chillers, the ones installed in 1998 and 1987, and the thermal storage tank would be maintained for emergency use when the Lake Source Cooling system was "down" and for use at peak hours of cooling demand in future years. The chiller installed in 1987 would be retrofitted with a new environmentally friendly refrigerant so that it could be part of the system.

Finally, Lake Source Cooling appeared to make sense environmentally. Less electricity would be used to generate air conditioning on campus, and thus the university would be using less fossil fuel to generate electricity and would pollute the environment less. The temperature of the water going back into the top of the lake would be warmer than the temperature of the water pumped up from the bottom of the lake. But the volume of this flow was so small relative to the size of the lake that the effect on the lake would be equivalent to its having received a few hours more sunlight a year. It was believed that this slight warming would have no adverse effects on the ecology of the lake.

Lake Source Cooling also had a number of disadvantages. First and foremost was the size of the initial investment required. The technology involved was simple. But about 2 miles of pipe that was over 5 feet wide would have to be purchased and installed beneath the lake's surface to reach a point at which the water level in the lake was deep enough to yield sufficiently cold water for the system to operate efficiently. Similarly, nearly 5 miles of supply and return pipe that was about 3.5 feet wide would have to be purchased and installed underground between the heat-exchange facility by the shore of Lake Cayuga and the main Cornell campus. That pipe would have to transverse a grade rise of over 450 feet as it passed under property owned by several local governments and the Ithaca City School District.

An initial estimate was that the costs of Lake Source Cooling would be in the range of $50 million. This estimate was later revised upward to about $55 million. There would, of course, be savings during the next fifty years because less electricity would be needed to cool the campus and because there would be no need to replace existing chillers or to install new ones to meet increased capacity needs. Nevertheless, Cornell's trustees were not about to embark upon a $55 million capital investment, rather than a $22 million capital investment (the initial costs of replacing existing chillers with new chillers), unless they were convinced that Lake Source Cooling made economic sense.

Undertaking Lake Source Cooling was also bound to create waves in the local community and to mobilize the environmental movement. Area residents not associated with the university tend to be suspicious of everything that the university wants to do and perceive that the university is always trying to take advantage of the local community. Cayuga Lake was rightfully viewed as an important natural resource in the community, and there fears were bound to be raised that the system would be environmentally harmful to the lake. To undertake Lake Source Cooling would require the university to get seventeen different permits and approvals, from multiple local, state, and federal government units, as well as to go through an exhaustive environmental impact review required by the federal and state governments. The university would have to mount an extensive, but subtle public relations campaign (so that the community would not feel that the university was trying to put something over on them), as well as a serious study of all the economic, technical, and environmental issues associated with the project.

Did Lake Source Cooling Make Sense?

To determine whether Lake Source Cooling made sense, the university established an internal oversight committee, on which I served, consisting of four university senior administrators. The committee reported regularly to a subcommittee of the Cornell trustees' buildings and properties committee. Cornell's Center for the Environment was asked to sponsor a scientific faculty oversight committee to do environmental reviews of the project. Similarly, outside consultants were asked to prepare environmental reviews. When potential environmental issues did arise, solutions were developed. Outside peer review consultants were also asked for their appraisal of the technical feasibility of the project and to suggest modifications.

Of great concern was the economics of the project. The economic benefits to the university would come from the university's expected annual future savings in utility costs from using Lake Source Cooling rather than the conventional chillers. They would also come from an estimated savings of $69 million that would otherwise have been spent on new and replacement chillers during the 2001–2030 period. The economic costs of Lake Source Cooling were its much larger initial capital costs. Would the future savings be large enough to offset the higher initial costs?

One of the members of the trustees' subcommittee was the chief executive officer of a utility company. He pointed out that the nationwide deregulation of the electric utilities' industry would substantially increase competition in the industry and would probably substantially lower future electric rates. Lower electric rates would mean that the annual savings in utility costs would be lower than the proponents of Lake Source Cooling initially might have projected.

Leading energy experts from around the region and the nation were asked to provide the university with their best estimates of the future path of electricity rates. Armed with these estimates, extensive financial analyses were undertaken to determine whether the project did make economic sense. These analyses depended on the assumptions made about the path of future electric rates, the cost of borrowing money (to finance the capital expenditures), the inflation rate, and the costs of construction, both of Lake Source Cooling and conventional chillers. For any set of assumptions that seemed to be reasonable, the same conclusion emerged. Financially, Lake Source Cooling would be a good deal for the university.

The exact details of the financial calculations and hence the financial savings that the university expected to reap are not public information. But if as a first approximation we assume that the extra cost of the initial investment would offset the savings from not having to invest in new and replacement chillers, the financial gain to the university would be the savings in electricity usage. In the initial year, these savings were about $1.2 million. If in the future electricity prices fall at a more rapid rate than the rate at which the demand for cooling on the campus grows, this amount would get smaller over time. In contrast, if the demand for cooling grows more rapidly than the rate at which electricity prices fall, this amount would get larger over time.

What does not incurring $1.2 million a year in electricity costs mean to the university? On the one hand, it could use this money to increase financial aid for students, pay higher salaries, or expand the size of the faculty and staff. Alternatively, it could simply not raise tuition by as much as it otherwise would have had to do.

If the university did not undertake the Lake Source Cooling project, its electricity costs would be $1.2 million a year higher. If it financed these higher costs solely by raising undergraduate students' tuition, the extra tuition increase would have to be more than $100. It would have to be this large because some fraction of it would be returned to students in the form of increased need-based grant aid. As discussed earlier, when tuition increases an extra $100, students' financial need also increases and thus so does their need-based grant aid.[2]

Faced with evidence of the economic viability of the project, the trustees' subcommittee unanimously recommended it to the full board of trustees and they voted to approve it in January of 1998. The project then moved into the stage of seeking the approval of local and state governmental units.

Seeking Approvals and Facing Environmentalists

A project of the scope of Lake Source Cooling must go through an extensive "permitting process." An extensive 1,500-page environmental impact statement was submitted to the key state agency, the New York State Department of Environmental Conservation (DEC), and in early January 1998 the DEC concluded that there were no environmental risks associated with the project. Even before this approval was received, the university had been working to win the support of a number of local governments through whose property the system would run.

One was the city of Ithaca and the university had to get permits from the city to tear up local streets and sidewalks so that it could install underground pipe for the system. Once the city was convinced that Lake Source Cooling would not harm the environment and that construction for it would create a large number of jobs for local construction workers, it agreed to provide the necessary permits. As a by-product, the city will receive about $1.2 million worth of new roads and sidewalks, which Cornell will provide when it rebuilds them after installing pipe. The city will also be able to use the time that the roads and sidewalks are torn up to make repairs on its own underground utility lines, thus saving itself the cost of having to dig up and replace the sidewalks and streets.

A second local government involved was the Ithaca City School District (ICSD). The university needed to run its lines underneath school district property and required permission from the ICSD to do this. One way to encourage the ICSD to grant this permission was to allow it to "tap" into the system, once it became operational, f _ _ the chilled water the district would need to cool several of its high school buildings. Allowing it to do so was estimated to save the ICSD about $100,000, which was what the district would otherwise have had to spend on a new chiller, as well as to save $24,000 a year in utility costs. The annual utility cost savings would accrue even though the portion of the high school buildings cooled would expand by a factor of four. The savings would result because the chilled water from the Lake Source Cooling system would be produced with only about one fifth the electric power usage of conventional chiller systems and because the university would provide the chilled water to the school district at almost a zero cost.

Although these savings to the school district were significant, the ICSD had long felt that the university was not making sufficient payments to it, in lieu of property tax payments, for the children of graduate students living in university housing who attend local public schools. This issue arose because university property that is used for purposes related to education, such as housing for students and their families, is not subject to state and local property taxes.

Spending by local school districts on public education in New York state comes partly from funds the state provides for each student and partly from local property taxes. Children of graduate students who live in university housing and attend public schools live on property that produces no property tax revenue to support the schools. The school district does receive state aid for these students, but the local share of the costs of educating them is borne by residents who pay local property taxes. Thus the ICSD has long believed that the university is imposing costs on all taxpayers that reside in the district and that a voluntary payment by the university to it, in lieu of taxes, would be appropriate.

Cornell has always maintained that it is under no legal obligation to make payments in lieu of taxes. But it does make contributions to both the city of Ithaca, where it is located, for fire protection services and to the Ithaca City School District. Cornell has also always maintained that these payments should be discussed independently of any other transactions that the university is involved in with local governmental units. As a result, substantial friction arose between the city and the university in 1994 when the city threatened to hold up building permits for important academic buildings until the university increased its payment in lieu of taxes to them.

Publicly, the university refused to allow its negotiations over Lake Source Cooling with the ICSD to influence its position on what it should pay the ICSD in lieu of taxes. Nevertheless, at roughly the same time that the ICSD agreed to provide Cornell with an easement to use its property, the university agreed to substantially increase its annual payment to the district, in lieu of taxes, from $100,000 to $300,000 a year over a three-year period. Although it would be sheer speculation to attribute the increased payment solely to the need for an easement, it is worth noting that this $200,000 is money that is obtained from student housing charges. Thus the increased university payments necessarily will lead to higher student housing rates. As will be discussed more extensively later, higher housing rates increase the financial need of students receiving financial aid and thus increase the grant aid paid to them by the university. As a result, both the university and its students will share in the costs of that extra $200,000 a year.

The final permits had to come from the town of Ithaca for the construction of the heat-transfer station. In another "unrelated transaction," the town made it known to the university that it would be very happy if the university donated to it for a town park part of a parcel of land, upon which a marina was located, close to where the pumping station was to be built. The university agreed to do so and to offer the town the first right to purchase the entire marina if it ever contemplated selling the rest of the parcel.

With all the necessary permits in hand, contracts were signed for the building and delivery of the miles of pipe and the components of the heat-exchange facility. However, various environmental groups and some individuals refused to believe that the university was engaged in a project that made sense both economically for it and environmentally for the area. A lawsuit was filed to try to halt the project, claiming that the town, the university, and the school district had violated various procedures in making their agreements. In late December of 1998, a state Supreme Court judge threw a number of these challenges out of court.

A group of ten local residents that had formed to try to stop the project was appropriately (from their perspective) named the Cayuga Lake Defense Fund. Earlier in the fall, when the noted consumer advocate Ralph Nader was on campus to give an address, the group enlisted his support to stop the project. Their focus was on potential environmental dangers that they saw in the project, even though the university claimed that virtually all of their concerns had already been addressed in the environmental impact statement. The group also never acknowledged the environmental benefits that the community, the region, and the planet would receive by the university's use of the efficient, ozone friendly, lake source cooling technology that burned far less fossil fuel than the alternatives.

After the group's challenge was thrown out, one member, a retired Cornell University professor said, "I was pretty sure it would probably fail but my motive was to delay the project with the hope that things considered damaging to the project would come out later to defeat it." Such a frivolous challenge serves only to increase the cost of the project to the university and hence ultimately to reduce the net savings that the university will obtain by undertaking it.

For example, suppose that through repeated challenges environmentalists were able to delay the project for a year. The university would have to pay an extra year's interest on the money it borrowed to purchase all of the miles of pipes that it required for the project (which have already been ordered and delivered). The cost of the miles of large pipe is in the range of $3 million. If financed through tax-exempt borrowing at an interest rate of 5 percent, the extra year's interests costs would be about $150,000. The university also has contracts for work with construction firms that undoubtedly call for large penalties if the university is not ready to have them begin their work at the specified time. Finally, the university would lose the savings in electricity usage that it had hoped to gain from the operation of Lake Source Cooling during that year. These savings are worth about $1.2 million a year. Thus delaying the construction of Lake Source Cooling would reduce the economic benefits of the project to the university. This in turn would reduce revenue for academic programs or cause student tuition levels to rise by more than otherwise would be the case.

In late January 1999, Cornell announced plans to begin construction of the Lake Source Cooling system on March 1, 1999. The first stage of the project, the construction and installation of the transmission pipes to and from the campus, began on schedule.

At about the same time, a local New York state assemblyman who is a strong supporter of the university wrote to the Department of Environmental Conservation. He asked the DEC to rescind, or temporarily suspend, the permit it had given Cornell until an investigation was undertaken of allegations of noncompliance by the DEC in their issuing the permit for Cornell to "discharge" the circulating lake water back into the lake. This issue had been raised by a national environmental organization, the Natural Resources Defense Council; Cornell has vigorously disputed all of the claims of this group. The assemblyman took no position on the validity of the claims, but undoubtedly thought that he had to write the letter to satisfy his supporters from the environmental movement. Many other local individuals and groups followed the assemblyman's lead and voiced their concerns.

Construction of the Lake Source Cooling system is projected to be completed in the first half of the year 2000, and the system is slated to be operational by the summer of that year. It appears that the ongoing efforts by environmentalists to halt, or at least slow down, the project have failed. If they had succeeded, they would have substantially added to the cost structure of the university. Even though they did not delay the project, they have succeeded in imposing significant legal and public relations costs on the university, costs that must be paid out of the revenues the university generates.

When Lake Source Cooling becomes operational, it will yield economic benefits to both the university and the local community. But the university's benefits will be smaller than might have been the case because some of the university's economic benefits have been shared with governmental entities (the donation of land, the increased annual payment to the local school district). Although it is possible that these "unrelated" agreements might have been made in the absence of the university's need for the governmental units' cooperation on the Lake Source Cooling project, a reasonable conjecture is that they are at least partially attributable to the project. The university's economic benefits will also be lower because of all of the extra legal and public relations costs that the environmental opposition has imposed upon it. Indeed, as indicated above, if the Lake Source Cooling system opening had been delayed a year, the costs to the university would have been substantial.

Local governments and the environmental movement see the university as a "fat cat" sitting on endowment and building assets valued at well over $4 billion. University administrators know that spending from the endowment is already fully committed. Reductions in the savings that Lake Source Cooling brings the university invariably will be borne by the university's students in the form of higher tuition levels or lower expenditures per student.

PART VIII

STUDENT LIFE

CHAPTER 17

Intercollegiate Athletics
and Gender Equity

NCAA Division I Athletics

Intercollegiate athletics teams are big business at many major universities.[1] Notre Dame University's football team, for example, generated revenues that exceeded its expenses by over $12 million in 1996–97. Individual teams and their conferences compete for millions of dollars in television revenue from the broadcast of men's football and basketball and, in recent years, women's basketball. Additional millions can be gained from appearances in major post-season bowl games in football and in the basketball tournaments sanctioned by the National Collegiate Athletic Association (NCAA). The further a team advances in the tournaments, the greater the financial reward to it and its conference.

Home football and basketball games are major events at many universities. The University of Michigan, for example, regularly fills its 107,500-seat stadium each Saturday that there is a home football game. Admittedly, Michigan's stadium has the largest seating capacity of any university stadium in the country, but others are not far behind. There is a certain prestige that comes from having the largest stadium. When the University of Tennessee at Knoxville added seats to its stadium to move into first place on the list of largest stadiums a few years ago, Michigan quickly renovated its stadium to add enough seats to regain the lead.

Many spectators at these events are students, but most are alumni, other friends of the university, and the general public. These varsity sports are big business and are used by universities as a way of building school spirit, linking alumni to the university, and generating revenue to help support the other varsity sports at the university. Varsity athletics are a major part of the development efforts at these universities. Even if the athletics department loses money on its operations, the claim is made that these sports are investments that generate considerable funding in the form of alumni contributions to the university as a whole.

Having a varsity team in a major sport that wins the conference title, or still better a major bowl game or a NCAA championship, can have a substantial effect on the revenues that flow to a university. It can also influence the quantity and quality of high school students that apply for admission to it. After Villanova won the NCAA title in men's basketball in 1985, the number of its accepted applicants who chose to attend the school skyrocketed, and the university found itself scrambling to find housing for all the extra freshmen that showed up.[2] Northwestern University's football team's trip to the Rose Bowl in January of 1996 led to a 30 percent increase in applicants in the next academic year and allowed the university to raise its admission standards. The average SAT scores of its entering students rose by almost twenty points, which helped vault it from thirteenth to ninth place in the *USNWR* rankings. Its licensing revenue for the use of its logo on sweatshirts, mugs, and the like, rose from less than $60,000 in 1994–95 to $600,000 the next year, a tenfold increase.

Duke is another selective private university that has used athletic success in men's basketball to help increase its stature as a national university. Applications for Duke's freshman class jumped by 15 percent the year after Duke reached the finals of the NCAA tournament in 1978 and increased another 19 percent after it again reached the Final Four in 1986. So, too, did Georgetown's applications soar after successful basketball seasons in the 1980s. A number of academic studies confirm that football bowl game appearances and appearances in the NCAA men's basketball tournament have a positive effect both on the contributions that universities receive from alumni and on the quality of their entering students.[3]

It is no wonder then that the competition for top college football and basketball players is extraordinary. All major universities that engage in NCAA Division I sports, with the exception of the Ivy League institutions and another set of eastern private institutions that constitute the Patriot League, award athletic scholarships to varsity athletes. Given the pressures to win, admission standards for athletes in the major sports are often lower than those for the student body as a whole, and the athletes' graduation rates are often much lower than the graduation rates for the university as a whole. For example, the average six-year graduation rate for the class that entered as freshmen in the fall of 1991 (the percentage who graduated by the spring of 1997) was 12 percentage points lower for Division I male basketball players, and 17 percentage points lower for Division IA male football players (those at institutions where the average attendance at home football games exceeds 20,000), than the rates for all male students at the same schools.[4]

The NCAA has responded to concerns about the lower graduation rates of varsity athletes by establishing minimum entrance and continued eligibility requirements for students receiving athletic scholarships.[5] Every institution is now required to report its athletes' graduation rate, as well as the rate for its undergraduate class as a whole. The NCAA also requires each Division I university to go through a certification process every ten years. This process addresses whether (1) the athletics program at the institution is in conformity with NCAA rules governing recruiting and the academic eligibility of athletes; (2) the university, rather than booster groups, is in control of the athletics department's finances; (3) athletes receive the same treatment as other students in academic areas and make satisfactory academic progress; (4) the university is complying with federal gender equity regulations and is providing equitable opportunities for minority students and staff; and (5) the institution is committed to the welfare of its student athletes.

Big-time athletics are not always a gold mine for universities. Although 71 percent of Division IA football programs produced revenues that exceeded their costs in 1996–97, the other 29 percent lost money. In cases where profits were produced, they were used to subsidize the rest of the institution's athletic programs and, in some cases, academic functions of the university. If we exclude the funding of varsity sports that was provided by the institution, the average Division IA institution lost over $800,000 on its intercollegiate athletic programs in 1996–1997.[6] Some observers believe that numbers such as these understate the losses the Division IA athletic programs actually suffer because they do not always accurately state the subsidies that institutions provide for their athletic programs. For example, often the operating and maintenance costs of varsity athletics' facilities are not included in the athletics department's budget.[7]

Varsity Athletics in the Ivy League

The Ivy League is unique among the athletic conferences that compete at the Division I level in the NCAA. The eight Ivy League institutions have agreed to prohibit athletic scholarships and each has decided to award undergraduate financial aid only on the basis of demonstrated financial need. Although some practice "preferential packaging" to attract outstanding students, the league prohibits preferential packaging based only on athletic prowess. The league rigorously monitors the academic qualifications of the athletes that its coaches recruit and requires that the academic ability of its recruited athletes reflect that of the student body as a whole.[8]

Although admission to the Ivy League schools is not based on any mechanical formula, either for recruited athletes or for students in general, the league closely watches an indicator of the academic qualifications of athletes on each school's varsity teams. This academic index for each student is a composite score based on the average of the student's mathematics and verbal SAT scores, the student's class rank, and the higher of the average of the student's SAT or achievement test (now called the SAT II) scores.

The scores for each school's athletes are confidential and cannot be reported here. However, across schools and over a recent sixteen-year period, recruited male athletes' academic indices averaged about 93 percent and recruited female athletes' academic indices about 95 percent of the average academic indices for the institution's freshman class as a whole. Put another way, these student athletes' academic credentials were, on average, within 7 and 5 percent of the average of the class as a whole, a very small difference. Indeed, at the school with the lowest average academic index for the class as a whole, the average recruited student athlete graduated in the top 20 percent of his or her class and had SAT scores that averaged 1300. Athletes at these Ivy League institutions truly are student-athletes.

The league also sets tight limits on the number of days that teams can be away from campus during the academic year and participation in varsity sports is not permitted during exam periods. Finally, the number of varsity athletic teams fielded by each of the eight Ivy League institutions is among the highest in the nation.

Table 17.1 presents a tabulation I made of the number of varsity teams at each Ivy League university and each university that is a member of two major athletic conferences, the Big Ten (actually eleven institutions) and the Atlantic Coast Conference (ACC) during the 1998–99 year. The numbers reported in the table are often different from what the institutions themselves report because I counted indoor and outdoor track and field, as well as swimming and diving, as one sport. I also treated cross-country as a separate sport.

The Ivy League institutions fielded between 26 and 38 varsity teams, with the average school in the league fielding 32 teams. In contrast, the ACC and the Big Ten fielded an average of 20 and 23 teams a school, respectively. The

Table 17.1   Number of varsity athletic teams at Ivy League, ACC, and Big Ten universities in 1998–99.

Ivy League		ACC		Big Ten	
Brown	36	Clemson	17	Illinois	18
Columbia	26	Duke	23	Indiana	20
Cornell	34	Florida State	17	Iowa	21
Dartmouth	32	Georgia Tech	14	Michigan	23
Harvard	38	Maryland	22	Michigan State	24
Pennsylvania	28	North Carolina	26	Minnesota	22
Princeton	34	N.C. State	19	Nothwestern	18
Yale	29	Virginia	22	Ohio State	32
		Wake Forest	16	Penn State	28
				Purdue	18
				Wisconsin	22
Average for the league	32		20		23
Average undergraduate enrollment in the conference	7,890		14,489		27,513

Source: The number of teams was calculated by the author from a search of the institutions' World Wide Web pages in February 1999. Indoor and outdoor track were counted as one sport, as were swimming and diving. Cross-country was considered a separate sport. If both women's and men's teams existed for a sport, that sport was counted as two sports. Undergraduate enrollments are for the fall of 1995 and come from WEBCASPAR.

difference in these numbers becomes even more striking when one considers the average undergraduate enrollment at universities in each conference. In the fall of 1995, the average undergraduate enrollment in the Ivy League institutions was under 8,000 students, while the average enrollments in the ACC and Big Ten were over 14,000 and 27,000, respectively. A much greater percentage of undergraduate students participate in varsity athletics at the Ivy League schools than at the Big Ten and ACC schools. Within the Ivy League, the percentages of students that are varsity athletes varies from over 20 percent at Princeton to about 9 percent at Cornell (the largest school).

Intercollegiate athletics is more a participation activity than a spectator activity for students at Ivy League universities. These institutions do not draw 100,000 spectators to their Saturday afternoon home football games. Indeed, the failure of most of them to draw an average of 20,000 spectators per game led the league to be placed in a lower classification, Division I-AA, for football. Without large revenues from their football program, the typical Division I-AA institution spent almost $2 million more on intercollegiate athletics in 1996–97 than it generated in revenue. If we view varsity sports as an integral part of undergraduate students' education, the failure of revenues to cover costs is not disturbing. Many of the activities conducted by selective private colleges and universities are subsidized by annual giving and endowment income.

Football is not the only sport that fails to attract many spectators in the Ivy League. At Cornell, except for men's hockey games, which are almost always sold out, spectators at intercollegiate events are often few and far between. To a basketball fan, such as me, this is great news—it means I can always walk into men's basketball games five minutes before the start of the game and find my favorite unreserved seat behind the basket empty. For the university's athletics department, it is not great news because these sports do not generate substantial ticket revenues and the empty seats in the stands do not aid in the competition to attract scholar-athletes to the university. In an effort to increase student attendance at games, the athletic department agreed in the mid-1990s to admit students for free to all athletic contests (except hockey games) in return for receiving an allocation from student activity fees. This allocation was set at a sum equal to the amount that the department had been receiving from ticket sales to students. To date, the plan has been only partially successful in expanding attendance.

The selective private universities that compete much more aggressively than the Ivies at the national level in football and basketball are members of major athletic conferences that contain predominately large state institutions. Among the thirteen schools ranked in the top ten (there was a four-way tie for tenth) in the *USNWR* 1999 ranking of colleges were the eight Ivies, MIT, Cal Tech, Stanford, Duke, and Northwestern. MIT and Cal Tech are specialized engineering universities that do not compete at the Division I level in most sports and also do not offer athletic scholarships. Stanford (Pac-10 Conference), Duke (ACC), and Northwestern (Big Ten) are each the only, or one of two, private institutions in their conferences. Public universities have long used success on the athletic field as a way of generating alumni and political support for their institution. To compete on the playing field with the public institutions in their conferences, Stanford, Duke, and Northwestern have all adopted the conference policy of awarding athletic scholarships.

Since the Ivy League schools do not offer athletic scholarships, what determines which of its schools have the most success on the athletic fields?[9] Table 17.2 presents information on the number of Ivy League titles that each institution in the league won during a recent sixteen-year period in all sports, in male sports, and in female sports. Harvard and Princeton have dominated the league, in terms both of total titles won and of men's and women's team titles won. Between them, the two institutions won over 45 percent of the Ivy League titles during the period. These are the two schools that have the highest endowments per student and whose student quality, as measured by the 25 to 75 percentile range in the SAT scores of freshmen, is also highest.

Top-quality academic students quite rationally want to go to the best undergraduate institution that they can get into, a fact that clearly gives Harvard and Princeton a leg up against many of their Ivy League competitors in the competition for top student-athletes. Their higher endowment per student also provides them with the resources to spend more on athletic facilities than their competitors and to provide more generous financial aid packages. Even if all the Ivies agree to provide only need-based financial aid, the richer institutions can offer more generous packages (more grants, fewer loans, and less work) for students with similar needs. Hence it is not surpris-

Table 17.2 Number of Ivy League varsity athletic titles won during the 1981–82 to 1996–97 period by each institution and the institution's 1996–97 endowment per student and SAT 25–75 percentile range.

| School | Number of titles won | | | Endowment per student (in $000) | SAT 25–75 percentile range |
	Total	Male	Female		
Brown	56	13	43	128	1290–1480
Columbia	27	24	3	173	1270–1470
Cornell	48	29	19	111	1250–1440
Dartmouth	58	32	26	249	1330–1520
Harvard	129	66	63	610	1390–1580
Pennsylvania	70	38	32	131	1270–1460
Princeton	135	74	61	776	1350–1530
Yale	55	30	25	526	1340–1530

Source: The 1997–98 Directory and Record Book of Ivy League Athletics (Princeton: Council of Ivy Group Presidents, 1997); *Cornell University 1998–99 Financial Plan: Operating and Capital, May 1998* (Ithaca: Cornell University, May 1998). *1999 America's Best Colleges* (Washington, D.C.: *USNWR*, August 1998). Last column, copyright © 1998, *U.S. News & World Report.*

ing that they most often win Ivy League titles. What is surprising is that Yale, which is the third richest school in terms of endowment per student, came in sixth out of eight during the period in Ivy League titles won.

As I pointed out earlier, the great increase in stock market prices and endowment values that took place during the late 1990s led the richer Ivy League schools—Princeton, Harvard, Yale, and Dartmouth—to announce vastly more generous financial aid packages for all students in 1998.[10] These new aid programs, which the poorer schools in the Ivy League could not afford to match, had the effect of substantially decreasing the attractiveness of the poorer schools to scholar-athletes who come from families whose income levels qualify them for grant aid.

In actuality, the "poorer" Ivy schools—Cornell, the University of Pennsylvania, and Brown—compete much more directly with Duke and Northwestern for students than they do with the richer Ivies. Scholar-athletes interested in competing in big-time football or basketball conferences will invariably choose Duke or Northwestern over the poorer Ivies. The 25 to 75 percentile SAT ranges for Duke and Northwestern were 1300–1480 and 1270 to 1450, respectively, roughly equivalent to the comparable ranges at the three "poorer" Ivies. To attend Duke or Northwestern so that they can compete in big-time football or basketball, rather than Brown, Cornell, or Pennsylvania, does not require student-athletes to give up anything in terms of the test scores of the students around them.

Scholar-athletes interested in competing in other sports weigh both the academic programs at the different institutions and their financial aid packages. For students with financial need, aid packages are particularly important, and the comparison for them would be between the athletic scholarships offered by Duke or Northwestern and the need-based financial aid packages offered by Cornell, Pennsylvania, or Brown. If preferential packaging for athletes were permitted in the Ivy League, the three Ivy institutions would be able to increase their grant aid packages and would then have a much better chance of winning the competition with Duke and Northwestern for scholar-athletes interested in participating in these other sports.

Why do the members of the Ivy League feel compelled to field so many different varsity athletic teams? One explanation is that because varsity athletics in the Ivy League are participatory rather than spectator activities, the institutions want to provide athletic competition opportunities for as many students as possible. However, these institutions also run large programs of intramural sports, supported through student activity fees, and club sports such as rugby and men's volleyball, whose teams compete with other institution's teams on a less formal and less expensive basis. Both types of programs provide multiple opportunities for students to engage informally in sports and should reduce the need for so many varsity sports teams. Why they do not do so will be discussed shortly.

A second, and perhaps better explanation, is that participation in varsity sports teaches valuable team skills to students, which are useful to them in later life. Participation in varsity sports also helps to "tie" students to the university. Many administrators and alumni from these institutions believe that varsity athletes who graduated from selective private universities, on average, both earn more and contribute more to their alma maters than other graduates of the institutions.

Gender Equity

Title IX of the 1972 Educational Amendments to the Civil Rights Act prohibits discrimination based on gender in programs of educational institutions that receive any funding from the federal government. Building on this legislation, in 1978 and 1979, the Office of Civil Rights (OCR) of the U.S. Department of Health, Education, and Welfare (now the Department of Health and Human Services) issued regulations that applied to intercollegiate athletics. In simple language, these regulations called for academic institutions to (1) provide opportunities for males and females to participate in intercollegiate competition that were roughly proportional to each gender's representation in the institution's undergraduate student body; (2) provide athletic scholarships to men and women roughly in proportion to their varsity athletic participation rates; and (3) provide equitable treatment in terms of the numbers of coaches and their compensations, the facilities provided for the athletes, and the recruiting and travel budgets of teams.

Proponents of gender equity in athletics faced a setback in 1984 when in Grove v. Bell, the Supreme Court ruled that Title IX applied only to the specific programs at educational institutions for which federal funds were received. For example, if an academic institution was receiving federal funding only for undergraduate financial aid programs and faculty research grants, this case implied that the institution was not required to pursue gender equity in athletics. However, in 1988, Congress passed the Civil Rights Restoration Act, which clarified that Title IX was intended to apply to all programs of academic institutions, including intercollegiate athletics. At that point, the pressure for compliance with Title IX's gender-equity requirements in intercollegiate athletics began to build.

The OCR allows institutions to demonstrate that they are in compliance with Title IX's requirements in participation opportunities by satisfying any one prong of a "three-pronged" test. First, and most direct, the institution may demonstrate that opportunities for males and females to compete in intercollegiate sports are in "substantial proportion" to the gender mix of the undergraduate student body.

If an institution has an undergraduate student body that is 45 percent female and 45 percent of its varsity athletes are female, the institution will satisfy the participation opportunity condition. But how close to the proportion of females in the undergraduate student body, the proportion of varsity athletes that is female must be for the institution to be in "substantial proportion" has never been stated exactly by the OCR or the courts, except in cases of allocation of athletic scholarships. More generally, while the courts have ruled in a number of cases that a 10 percentage point differential (that is, say 35 percent of the athletes being female in the example above) is not substantial compliance, many observers believe that a 3 to 5 percentage point differential might be.

If an institution fails to meet this first test, it still may be found to be in compliance if it demonstrates a history and continued practice of moving toward substantial compliance in the provision of athletic opportunities for the underrepresented gender. The key point here is that the institution must both have begun efforts to remedy the inequity and have a plan to continue remedying the inequity until substantial compliance is achieved.

Finally, if an institution fails to meet either of the first two tests, it still may be found to be in compliance if it demonstrates that the interests and abilities of its underrepresented gender is fully met by its existing set of male and female athletics programs. Merely asserting that this is true is not sufficient and, to my knowledge, no college or university has ever been declared in compliance on the basis of meeting this third test. Indeed, in a major court case that went as far as the Supreme Court, it was declared in 1997 that Brown University's assertion that its programs met this test was inadequate, and Brown was ordered to provide the courts with a plan to bring the university into compliance. The Brown case resulted from a 1991 decision by the university to drop women's volleyball and gymnastics as part of a series of budget-saving cuts.[11]

The Brown case, along with suits by female athletes at other universities, produced pressure for institutions to do more to achieve gender equity. For example, Cornell planned on eliminating men's and women's gymnastics and men's and women's fencing in 1993–94 to bring an athletics department budget that was long in deficit back into balance. The threat of a suit by some female athletes, which came on the heels of the initial federal district court decision in the Brown case, was sufficient to induce Cornell to continue the female programs, although it did drop the two male sports.

A further reason to take the establishment of gender equity seriously was supplied in 1993 when the NCAA instituted its certification process for all Division I institutions with athletics programs. Of key importance is that to be certified, an institution must have had a plan to achieve gender equity and must have demonstrated that substantial progress had been made by 1999 (for reviews undertaken after that date). Failure to be certified prevents an institution's teams from appearing in any NCAA tournament competitions, which would have negative implications for the institution both financially and for the recruiting of student athletes.

The Equity in Athletics Disclosure Act, which became effective in October 1996, requires colleges and universities to report annually where they are in their gender-equity efforts. Comparisons for 1996–97 are found in Table 17.3 for the Ivy League institutions and for the universities in the Big Ten and the Atlantic Coast Conference.

On average, the Ivy institutions were closer to achieving gender equity than their counterparts in the other conferences. The average Ivy institution's percentage of female varsity athletes was 8 percentage points less than its percentage of female students, and its percentage of varsity athletic expenditures that went to female teams was 12 percentage points less. The differences were 9 and 22 percentage points for the ACC institutions and 10 and 17 percentage points for the Big Ten institutions. Duke and Northwestern, the two highly selective private institutions in the latter two conferences, did more poorly on gender-equity measures than did the average Ivy League institution.

The numbers in this table suggest that, as of 1996–97, most institutions in the three conferences failed the first prong of the test for compliance with gender equity. However, as long at they were moving in the right direction and had plans to achieve substantial proportionality, they still could be judged in compliance. At Cornell, for example, the percentage of varsity athletes that were female increased from 37 percent in 1996–97 to 43 percent in 1998–99. This placed Cornell's female percentage of varsity athletes within 5 percentage points of its percentage of female students.[12]

It is useful to contrast efforts to achieve gender equity in intercollegiate

Table 17.3   Gender equity in varsity athletic programs at Ivy League, ACC, and Big Ten universities in 1996–97.

	Female percentage of				
	a Under- graduates	b Varsity athletes	c Varsity operating expenses	d (a − b)	e (a − c)
Ivy League					
Brown	54	49	44	5	10
Columbia	62	37	31	25	31
Cornell	47	37	41	10	6
Dartmouth	48	46	41	2	7
Harvard	45	40	39	5	6
Pennsylvania	49	37	32	12	17
Princeton	46	41	36	5	10
Yale	48	47	40	1	8
Conference average				8	12
ACC					
Clemson	45	39	14	6	31
Duke	49	37	25	12	24
Florida State	55	42	34	13	21
Georgia Tech	28	28	26	0	2
Maryland	48	40	21	8	27
North Carolina	60	43	25	17	35
N C State	39	39	29	0	10
Virginia	53	42	24	11	29
Wake Forest	50	39	27	11	23
Conference average				9	22

athletics with more general efforts to eliminate gender and race discrimination in employment. If an employer is systematically not hiring qualified females or underrepresented minorities, the public policy remedy is to require the employer to hire more qualified employees from these groups. The employer is not expected to increase the company's overall level of employment, but rather to hire more qualified women or minorities and hence fewer white males. Hence, antidiscrimination in employment legislation may restrict the opportunities of some white males; but these restrictions are

Table 17.3   (continued)

| | Female percentage of | | | | |
	a Under-graduates	b Varsity athletes	c Varsity operating expenses	d (a − b)	e (a − c)
Big Ten					
Illinois	47	33	30	14	17
Indiana	54	42	31	12	23
Iowa	54	39	36	15	18
Michigan	50	45	42	5	8
Michigan State	53	37	37	16	16
Minnesota	50	39	31	11	19
Northwestern	51	40	33	11	18
Ohio State	47	42	31	5	16
Penn State	45	40	23	5	22
Purdue	46	38	36	8	10
Wisconsin	52	42	28	10	24
Conference average				10	17

Source: The data in columns a, b, and c are from *The Chronicle of Higher Education,* April 13, 1998. Data were reported by the institutions under the Equity in Athletics Disclosure Act, which took effect on October 1, 1996. The numbers in columns d and e were computed by the author.

seen as being nothing more than removing unfair advantages that the white males had because the employer was previously discriminating in favor of them.

Nothing in the Title IX legislation requires academic institutions to increase their overall expenditures on varsity athletics to comply with Title IX. While increasing the number of female teams, or the number of females participating on existing female teams, will enhance female participation, reducing the number of male teams or the number of males participating on existing teams will also move an institution toward compliance. If the legislation had required that compliance be achieved only through increasing female participants, it would have been a form of unfunded mandate, which would directly have increased the costs of colleges and universities.

Nationally, there is evidence that compliance efforts have led both to the expansion of opportunities for women and the contraction of opportunities for men. One national study found that between 1978 and 1996, NCAA Division I schools added 1,658 new women's programs. During the same period, however, 927 new men's programs were created and 853 existing men's programs were dropped.[13] At Cornell, men's fencing and gymnastics were dropped in 1993–94 and women's softball, equestrian competitions, and squash were added during the 1993–94 to 1995–96 period. Cornell went from having 20 male and 15 female sports in 1992–93 to having 18 male and 18 female sports in 1998–99.[14] Given the vast size of men's football teams and the amount of money spent on them, to achieve gender equity will require a larger number of female teams than male teams at many institutions that have men's football programs.

Adding female teams is the most expensive way to achieve gender equity. Cheaper ways are to reduce the number or size of male teams and to add more females to existing female teams.[15] One may think that reducing the size of the men's basketball team from 15 to 12, for example, would not be a big deal, because the last 3 players spend virtually all of their time sitting on the bench. But such thinking ignores the enjoyment that many players get from being a member of a team and practicing and traveling with it, even if they never play. It also ignores that injuries can quickly deplete a team's strength and leave a coach wishing that players 13 through 15 were still on the team.

At Cornell, all four strategies are being pursued to try to achieve gender equity. Gender-equity efforts have had real financial costs because the university has not been able to bring itself to deeply cut male athletic programs. While I was a vice president, a proposal was on the table to eliminate men's baseball. The reason given was that with the Ithaca climate, Cornell is never going to be a powerhouse in baseball. Cornell last won an Ivy League title in baseball in 1977, and if men's baseball was eliminated, the baseball field could be converted to a women's softball field. The university could thus save the construction and maintenance costs of a new softball facility.

That proposal was killed by negative alumni reaction. Instead, increased contributions from alumni were solicited to help fund men's baseball. Whether these new contributions will be sufficient to fully cover the costs of the men's baseball program is an open question, as is whether they came from contributions that otherwise would have gone to some other part of the university. Although the new women's softball field was also funded through contributions, these contributions may not prove sufficient to cover the annual cost of maintaining the field. Moreover, the failure to eliminate men's baseball means the university must further increase its expenditures on female sports to achieve gender equity.

Sometimes gender-equity requirements add to the cost of existing women's sports. Gender equity requires that Cornell's male and female crew teams have the same quality of locker facilities at the Cayuga Lake inlet where they train and compete. Currently the male facility is much larger than the female one. Hence the athletics department decided that it had to construct a new female locker facility. I suggested that one way to avoid that cost was to rotate the existing facilities. The male team could occupy the larger facility in alternate years. This suggestion was not taken seriously— the department claimed that it would disadvantage Cornell in the competition for scholar-athletes interested in crew.

Crew is an interesting example of how the argument that "we need to have (fill in your favorite example) to remain competitive for top students" can be carried to almost an absurd extreme. Very few high school students participate in crew. The crew coaches at Cornell religiously attend swim team tryouts to try to recruit for their sport swimmers who are not quite good enough to make the swim team, but have a physical build that indicates they have the potential to be good in crew. Cornell requires that all students pass a swimming test, and the crew coaches also attend the swim tests, look at all the students' physiques, and try to recruit prospects. Finally, the coaches are omnipresent at freshman registration, trying to market the team to new students. The coaches then take the novice rowers that they have recruited and train them. By the time many of them are juniors and seniors, they form the skilled nucleus of the varsity team.

Crew is a wonderful sport. But most of the participants on Cornell's team come to the university without having the faintest idea that they will be involved with the sport. Hence the argument that Cornell needed the new locker facility to attract student-athletes is hard to take seriously.

The athletics department also requested permission, while I was a vice president, to build a new indoor squash facility to help retain a "world-class" squash coach that it had hired. Since the department's budget was perpetually in deficit, it was hard for me to grasp how adding a new facility, which would be primarily used by a small group of male and female varsity athletes, was necessary for the institution. Although rules changes had made the university's existing squash courts too small for national competition, the institution did have the option of dropping the sport. Only about 30 of Cornell's more than 1,000 varsity athletes were on the squash team in 1998–99, and the majority of these were males. Hence, eliminating the sport would have *improved* gender equity at the university.

When the squash coach decided to leave Ithaca, I thought that the pressure to have the new facility would diminish. Not the case! The department then argued that it needed the new facility to remain competitive for the top male and female squash players that it was trying to attract. Apparently the fear that a few top students would not come to Cornell because of the lack of a new squash facility was persuasive. The facility is being built with gifts, the department will have to maintain it, and the deficit of the department will most probably grow still larger.

Not surprisingly, as I wrote this chapter, pressure from trustees and key alumni was being brought to bear on the Cornell administration to increase expenditures on varsity athletics. The argument being made was that the department must be underfunded if it was perpetually running a deficit. Further, better funding of athletics would, proponents argued, translate into improved varsity team records, more alumni donations, and would make the institution more attractive to all potential students. No one suggested the obvious alternative: that Cornell could reduce the department's deficit by reducing the number of intercollegiate sports in which its students participate.

Why is a world-class squash facility, a new female crew locker facility, and a new women's softball field so important to Cornell? One reason is that selective private universities want to be the best at everything that they do. Another is that alumni pressure (and the implied threat of withholding contributions) makes it difficult for university administrators to cut any program that alumni care about. And a third reason is the claim that the failure to build these facilities would place the university at a competitive disadvantage in its quest for students. Although universities may blame gender-equity legislation for increasing their costs, in fact it is conscious choices by the institutions to achieve gender equity primarily by adding rather than by subtracting, and by building new facilities rather than sharing existing ones, that leads to the increase in costs.

I note with envy that Columbia, the Ivy League institution with the fewest number of varsity sports teams, experienced a much greater growth in undergraduate applicants than Cornell has over a number of recent years. Columbia also has seen its entering classes' test scores rise relative to Cornell's entering classes' test scores. Much of the credit for Columbia's good fortune is due to the resurgence of New York City as a place to live. But Columbia's administration also appears to understand that stressing varsity athletics is not a necessary, or even a sufficient, condition for improving the quality of students that attend a selective private university.

CHAPTER 18

Dining and Housing

Student dining and housing are enterprise units at Cornell. They are expected to fully cover their operating and capital costs and receive no subsidies from the general operating budget of the university. One might conclude from this description that their operations have no impact on the rest of the university. Nothing could be further from the truth.

Dining

Cornell is widely reputed to have one of the best dining services for students in the nation.[1] Students may choose from a variety of plans—the most comprehensive one covered twenty meals a week and cost $1,510 per semester in 1998–99. That year there were four separate dining facilities located in the residential units that ring the campus and one more dining facility near the center of the campus, where most of the academic buildings are. Students enrolled in meal plans were free to eat as much as they wanted at each meal at these five facilities. There were also twelve other dining facilities on campus where food was sold on an à la carte basis. At five of these twelve facilities, students enrolled in meal plans received credit for up to a specified dollar amount per meal.

The menus vary daily at each dining hall and also vary across dining halls. Each of the dining halls offers five entrées for dinner, including a vegetarian main dish. Students on the meal plans are free to eat in any unit. With menus varying across the units, some students choose where they will eat on a particular day on the basis of what is being served at each dining facility that day. Several times each semester guest chefs are brought to the campus from famous restaurants around the nation to serve dinners from their restaurants. There is no extra charge to students on the meal plans for these Cross-Country Gourmet program dinners. Members of the faculty and staff who are willing to pay "big city" prices may also attend them.

Many Cornell students like to sleep late and finish their classes by early afternoon. Interestingly, many professors have the same aversion to early morning and late afternoon classes. Hence classes at Cornell tend to be clustered between 10:00 A.M. and 3:00 P.M. Cornell's campus being large, there is a fifteen-minute break between classes to ensure that students can move from one building to another for classes. Because residential units are located around the perimeter of the campus and may be as much as a fifteen-minute walk from classroom buildings, most students prefer to eat lunch in central campus dining facilities.

These preferences put a lot of pressure on the capacity of these facilities, but the dining system worked well until the decision was made to renovate Sage Hall in 1995–96. A dining facility in the basement had been serving approximately 1,200 lunches a day. Once that facility was closed, long lines appeared at lunchtime at the other central campus facilities. Some of the displaced diners could have been accommodated at the other central campus locations, but the total number of diners displaced was too large to accommodate all of them at these facilities.

The university immediately began to consider how to handle this problem. As an economist, I naturally suggested using a price system. The dining facilities located near the residence units had considerable unused capacity at lunchtime. To encourage students whose schedules allowed them to return to the residence hall dining facilities for lunch to do so, I suggested that Cornell provide substantial discounts to students who ate in them at lunchtime. For example, if each student who ate lunch in one of these facilities was given a $2 a day rebate, over the course of a five-day a week, fifteen-week semester, students taking advantage of the option would save $150 a semester. I also suggested that the university should compute its financial aid packages on the assumption that students were not taking advantage of this option so that students receiving Cornell grant aid would actually receive cash payments for choosing this option.

The staff of Cornell Dining, the enterprise unit that provides food services on campus, did not look favorably on my suggestion. They thought that providing rebates would reduce their revenue and force them to raise prices. They worried that many students would not have sufficient time to go back and forth to the residence halls for lunch. I suggested running campus buses back and forth to the residence units during the midday hours more frequently to facilitate use of the residence hall dining facilities. This suggestion was explored, but rejected, because a survey of students indicated that they would prefer to stay near the center of the campus for lunch.

How much weight should administrators give to such preferences in making decisions at the university? I, for instance, would prefer to live in a community that has a more temperate climate than Ithaca's and better air service to major cities. But those preferences have not kept me from remaining a faculty member at Cornell for over twenty-five years because there are many other aspects of Cornell that are much more important to me than Ithaca's climate and airline connections.

Cornell's administration knew from periodic surveys it conducts of accepted freshman applicants (both those that enroll and those that go elsewhere) that the major factors that attract students to the university are its academic strength and the opportunities that a Cornell diploma opens up for post-graduate employment and education. The same surveys indicate that accepted applicants often rank Cornell best among the institutions they are considering in terms of student dining, but they also show that dining plays a very minor role in their decisions whether to enroll at the university. Hence even given the preferences of students for central campus dining options at lunchtime, it is unlikely that Cornell would lose many prospective students if more central campus dining were not offered.

Cornell Dining does not think along these lines. Like other student service units on campus (such as athletics, housing, and health services), it seeks to provide services that satisfy student preferences. Its goal is to maximize student satisfaction, subject to the financial constraint of not running a deficit. Cornell Dining does understand that dining rates must be approved by the central university administration and that it is under pressure to keep the rate of increase in dining rates low. As long as it can achieve the latter, it is free to pursue its own objectives.

So what was Cornell Dining's preferred solution? Much to my surprise, Cornell Dining had a reserve of approximately $9 million that had been set aside from previous years' revenues to protect against the contingency that another dining facility would have to be built on the central campus. That sum was estimated to be sufficient to expand an existing facility in Willard Straight Hall, a historic building on the campus. But faced with the difficulties that would be involved in trying to maintain the integrity of the architectural design of a historic building and the objections that would be raised by historic preservationists, plans to renovate the building were abandoned, at least temporarily.

My opposition to the expanded facility was based on economic grounds. Although Cornell Dining's reserves might cover the construction of the new facility, they would not cover the operating and maintenance costs of the new space. Unless the overall usage of Cornell Dining facilities increased by enough to generate sufficient additional revenue to offset these costs, the costs would be reflected in higher dining rates.

Higher dining rates increase the total costs of attending the university. It is the total cost of attending the university, not its tuition and fees, that influences accepted students' decisions to attend Cornell. It is also the total costs that determine the financial aid that is provided for students. For students receiving grant aid from the university, every dollar increase in dining costs automatically increases their grant aid by a dollar. So higher dining rates will lead to increases in the university's financial aid budget unless the university compensates for the higher rates by reducing its planned tuition increase by an equivalent dollar amount. Increased financial aid costs or reduced tuition revenues both mean that less money will be available to spend on the academic functions of the university.

I quickly calculated that if the $9 million dining reserve was instead invested by Cornell Dining and it yielded the department a 5 percent annual return, this would provide them with $450,000 a year in additional revenue. These funds could be used to defray the costs of the type of rebates that I suggested. That amount of money would be sufficient to provide $300 annual rebates to 1,500 students. If that many students ate lunch in the residence hall dining facilities (remember that the rebate would be paid to all students who ate there, including ones who would have eaten there anyway), the strain on central campus dining facilities at lunchtime would be reduced. Cornell Dining would not lose money, and no extra utility and maintenance costs would be added to its budget. Hence no additional pressure would be put on dining rates.

Economic logic often does not carry the day in discussions of issues such as this because of administrators' preoccupation with satisfying students' preferences. Fortunately, from the perspective of students, another alternative was found that did lead to the expansion of central campus dining. This alternative involved drastically reducing the size of the faculty club and converting the vacated space into an additional student dining facility.

Cornell's School of Hotel Administration is located almost directly in the center of the campus. For years, the faculty club, called the Statler Club, was located in a cafeteria-style facility in the basement of the Statler Hotel, which is part of the hotel school. Club members ate their lunches in this lower-level facility and then went upstairs to a lounge to drink coffee and discuss the issues of the day. The availability of free coffee upstairs "encouraged" club members to vacate the dining area quickly, and this rapid turnover of seats permitted many of the university's faculty members and professional staff to be accommodated at lunchtime. For the privilege of having this private dining area, members of the Statler Club paid modest annual dues that went to the hotel school to cover the cost of the coffee service and to serve as "rent" for the space. This was one of the few places on campus where a charge for space did exist.

During the 1980s, the Statler Hotel was demolished and a new Statler Hotel was constructed on the same site. Membership in the Statler Club declined during the years that the club was in "exile" in a building that was not as centrally located. When the new Statler Hotel opened, club members found that the rent for the club's space had risen considerably. As with many new buildings that universities construct, the new Statler Hotel had proved to be more expensive than was planned and fund-raising efforts had not been as successful as hoped. Faced with a $10 million debt on the building, for which it was responsible under the budget structure that treats the school as a tub, the school had decided that it needed to raise the rent on the club's space. The increased rental payments would provide needed funds to help the school cover its annual interest payments and pay off the debt itself.

Membership in the Statler Club, which had begun to decline while the club was in exile, continued to decline. Whether this continued decline was due to the increase in dues, an increased availability of alternative places for faculty to eat on the campus, or a change in faculty lifestyles that reduced the need for a faculty club is not totally clear.[2] What was clear was that the Statler Club's revenues were insufficient to cover the rent it was being charged. The club's deficit, which at one point cumulatively exceeded $300,000, reached over $60,000 a year, and the responsibility for covering this deficit fell to the central administration. Since the provost was already paying the membership fees for emeritus professors, who are major users of the Statler Club, he thought that in tight budget times the university could not afford to continue to cover the deficits. To do so would continue to drain money from the academic side of the university.

One of my most unpleasant tasks as vice president was to tell the officers of the Statler Club that their space was going to be drastically reduced. The main basement dining facility in the hotel was converted to a general cash dining room. An agreement was reached between Cornell Dining and the hotel school that permitted students on meal plans to purchase lunch in this facility on an à la carte basis. If their bills exceed a specified maximum limit, cash payments are due for the excess. This option has proven popular, and the students who use this dining facility rate the quality of the food served at it very highly. Meanwhile, the Statler Club has been reduced to offering a limited soup and salad bar menu in an area with much less seating than it formerly had. Use of the club by the faculty has declined still further, and for all practical purposes, the university no longer has a faculty club.

This is not, however, the end of the story. In 1998–99, after I had already returned to the faculty, Cornell's Department of Campus Life announced that a comprehensive study of all food services on campus was being conducted in response to concerns voiced by the students and staff. I am usually not a betting man, but I am willing to wager that one of the major recommendations of this study will be the creation of more central campus lunchtime dining areas. Inevitably new facilities will be built, they will add directly to the costs charged for dining, and they will indirectly lead to an increase in the university's financial aid costs.

One last issue relating to dining. Dining workers at Cornell are among the lowest paid workers on campus. On an activist campus such as Cornell, faculty and student groups have often taken the side of these workers in their contract negotiations with the university. During the 1996–97 round of negotiations, well-organized groups of faculty and students argued that the university should pay dining and all other employees at least a "livable wage." That wage was determined by a local credit union, which estimated what it would cost an individual to live modestly in the community. In 1996, the livable wage for an individual was estimated in the Ithaca area to be about $16,500 a year. This translates into an hourly wage of $8.25 for an employee working 2,000 hours a year.[3]

Many dining employees work considerably less than 2,000 hours a year because there are no students on campus during intercession periods and student enrollment is much lower during the summer than it is during the academic year. Although the university attempts to place dining workers in other seasonal jobs when their services are not needed in dining facilities, it is not always successful in these efforts. Hence to pay a livable wage to many dining workers would require paying considerably more than $8.25 an hour. Even this hourly rate was much higher than what many dining workers were making before the negotiations.

Neither the faculty nor the students who support the livable wage concept volunteered that they would be willing to pay for higher salaries for dining workers by respectively agreeing to lower salary increases or higher tuition levels. Instead, they argued that funds could surely be found within the billion-dollar budget of the university. Would that it were so easy. Cornell Dining is an enterprise unit and when its workers' wage rates go up, unless cost-saving changes in how dining operates can be implemented, these wage increases are passed on to students in the form of higher dining rates.

Politically, the livable wage concept is a very potent bargaining tool for the union at Cornell. Cornell receives considerable political support from organized labor in New York state because of the efforts of the extension division of Cornell's School of Industrial and Labor Relations to provide training programs for union members throughout the state. The union movement often lobbies the New York state legislature and the governor for financial support for that school and Cornell's other three statutory colleges, as well as for programs such as tuition assistance for low-income students that benefit the university as a whole. To be seen as opposing a concept such as the livable wage that is important to the labor movement might be politically very costly to the university.

The average negotiated salary increase given unionized staff that year was roughly equal to the average salary increase that nonunion staff at the university had been granted, about 4 percent. The university did agree, however, to distribute the increases for unionized workers in such a way that lower-paid workers received higher percentage increases. Although a livable wage was not achieved, great progress was made as the minimum hourly wage for new unionized workers was increased substantially to $7.75.

Dining employees are concentrated at the lower end of the union wage scales. As a result, the average wage of dining employees rose by considerably more than 4 percent that summer. When new dining rates were announced for the 1998–99 academic year, the first setting of dining rates after the contract settlement, the rates were 6 percent higher. The university had worked hard to keep the rate of endowed tuition increase between 1997–98 and 1998–99 at 4.3 percent, which was still more than 2 percentage points more than the rate of increase in the consumer price index. The more rapid increase in dining rates increased the costs of attending Cornell, and this increase, in turn, increased the grant aid that the university provided to students under its need-based financial aid program. This left fewer funds available for the academic side of the university.

Undergraduate Housing

Cornell University's housing policy for undergraduate students is in transition. In 1995–96, 44 percent of its undergraduates lived on the campus in university-owned housing. Cornell ranked fifteenth out of sixteen private and public institutions that it competes with for undergraduate students on this measure. Many of the competitor institutions house over 80 percent of their students on campus in university-owned housing.

On-campus housing was guaranteed for all freshmen that wanted it but upper-class students had to bid for available spots. About three quarters of the latter chose not to do so. Most of these students lived in fraternities or sororities, or in off-campus apartments or older houses within walking distance of the campus. Others lived short car rides away from the campus, taking advantage of the lower rental prices for units farther away from the campus.

Exit interviews conducted with graduating seniors, as well as more formal surveys of the senior class, indicate that many of Cornell's seniors view living off campus as one of the best parts of their college experience. It enables them to learn a set of life skills that many did not have when they first arrived at Cornell, such as negotiating leases, furnishing apartments, shopping for food, and cooking. Often they assert that these experiences helped to prepare them for their post-college lives.

Freshman and upper-class students who remained on campus had a wide variety of housing from which to choose. North of the campus, about a five-minute walk from the central campus, was a set of housing units that included classic Gothic halls, high-rise buildings with suites, and modern townhouse apartments. Over half of the university's on-campus housing was in this area, called North Campus.

West of the campus, down a steep slope from the main academic buildings, were the West Campus housing units. These included more classic Gothic halls, as well as a set of more modern looking university halls. For the most part the newer buildings were configured in traditional dormitory style: double rooms spread out along a corridor, with communal bathrooms and some common areas. About one third of the students living in on-campus housing resided on the West Campus.

Just south of the campus is an area called Collegetown. An easy walk from West Campus, this several-block area includes numerous restaurants, coffee shops, bars, and stores. Also in this area were two dormitory style housing units that housed about 10 percent of the on-campus students.

In addition to the option of living in conventional living units in these three areas, students also had the option of living in one of ten program, or theme, houses. These included Ecology House, Just About Music (JAM), Language House, the Holland International Living Center, the Multicultural Living and Learning Unit, Akwe:kon (American Indian House), the Latino Living Center, the Ujamaa (African American Culture) Residential College, and the Transfer Center. Each of these program houses brought together students with similar interests. Approximately 20 percent of on-campus students lived in program houses. In the main, the program houses were located on West and North Campus.

Although Cornell's undergraduate students liked the freedom of choice and range of options that the university's housing program provided, the trustees, the administrators, and the faculty had serious concerns about Cornell's housing program. The "personalities" of West Campus and North Campus had become very different. The former, close to many of the university's fraternities and sororities, developed a reputation for having a very boisterous atmosphere and housed predominately white students. The latter was quieter, and over half of its students were Asian American, international, and underrepresented minority students. Two of the three ethnic program houses, Ujaama and Akwe:kon, were located on North Campus.

Some people believed that the pattern of where students chose to live, as well as the very existence of the ethnic program houses, was defeating one of the purposes of Cornell, a diverse student body. The university wants to bring students with diverse backgrounds together so they can interact and learn more about other people's values and perspectives.

In actuality, only a small fraction of the underrepresented minority students lived in program houses, and these students were exercising the same freedom of residential choice given all other students. A complaint that the university had a segregated housing system, lodged by the New York Civil Rights Coalition, was dismissed for this reason after an investigation by the Office of Civil Rights of the U.S. Department of Education.[4]

Another concern related to the connection between the academic side of the university and students' lives outside the classroom. Although the university had attempted to integrate the two through programs where faculty members lived in residence units and faculty fellows regularly visited residence halls and interacted with students, these programs did not reach the majority of upper-class students who lived off campus. The lack of integration of student life and academics was thought to discourage potential students who were interested in gaining that type of college experience by attending Cornell.

Finally, Hunter Rawlings had become president of Cornell in July of 1995, about the time that Duke University had restructured its housing to create a freshman campus to invigorate the intellectual atmosphere on its campus.[5] Attempts to integrate the academic and student life sides of campuses were going on at many selective institutions. President Rawlings believed that to remain competitive in the market for top students, especially those interested in arts and science degrees, Cornell would have to take actions to improve its living and learning environment.

In March 1996, after receiving a report from a joint faculty, student, and staff committee, Rawlings publicly announced his interest in undertaking such actions. He indicated that he wanted to provide a similar freshman year experience for all students and suggested that to help achieve this, he was going to gradually limit the number of freshmen that could live in program houses. Freshmen would still be able to participate in the cultural activities at the houses; they simply would not be able to reside in them.

Reaction on the campus was predictably negative. The ethnic program houses saw his statement as a veiled attempt to eliminate them from the campus, and protests by underrepresented minority students and their supporters followed. The general student body was aghast at the possibility of any reduction in students' freedom of choice.

After several additional months of discussions and deliberations, Rawlings decided to move toward housing all freshmen on North Campus, in effect creating a freshman campus similar to the one that Duke had created several years earlier. Freshmen would be allowed to live in program houses, but only if the houses were moved to North Campus. In addition, the program houses would be required to limit freshmen to no more than 50 percent of their residents. Whether sophomores, juniors, and seniors will want to live in a program house that is located in the midst of the entire freshman class is still an open question.

Rawlings also proposed renovating the West Campus residence halls to make them more desirable residence options for undergraduates after the freshman year and guaranteeing housing on campus for any transfer student or sophomore who desired it. Finally, committees of members of the faculty and student life staff were appointed to decide on ways to make the residence units part of the intellectual life of the campus and to break the divide that existed between what went on in the classroom and outside it. Discussions by these committees led to plans for some of the West Campus units to evolve into residential colleges, similar to those that have existed at Yale for generations. Rawlings's compromise plan was hailed by most on the campus as a stroke of genius and the Cornell trustees unanimously approved it in May of 1997.

The program could not be implemented right away because the existing North Campus housing stock did not have sufficient capacity to house all freshman students and the residents of the program houses. Planning began to construct additional housing and dining facilities on North Campus. Planning also began to convert West Campus's primarily dormitory style facilities with double rooms into facilities containing suites and semiprivate bathrooms, more single rooms, more cooking facilities, and more common study and recreation space.

To encourage more faculty participation in student life, plans to house more faculty in both the North Campus and West Campus housing units had to be developed, and apartments for faculty members and their families were included in the design of new buildings and renovation projects. This, along with the fact that many double rooms would eventually be replaced on West Campus by single rooms, meant that the net number of new housing units created for students on campus would be less than the 560 new beds that were to be added to North Campus. The cost of the North Campus construction program alone was estimated in the fall of 1998 to be about $65 million. A year later the renovation cost of the West Campus was estimated to be in the range of $200 million.

How were these costs to be covered? The university did not have the flexibility to substantially raise residence hall room rates. To do so would provide an increased incentive for upper-class students to live off campus. It would also increase the total cost of a student's attending Cornell and hence the university's financial aid costs. Even if the renovated West Campus housing units operated at very close to capacity, the existing structure of residence hall rental rates would not be sufficient to cover all of the operating, maintenance, and debt service costs of the new and renovated facilities.

The university's senior administrators worked quietly behind the scenes with potential donors and developed ways to finance the debt from the North Campus project, which enabled that project to go forward. Construction began in the fall of 1999. The presence of freshman students on North Campus is gradually being increased, and it is projected that all the new facilities will be completed in time for the start of the 2001–2002 academic year. All freshmen will be living on North Campus at that time. The new residence halls will have air conditioning, and the hope is that this will help the university expand its usage of the campus during the summer months.

On October 8, 1999, Rawlings announced that the university had received a $100 million pledge from an anonymous donor to help defray the cost of transforming the West Campus. Although the timing of the receipt of this future gift was not specified, it is reasonable to assume that it also will be used to help finance the debt.

Concern has been expressed by some faculty members that the financing of the debt from the two projects involves using gifts to the university that otherwise could have been used to strengthen academic programs. The administration denies that this is the case, but the funding sources remain confidential, so it is not clear if this concern is valid. Other faculty members are concerned that the expansion of academic programming in the residence halls, including expansions of the faculty-in-residence and faculty fellows programs, will also deprive the core academic departments of resources. The administration's belief is that these increased costs can be funded through external gifts, but again there is concern over whether such gifts will come at least partly at the expense of donations to the university's core academic programs.

As a Cornell vice president at the time the plan was developed, I was concerned that the plan assumed very high occupancy rates for the West Campus housing units that will be renovated in the future. With the addition of 550 new beds on North Campus and the shift of all freshmen to North Campus, several hundred more upper class-students will have to choose an on-campus housing option for these occupancy projections to be satisfied.

Cornell wants to increase the number of upper-class students living on campus, and it is betting that if improved on-campus housing is available to students, more will decide to live on campus. The university did conduct a survey of upper-class students to learn the attributes that the students would need to see in campus housing for them to consider returning to live on the campus. But this survey did not do any formal analysis of the number who actually would do so. Hence the renovation of West Campus is based on a *Field of Dreams* type of hope: build it and they will come.

At the same time plans are being made for these renovations, a number of new high-rise apartment buildings are being built in, or planned for, the Collegetown area by private developers. Since the university has no plans to expand its enrollments, these new Collegetown apartments, which will compete both with university-owned housing and privately owned off-campus housing, will make it difficult for the university's optimistic occupancy forecasts to be met. If they are not, for its residence hall operations to avoid a deficit, Cornell would either have to increase its housing rates (a move that might further reduce occupancy rates and be self-defeating) or provide a subsidy to housing from its general operating budget.

Either action would reduce the funds available for the university's academic programs. The former would do so by increasing the total cost of attending the university, which would in turn increase the university's financial aid costs. The latter would directly reduce the availability of university funds for other purposes. If competition from the local Ithaca housing market causes Cornell's projections of future rates that it can charge for housing to be too high, housing will similarly run a deficit.

It is reasonable to assume that Cornell will not starve its academic programs if its optimistic projections about housing occupancy rates fail to materialize. It is the academic reputation of the university that is most important in convincing top students to enroll. Hence efforts to remain competitive for top students will eventually lead to the need for additional tuition revenue to replace any funds that have to be diverted to student housing from the academic side of the university. So Cornell's new housing initiative may well eventually lead to higher tuition rates. Although housing and dining are enterprise units at Cornell, their behavior directly and indirectly affects the rest of the university.

PART IX

CONCLUSION

CHAPTER 19

Looking to the Future

Why Costs Continue to Rise at Selective Private Institutions

Simply put, cost increases at selective private colleges and universities are driven by the desires of these institutions to be the very best that they can be. Competitive pressures have caused their focus on pushing back the frontiers of knowledge and providing high-quality education to widen to include providing the very best student living, dining, and athletics facilities. This only exacerbates the cost pressures that the institutions face. In our increasingly winner-take-all society, each institution understands the importance of remaining among the set of institutions considered truly selective. Hence each strives to maintain or improve its position, rather than to reduce its costs.

As I have demonstrated throughout this book, these cost pressures have been increased by actions that the federal government has undertaken. These actions include the Justice Department's suit that led to the consent decree that prevents Ivy League institutions that have accepted the same applicants from meeting to discuss the financial needs of those applicants and the government's continual efforts to reduce the indirect cost rates associated with sponsored research. They have further been increased by the behavior of local governments, the institutions' systems of shared governance, the ways the selective universities organize to allocate resources and raise funds, the ways they select and reward the academic leaders of their colleges, and the growth of publications that numerically rank institutions.

The benefits that students obtain from attending these institutions are not diminishing. If anything, they are increasing. As a result, students continue to flock to them, and competition for positions in their entering classes is at an all-time high. As long as lots of high-quality applicants keep knocking at their doors and accepting offers of admission, the institutions have little incentive to try to hold down costs. Rather, each continues to focus on attracting more resources so that it can maintain and try to improve both its absolute quality and its relative position among the selective institutions.

Is there any hope that the institutions themselves will end this arms race of spending or at least moderate their rate of tuition increases? The market leaders, the most selective institutions with the highest endowment per student and tuition levels—Princeton, Harvard, and Yale—will provide the answer to this question. For if these institutions slow down their rate of increase in tuition, the other selective institutions will eventually have to do so also.[1] The lesser selective private institutions cannot get away for long with charging higher tuition to their full-paying students. If they attempt do so, they will run the risk of increasingly losing the best of these students to their better-endowed competitors.

In 1997–98, the average tuition and fees at Princeton, Harvard, and Yale was slightly under $23,000. The comparable average for Cornell and Pennsylvania, two of the lesser-endowed selective private universities, was around $22,500. Although there is some room in the short run for the latter institutions to increase their tuition at higher rates than the former institutions do, once their tuition levels come closer to those of their richer counterparts their freedom to do so will diminish. It will be very hard for them to justify to their constituents that their students should pay more than students pay at the richer institutions. Although they have greater need for tuition revenue, they devote fewer resources to educating each student than do their better-endowed counterparts.

If the better-endowed institutions slow down their rates of tuition growth, so eventually will the lesser-endowed selective private institutions. Such a slowdown will, however, only intensify the efforts of the institutions to obtain revenue from other sources. Campaigns for giving to support annual operations, to increase endowments, and to fund capital projects will continue. The institutions will become wealthier and wealthier.

Why Society Should Care

Why should society care about the tuition levels at these institutions? Although people with modest incomes can only shake their heads in disbelief at new homes that cost over $1,000,000, or luxury cars that cost over $50,000, very few people would propose that price ceilings be placed on homes or new cars. Most of us believe that the wealthy have a right to spend their money however they please. If they feel compelled to spend exorbitant sums on conspicuous consumption and "to buy the best," so be it.[2]

Of course, those of us with income levels that do not permit such expenditures see little reason why we should subsidize such purchases. Similarly, we see little need for us to subsidize the vacation homes of the wealthy. Such reasoning provided the rationale for Congress's adopting limitations in the deductibility of mortgage interest payments in the federal personal income tax statute during the late 1970s and early 1980s. In particular, the mortgage deduction was limited to an individual's primary residence and a cap was placed on the maximum amount of mortgage interest that can be deducted.

The final report of the National Commission on the Costs of Higher Education rejected the notion of placing any controls on the tuition levels that American colleges and universities charge, arguing that such controls could be "destructive of quality in higher education."[3] The commission understood that the nation benefits from having so many of the world's very best private institutions of higher education located in the United States. It grasped that the constant efforts of these institutions to push back the frontiers of knowledge and improve their quality yield vast benefits to society that transcend the benefits received by the students who study at them.

How much we as a society should be willing to pay for these benefits is another question. The selective private institutions benefit from a large number of tax advantages that accrue to them under federal and state tax statutes. Contributions made to them by individuals and corporations are deductible from federal and state personal and corporate income taxes. A large body of research demonstrates that the tax deductions received for charitable contributions cause giving to be higher than would otherwise be the case.

The income that the institutions earn each year from their endowments is also not taxed. Similarly, the property the institutions own that is used for educational purposes is exempt from local property taxes. Finally, they can often borrow funds at lower, tax-exempt interest rates. Because of these tax exemptions at the federal, state, and local level, the public at large is subsidizing the activities of these institutions to the tune of literally billions of dollars of lost tax revenue each year.

The public's willingness to bear such costs is based on the belief that these institutions yield broad benefits to society as a whole. In the future, however, it will not be sufficient for the selective private institutions to justify this support by referring to the value of the research that they produce or to the value that society places on having high-quality private educational alternatives. Instead, to maintain broad public support, these institutions will have to continually demonstrate that they remain accessible to students from all socioeconomic backgrounds. They will be able to continue to raise their tuition levels at rates greater than the rate of inflation only if they increasingly provide need-based financial aid to students from lower- and middle-income families so that these students can continue to attend them.

The competition for top students is likely to lead more of the institutions to award merit aid to students who have no financial need. But even as the institutions devote more resources to merit aid, it will remain absolutely essential that they maintain, and strengthen, their need-based financial aid programs. Most of these institutions sincerely believe that the educational process is improved if students are exposed to other students from a wide variety of socioeconomic backgrounds. Most also genuinely believe that they have an obligation to try to assure that the future leaders of our nation, many of whom attend them, come from all segments of our population. Hence they will want to maintain need-based aid policies independently of the political reasons for doing so. But if they do diminish their commitment to need-based aid, they will lose public support and that would probably prove very damaging to them politically.

Increased merit aid, coupled with the maintenance of need-blind admissions and need-based financial aid policies, will probably require them to devote an increasing share of their budgets to undergraduate financial aid. The richer institutions, such as Princeton, Harvard, and Yale, may be able to finance their increased financial aid costs out of increased endowment spending. The less well off members of the group, such as Pennsylvania, Duke, and Cornell, will face some very difficult tradeoffs. Some will be unable to afford to simultaneously maintain their academic quality, the socioeconomic diversity of their students, their faculty salaries, and the research support that they provide for faculty members. Something will have to give. It will not be easy to be senior administrators at many of these institutions in the years ahead. The pressure for the institutions to operate more like businesses and for the administrators to make hard choices will intensify. The institutions' faculty members will have to understand that tradeoffs exist and some things must be given up.

If the institutions fail to maintain their accessibility and their endowments continue to grow, it is reasonable to assume that the various levels of government will not sit idle. Proposals to limit tax exemptions on endowment income and the deductibility of contributions to private colleges and universities may emerge that are analogous to the caps that now exist on mortgage tax deductions. Limitations conceivably could be based on the size of an institution's endowment per student, as well as on the size of the contribution being made.

Similarly, attacks on the low levels of the spending rates from selective private institution's endowments will grow. Private foundations are required to spend at least 5 percent of the value of their endowments each year to maintain their tax-free status. Educational institutions face no such regulation. Many spent less than this percentage throughout the 1990s. Although there were good reasons for their having done so, selective private institutions that continue to raise tuition by much more than the rate of inflation, that back off of their commitment to maintain accessibility, and that continue to exhibit large endowment growth, may well be courting potential disaster. They will be almost "asking" to be regulated.

Attacks on the tax-exempt status of their property will also be likely to increase. The process of nipping away at this advantage, via taxing income from enterprises that are alleged not to be directly related to the educational mission of the institution, has already begun as localities strapped for cash go after visibly wealthy, large tax-exempt organizations. At Cornell, for example, the revenue generated by the hotel school's "teaching hotel" on campus is now subject to state and county sales taxes. Similar efforts have been reported nationwide to tax the earnings that institutions receive from the sale of "luxury boxes" in football stadiums.[4]

A more serious attack was narrowly averted in 1995 when a Pennsylvania state appeals court overturned by a vote of four to three a lower court decision that would have removed the tax-exempt status of Washington and Jefferson College.[5] The Pennsylvania State Supreme Court had ruled a decade earlier that to qualify for tax exemptions it was not sufficient to be a nonprofit organization. To qualify, a nonprofit organization had to provide a substantial portion of its services at no charge and to benefit an indefinite class of individuals who were deemed worthy of charity. Although the appeals court held that Washington and Jefferson College met this test, selective private colleges that back away from their commitment to accessibility should be forewarned.

What Government Can Do to Help

Although most of the responsibility for the increase in costs and tuition at selective private institutions is due to each institution's quest to be as high in quality as it can, as I have shown throughout the book, federal and state government policies have played a role. There are some actions that both levels of government can take that would help moderate cost increases at the selective private institutions and possibly slow down their rate of tuition growth.

To turn first to the federal government, federal grant aid for needy students seeking to attend public or private institutions has not even kept up with the rate of inflation since the program began in the early 1970s. Figure 19.1 makes this point clear by plotting how in constant 1997–98 dollars (adjusted for inflation) the maximum actual Pell (Basic Educational Opportunity Act) grant that students were eligible for changed between 1973 and 1997. The maximum actual grant has changed over time both because Congress has changed the statutory maximum grant level and because the funding authorized by Congress in some years has not been sufficient to pay needy students all that the program formula indicates they should receive. In those years, all grant amounts are reduced proportionately and the maximum actual grant awarded is less than the legislatively adopted maximum grant.

Viewed in constant 1997–98 dollars, the maximum actual grant level rose

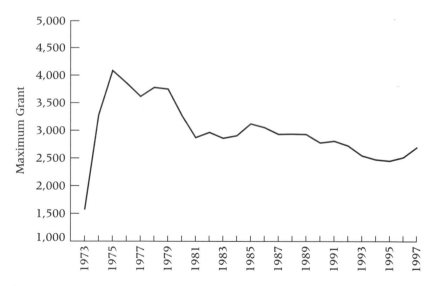

Figure 19.1. Maximum actual Pell grant in 1997–98 constant dollars, 1973–1997. (Source: *Trends in Student Aid* [Washington, D.C.: The College Board, 1998]).

from about $1,500 at the program's inception to over $4,000 in 1975. Since that date it has declined considerably. After falling to under $2,500 in the mid-1990s, it rebounded to $2,700 in 1997. This is still well below the grant levels that existed in the late 1970s or even in the 1980s. Part of the reason for the declining grant per student is that the program was expanded to include private for-profit, nondegree-granting institutions and thus more students had to be funded out of any given budget. In addition, federal loan programs were expanded without concomitant increases in the grant program budget.

The failure of the maximum level of grant aid to keep up with inflation is one of the reasons that tuition levels at selective private universities have risen so much over the past two decades. These institutions replaced aid that would previously have come from the government with their own internal funds. Although sometimes these funds could come from endowment income, often they had to come from tuition revenue, and this drain necessitated a greater increase in tuition than would otherwise have been the case.

This is not the only, or even the major, reason why tuition increases outpaced inflation. However, if the federal government is committed to helping to guarantee the accessibility of these institutions to students regardless of the students' family income levels, its commitment to providing need-based financial aid to low-income students should not be diminished in real terms. Although we should not necessarily expect federal grant levels to keep up with tuition increases if the institutions persist in raising tuition by more than the rate of inflation, federal policy should at least keep the maximum actual Pell grant level constant in real terms. This would reduce some of the pressure that the institutions face to raise tuition each year.

As my discussion of research costs showed, over the last decade the federal government has also relentlessly placed pressure on the selective private research universities by reducing the indirect cost rates that they can claim on their externally sponsored research projects. The indirect costs that universities receive on grants and contracts are reimbursements for expenses actually incurred. As the reimbursements decline, the institutions can attempt to reduce some of their expenses, but most of the expenses go directly toward supporting the institutions' research infrastructure. Given the goal of these institutions to remain at the frontiers of science and to maintain their preeminence, invariably they must seek other sources of funds to support these activities. When unrestricted resources of these universities, such as endowment income or gifts, are used for these purposes, more pressure is generated to raise tuition to support their educational missions.

This is not the place to enter into a complete discussion of what our nation's policies should be for the support of university-based research. It seems clear, however, that the current system of indirect cost reimbursements, which depends heavily on calculations by the institutions of what their research infrastructure costs are and then negotiations between their auditors and the government's auditors, has outlived its usefulness. A simpler approach, in which the federal government agreed to provide each university with a constant percentage markup, or overhead payment, on its direct cost research volume would make much more sense.[6]

This would provide institutions with an incentive to reduce their administrative support costs, because any reductions would mean an infusion of money in the form of freed-up dollars rather than the loss of government reimbursements. It would reduce the level of auditing activity that goes on at universities and in the federal government, thereby providing cost savings to both. It would also provide the institutions with an additional incentive to expand their research volume and thus to be better at what they are doing. Finally, institutions would be freed from the constant downward pressure on indirect cost rates, which in turn would reduce the pressure that their research infrastructure costs place on tuition.

If this is such a good idea, why hasn't it been adopted? One reason is that the major private research universities as a group stand to lose from it in the short run. Their indirect cost rates tend to be higher than the indirect cost rates at public research universities, because state governments do not always require their public universities to reimburse them for the construction costs of new research facilities. Any single national overhead rate would undoubtedly be an average of what the public institutions and the private institutions currently charge. Thus while in the long run such a policy is desirable, in the short run it might increase, rather than decrease, pressure on the selective private institutions' tuition levels.

In addition, the research universities argue that such a reimbursement scheme would discourage institutions from undertaking research that makes heavy use of costly elements of the infrastructure. Institutions that specialize in research that is relatively cheap to support would benefit relative to institutions that specialize in research that is relatively expensive to support. This objection can be addressed by allowing the reimbursement rate to vary with the mix of projects that an institution undertakes. Each project that the government supports can be given a weight by the government that reflects its perception of the relative infrastructure cost of undertaking that type of research and this weight can then be used to adjust the indirect costs that the government will assume for that project.

A final action that the federal government should undertake is to promote regulatory reform that reduces cost pressures on the research universities. Without sacrificing the objectives of regulations in areas such as environmental health and safety, ways should be developed to reduce the costs of compliance that the institutions face. This is not a novel suggestion; responding to a report from representatives of a number of federal agencies, President Clinton in April 1999 charged the group to devise a set of recommendations to help achieve this.[7]

State governments can also take helpful actions. Although attendance at selective private colleges and universities is one route to economic success and leadership positions in our society, it is not the only route. Indeed, as long as there are good public higher educational alternatives in each state, concern about the behavior of the selective private institutions is really overblown. After all, less than 6 percent of American college graduates are educated at the selective private institutions. I am among the many proud graduates of public institutions of higher education who can attest to the roles that these institutions historically have played as vehicles of upward mobility, providing their graduates with the wherewithal to achieve economic success and qualify for leadership positions.

Sadly, as the National Commission on the Cost of Higher Education indicated, state support for higher education has not been as consistent as it should be, and state appropriations per student have diminished in real terms in some states. Figure 19.2 demonstrates this point in graphic terms. It plots the national level of state appropriations for public universities per full-time equivalent student nationally during the 1969 to 1995 period. All appropriation figures are in constant 1992 fiscal year dollars, so the effects of inflation have been removed.

State support for public higher education varies with the finances of state governments. Between 1969 and the mid-1980s, state support per full-time equivalent student increased by about 50 percent in real terms. But between 1988 and 1994, state support per full-time student declined by about 10 percent in real terms before beginning to increase again in 1995. During these years, the real level of expenditures per student at the selective private institutions was increasing at a substantially more rapid rate.

To try to maintain their level of quality, many state institutions raised their tuition levels. Tuition has increased relative to state appropriations as a source of funds. Many have expressed concern that these tuition increases have reduced the accessibility of the public institutions to lower- and middle-income students. Indeed, it was the increase in tuition at these public institutions, rather than the increases at the selective private institutions, to which the national commission paid the most attention. Yet in spite of these tuition increases many of these institutions have declined in quality. Their faculty salaries have declined relative to faculty salaries at the private institutions, a fact that has made it more difficult for them to attract and retain top faculty. Class sizes also have risen at many, and by the late 1990s students at some of them were complaining that reductions in the number of courses offered were preventing them from taking all the courses that they needed for graduation within a four-year period.

State governments face many competing demands for their limited funds. When federal marginal tax rates were substantially reduced during the Reagan years, the federal income tax deductions that taxpayers receive for the

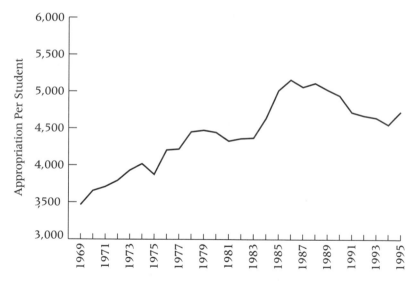

Figure 19.2. State appropriations to public higher educational institutions per full-time equivalent student in constant 1992 dollars, 1969–1995. (Source: Author's computations from state appropriation data given in the CASPAR System and full-time equivalent student data given in *Digest of Education Statistics* [Washington, D.C.: National Center for Education Statistics, 1997], table 200).

state income taxes paid by them became worth less to the taxpayers. For example, suppose a taxpayer was in the 50 percent marginal tax bracket before the Reagan tax cuts; each $1,000 that she paid in state income taxes would reduce her federal personal income tax liability by $500. But if her federal marginal tax rate fell to 35 percent, after the tax cut each $1,000 that she paid in state personal income taxes would now reduce her federal personal income tax liability by only $350.

Not surprisingly, pressure for reductions in state income tax rates increased after federal marginal tax rates were reduced, and state income tax rates subsequently were cut in many states. This action caused reductions in the growth rate of state tax revenues at the same time that states were facing demands for increased funding for the Medicaid program, welfare expenditures, and the criminal justice system. As a result, public higher education could no longer count on the same increases in state support that it had received in the past.

In my view, this reduction in the priority of state support for public higher education was a serious public policy mistake. State governments need to be educated so that they understand the role that higher education plays in economic development and in boosting the incomes of state residents. The states need to restore the priority that they previously gave to public higher education and assure that high-quality public higher educational opportunities are provided in at least the flagship institutions in each state. Some states have begun to do even better and have begun, or expanded, honors colleges within a number of their larger public institutions to make high-quality public education available to more students.

Such actions are important because by far the majority of American students are educated at public higher educational institutions, and hence the quality of these institutions goes a long way toward determining the average quality of American higher education. In addition, the better the public educational alternatives are, the more sensitive the demand for positions at the selective private colleges and universities by full-paying students will be to the tuition levels that the selective private institutions charge. Expanding high-quality public higher educational alternatives will cause the selective private institutions to be much more cautious about raising their tuition levels.

Sadly, it is unlikely that sufficient funding will come from state governments in many states to boost public higher education to the level of support at which it should be operating. Hence, to assure the quality of the public institutions, it may be necessary for many of them to move to a higher tuition policy and for them then to guarantee access to lower-income residents by providing need-based financial aid. This will require them to aggressively engage in fund-raising campaigns to raise private funds for financial aid. Put another way, improving the quality and maintaining the accessibility of the public higher education system may depend upon these institutions' mimicking some of the behavior of the selective private institutions.

A second thing that state governments can do relates more directly to the selective private institutions. When I discussed Cornell's parking and transportation demand management program and its Lake Source Cooling project, I illustrated how tensions between local government and educational institutions can lead to delays in the institutions' construction projects that increase the projects' costs. These tensions flow largely from the institutions' tax-exempt status.

The institutions also often find themselves having to negotiate with local governments over the contributions that they will make in lieu of taxes to the localities, which in itself seems to defeat the purpose of their being granted tax exemptions in the first place. During these negotiations, the institutions are quick to point out that property values in a community are higher because of their presence. They also emphasize that their students and employees bring considerable purchasing power to the community and are a source of revenue for local businesses. Finally, they note that they provide services to the community in the form of culture and entertainment. The communities in turn point out that these benefits do not fully compensate the communities for the additional services that they must provide because of the presence of the institutions. Elementary and secondary education and police and fire protection are but a few examples.

Relations between academic institutions and their communities would be far smoother without the constant irritant of the tax revenues the communities are foregoing. Some states, for example New Jersey, at least partially compensate local governments for local property tax revenue lost owing to the presence of any state property, including public colleges and universities, in the community. Others, such as Connecticut, also provide compensation to localities that host private higher educational institutions. New Haven, for example, receives considerable revenue from the state of Connecticut to compensate it for the property tax revenue it loses because of the presence of Yale University in its community. Subject to some limitations, the compensation rate is set at 20 percent of the assessed value of state property and

60 percent of the assessed value of tax-exempt private college and university property in Connecticut.[8]

Other states might well consider emulating the Connecticut program. A justification for a state's compensating localities in which private higher educational institutions are located is that unlike other nonprofit institutions, such as churches, higher educational institutions are not uniformly located across communities. Furthermore, the benefits that these institutions bring to the state transcends the benefits to the communities in which they are located. Although some of the benefits accrue locally in the form of higher volumes of economic activity and thus higher sales tax revenues, the localities in which the institutions are located are not fully compensated for their lost property tax revenue and the additional services that they must provide. Some of the benefits that accrue to the state as a whole, in terms for example of the higher state income tax revenue that is associated with a more educated workforce with higher earnings, should be directed back in the form of state payments to the communities that house the institutions.

To the extent that state programs to recompense communities for the presence of educational institutions improve the relations between private colleges and universities and the communities in which they are located, they will permit the institutions' construction projects to proceed with less delay and at lower costs. To the extent the institutions are not compelled as much to make "payments in lieu of taxes" to local governments, they will achieve some savings in costs. These can be used to moderate tuition increases, or to invest in projects in the local community that make sense both to the university and to the community.

What the Institutions Can Do

Although federal and state governments can take actions that will help reduce the cost pressures that selective private institutions face, ultimately it is the institutions themselves that must take actions to moderate their costs and their rate of tuition increases. It is important to distinguish between cost increases and tuition increases because gaining control of the latter is more likely to occur than gaining control of the former.

Each of these selective institutions is engaged in the equivalent of an arms race of spending to improve its absolute quality and to try to improve its relative stature in the prestige pecking order (or at least not see it diminished). Consequently, no institution will unilaterally reduce its rate of growth of spending—to do so would invite reduced prestige. Indeed, the popular *USNWR* annual rankings of selective private institutions depend heavily on the spending per student that each institution undertakes. An institution that unilaterally reduced its rate of growth or, even more drastically, its level of spending would pay for it dearly in the subsequent year's ratings.

Moreover, the selective private institutions do not have the option of banding together and voluntarily agreeing to limit spending. Similarly, they do not have the option of voluntarily agreeing to limit the fraction of their classes that they admit through an early decision process. Doing either probably would be viewed as an attempt to reduce competition and thus be considered a violation of the consent decree. Even if the most selective members of the group reduced their spending on activities such as student recruiting, the lesser selective institutions have an incentive to continue such spending to gain a competitive advantage and increase their attractiveness to students. So attempts to obtain agreement on spending limitations would be highly unlikely to prove effective.

In contrast, if all selective institutions valued reducing the growth rate of tuition relative to the rate of inflation, there could be a social benefit from their banding together and agreeing to limit tuition and fee increases. If the very best and wealthiest institutions voluntarily decide to do this, the others will eventually have to fall in line. If the best do not unilaterally do this, a voluntary agreement to limit tuition increases would probably enhance the public's perceptions of the selective private institutions. Given that tuition increases are the major discretionary source of revenue available to fund faculty salary increases on most of their campuses, agreeing to limit tuition increases will not be an easy thing to accomplish. Moreover, a spending race would still take place as the institutions aggressively seek to increase other revenue sources. But the public would be happier about the behavior of these institutions because public concern lies primarily with how much the institutions charge for tuition, not with how much they spend.

Could the institutions voluntarily agree to limit their tuition and fee increases to, say, the rate of inflation in the previous calendar year, or the rate of inflation plus 1 percent? In part that depends upon whether this would be considered a violation of the consent decree. Institutions' voluntarily agreeing to raise tuition at rates that are much lower than their previous rates would seem to be in the social interest. But whether the Justice Department would view such cooperation as an antitrust violation is unclear. At the very least, it would be productive for representatives of some of the institutions to have discussions with the Justice Department about how it would react to such a voluntary joint agreement.

If the selective private institutions cannot voluntarily agree to limit their tuition increases, or if the most selective and wealthiest of them do not lead the pack in doing so, then a slowdown in tuition growth is unlikely to occur. Without the discipline on holding down spending and tuition that is imposed externally at many public institutions, no senior administrator at a selective private institution wants to be blamed for his or her institution's falling behind its competitors.

Furthermore, any senior administrator who recommends holding down spending, or even worse cutting spending, risks incurring the wrath of the faculty. Holding down spending increases may lead the institution's faculty salaries to fall behind the salaries of their peers at other institutions, and any such decrease will diminish faculty members' attachment to the institution and make it more difficult for the institution to recruit and retain top faculty. If reductions in spending growth or spending cuts are made across the board, they will not strengthen the institution. If, after joint faculty and administrative deliberations, cuts are directed at areas believed to be weak or of less importance, the institution runs the risk that the sense of community that exists among its faculty members will be damaged. The institution will become less collegial and faculty members will increasingly worry about what's best for them and their unit, rather than about the welfare of the institution as a whole.

So what can the institutions do? Trustees play a very key role in the process because they have the final responsibility for the institution's financial matters. If the trustees of an institution place a high value on keeping tuition increases low, they should impose the fiscal discipline at the institutions that state legislatures and governors impose on public institutions. Trustees of the selective private colleges and universities want their institutions to be of as high a quality and as highly rated as possible. But if they value keeping tuition increases low, they should demand that resources for improvement come from the generation of new revenue streams and from the savings achieved through increased efficiencies on both the academic and nonacademic sides of the institution. Unless trustees provide the leadership for such actions, they are unlikely to occur. Rice University is one selective private institution where historically the trustees have provided such leadership.

How selective private universities organize themselves for fund-raising and budgetary purposes, as well as how they select and reward the academic leaders of their individual colleges, goes a long way toward determining whether the institution can establish university-wide priorities, eliminate overlap, and achieve efficiencies. In particular, budget structures need to be established that give the central administration of a university some control over resources so that it can use these resources to encourage its colleges to collaborate and pursue institution-wide objectives, rather than allowing each college to go off on its own. Treating each college as a tub on its own bottom provides incentives for the colleges to generate revenues and monitor their own costs. But such a system is also almost guaranteed to lead to balkanization, unnecessary duplication, and higher overall costs for an institution.

Similarly, compensation structures should be established for academic deans, as well as vice presidents in charge of nonacademic units, that make clear that they are responsible both for the welfare of their unit and for that of the entire institution. These administrators should understand that they are expected to place high priority on cooperating in university-wide efforts to achieve efficiencies and reduce costs. Indeed, it should be explicit that their annual compensation, as well as the decision on their reappointment when their terms expire, will be heavily dependent on how well they perform on these dimensions.

To accomplish this at many institutions is much easier said than done. Trustees are graduates of particular colleges within the university and their loyalty is often primarily to the college from which they graduated, not to the university as a whole. Deans and even individual faculty members have been known to talk to trustees when the central administration is contemplating actions that the dean or faculty member feels will be disadvantageous to his or her unit. The trustees in turn put pressure on the central administration not to take the action.

Accordingly, central administrators will have to do a better job of explaining to trustees and to key alumni supporters of each of their colleges that what is best for the individual unit is not necessarily best for the institution as a whole. They will have to devote more time to discussion with constituents about the importance of the units' cooperating to help achieve cost reductions.

Trustees and administrators at these institutions must also realize that if they do not undertake efforts to improve the efficiency of their academic and nonacademic activities and reduce their costs, they risk eventually losing some of the support that they receive from their corporate supporters. Given the efforts that corporations are making to cut costs, academic institutions cannot appear to be wasting resources. Trustees should thus demand that their administrators regularly report their progress at achieving cost savings. Administrators should in turn regularly seek out ways to achieve cost savings.

One way to achieve this is to share more resources between institutions. For example, Yale, Columbia, and the New York Public Library are in the process of building a single off-campus library storage facility that will house rarely used books from the three libraries. Delivery of a needed book will be guaranteed to users at any location within twenty-four hours. By pooling their collections in one place, the three facilities can deacquisition duplicate copies and thereby achieve considerable cost savings.

There are many other ways in which institutions can share resources. I have already given examples of how specialized courses can be taught simultaneously to students at multiple institutions by a faculty member from one institution through the use of distance learning technologies. Administrative savings can be achieved if institutions combine some of their "back office" operations. For example, if multiple organizations share a common purchasing office, it is likely that they will be able to achieve economies of scale and negotiate better prices with suppliers.

Cost savings can also be achieved by seriously reexamining each thing that an institution is doing and asking how it contributes to the mission and quality of the institution. Institutions regularly develop innovative programs, but only occasionally evaluate them after a trial period to see whether they are worth keeping. New initiatives should have "sunset clauses" requiring that a decision be made for them to continue or not after a trial period.

Existing programs and departments should also be periodically evaluated. These evaluations should be used to determine if their scale should be changed or if they should be gradually eliminated. A system of reviews of this type will probably reduce collegiality among faculty members. But this may well be the price the institutions must pay to assure external constituents that they are responsible stewards of the resources with which they have been provided.

The tenured faculty members at these selective private institutions will also have to grasp that efforts to maintain or increase the quality of their institutions cannot continually be borne by undergraduate students in the form of tuition increases that continually exceed the rate of inflation. Faculty members will have to participate in responsible management of their institution's resources by becoming actively involved in program reviews. They will have to participate in efforts to generate additional revenue through expanding professional master's, continuing education, and executive education programs, through increasing the enrollment of transfer students, through developing distance learning programs, and through participating in development and alumni relations activities. The precise revenue-generating activities that will take place will differ from institution to institution. But the faculty at each institution needs to understand that it has a responsibility to help its institution to prosper.

Some faculty members will argue that they already generate revenue. After all, it is their reputations and academic accomplishments that attract students and research support to their institutions. These faculty members are certainly correct. But given the pressure on many of these institutions, expanding revenue sources and cutting costs is the only way that the institutions can avoid continually raising tuition by more than the rate of inflation. Faculty members will need to view themselves more as responsible institutional citizens and less as independent entrepreneurs.

CHAPTER 20

A Final Thought

When Frank H. T. Rhodes retired as president of Cornell University in 1995, the Cornell faculty honored him by holding a conference. Distinguished current and former presidents of selective private universities and high-level government officials presented papers that were later published in a volume I edited titled *The American University: National Treasure or Endangered Species.*[1] Although the authors discussed the many challenges that research universities face in the years ahead, they uniformly agreed that the institutions were national treasures.

The same could be said about America's selective private liberal arts colleges. Together these institutions stand atop the greatest higher educational system in the world. As we enter the twenty-first century, these are institutions that Americans can truly be proud to have within their nation's borders.

But if they continue to raise their tuition by 2 or 3 percentage points more than the rate of inflation, as they have done throughout much of the previous century, they may further erode their already waning public support. This in turn may lead to public policy changes that will not be in the institutions' best interests. Hence the institutions had better seriously contemplate what their future tuition policies should be.

There is a temptation among some faculty and administrators at these institutions to believe that the excellence that the institutions represent is well understood by the public and that no one will seriously take actions that are disadvantageous to them. Government policies that have hurt their institutions in the past, such as reductions in indirect cost rates and the failure of the maximum level of Pell grants to keep up with inflation, are thought by these individuals to be only federal responses to tough budgetary situations. These same faculty members and administrators even express the belief that with a sustained upturn in the economy, federal treatment of higher education will improve.

Economists are notoriously bad at predicting the future, although their predictions are probably no worse than the predictions of meteorologists. But one need only look at how public and private policies that influence America's major hospitals and medical schools, which are also thought to be the greatest in the world, have changed in recent years to become less sanguine about future public support for higher education.

The growth of managed-care health systems has reduced the revenues that the medical colleges receive from their physicians' practice plans, which in turn has limited the resources that they have to support biomedical research and the training of new doctors. Financial cutbacks in Medicare reimbursements, occasioned by the financial difficulties faced by that insurance system, have caused a cutback in Medicare reimbursements to hospitals, reimbursements that also help to support the operations of major medical centers. As a result, America's great hospitals and medical centers are scrambling to stay afloat, undergoing major changes and constantly devising ways to reduce costs and increase their efficiency.

America's selective private colleges and universities may never find themselves in as rapidly changing an environment as the medical centers have faced. But the medical centers' experiences suggest that selective private higher education is not immune to changing public concerns and policies. It would be very prudent for these institutions to think more now about increasing the efficiency of their operations and holding down their costs.

APPENDIX

NOTES

ACKNOWLEDGMENTS

INDEX

Defined Benefit and Defined Contribution Retirement Plans

A *defined benefit* retirement plan provides a retiree with an annual retirement benefit that is specified to be a function of the individual's salary and years of service. A simple form of defined benefit plan is given by the formula

$$B = kts,$$

where B is the individual's annual retirement benefit, k is a measure of the generosity of the plan, t is the individual's years of service, and s is the individual's average salary over some specified period of time. Under the defined benefit retirement plan in effect for statutory college faculty at Cornell, k is .02 and s is the average of the individual's three highest annual salaries. Hence a statutory faculty member who retired after 30 years of service would receive an annual pension equal to 60 percent of the average of his or her three highest years of salary.[1]

Defined benefit plans provide incentives for retirement because the later the retirement age, the smaller the number of years that the retirement benefit payments will be made. If we ignore issues relating to salary increases, after some age the increase in the annual benefit level the faculty member would get from working 1 more year is more than offset by the loss of 1 year's retirement benefits from delaying retirement. Thus after some age, failing to retire reduces the individual's lifetime value of retirement benefits. In addition, maximum percentage benefit levels can be specified, which, after some point, eliminate the increase in annual retirement benefits that comes from working 1 more year. For example, the maximum benefit percentage under the statutory defined benefit plan is 37.5 years of service. Working additional years does not increase the employee's annual retirement benefit level.

Retirement incentive programs can be straightforwardly developed within defined benefit systems. For example, several retirement incentive programs in Cornell's statutory colleges provided a faculty member with an additional month's service credit for each year worked, if he or she retired within a prescribed period of time. Hence faculty members who had been employed for 24 years received an additional 2 years of credit. For an individual with an "average salary" of $80,000, this would lead to an increase in annual retirement benefits of $3,200 a year (.02 × 2 × $80,000). If the faculty member turned down the retirement incentive, in the absence of salary increases the faculty member would have to work 2 more years before he or she could receive the same annual retirement benefit, which he or she would then collect for 2 fewer years. Thus the programs provided a strong incentive to retire.

Under *defined contribution* retirement systems, each year the employer contributes a specified percentage of the employee's salary to a fund, which is then invested to provide benefits at retirement for the employee. The fund "belongs" to the employee, so that as long as the market return on the assets in the fund is positive, the value of the fund is larger the later the age at which an employee retires. Pure defined contribution plans thus do not provide strong economic incentives to retire for faculty members, because delaying retirement leaves the faculty member with a larger retirement fund.

Retirement incentive programs under defined contribution systems typically provide for additional employer payments to the employee if the employee retires within a prescribed interval of time. These additional payments are subject to federal and state income taxes, however, in the year they are made. Several retirement incentive programs for statutory college faculty provided for an additional payment of .15 of 1 month's salary. To continue with the example above, a faculty member with 24 years of service and an $80,000 annual salary, would get a payment of $24,000: .15 × 24 × (80,000 ÷ 12). After federal and state income taxes were deducted, which I assume would average 23 percent, the faculty member would have about $16,000 to invest in an annuity.

But if the faculty member worked 1 more year, the university's retirement contribution for the year, plus the earnings that would accrue from all the assets already in the employee's account, would far exceed the value of the lump-sum payment. To see this, note that if the employee's salary had averaged $60,000 and that if 10 percent had been contributed by the state to his or her retirement account each year, after 24 years, the value of the account (even if we ignore all of its investment returns!) would be $144,000. If the investment return in this tax-sheltered account were 10 percent in the next year, the earnings of $14,400 would almost equal the value of the incentive. Once we factor in tax-sheltered investment earnings on all contributions to the account over the previous 24 years, as well as the next year's payment by the state into the account of $8,000, we can easily see how ineffective this defined contribution retirement incentive was. In addition, working 1 more year delays the withdrawal of any of the assets for a year. Not surprisingly, very few eligible statutory faculty members who were enrolled in the defined contribution program participated in the statutory college retirement incentive program.

Notes

1. Why Do Costs Keep Rising at Selective Private Colleges and Universities?

1. Susan S. Hill, *Science and Engineering Doctorate Awards* (Washington, D.C.: National Science Foundation, 1999), table 4.
2. Henry Rosovsky, *The University: An Owner's Manual* (New York: Norton, 1990), chap. 2.
3. William G. Bowen, *The Economics of the Major Private Research Universities* (Berkeley, Calif.: Carnegie Commission on Higher Education, 1967).
4. *Trends in College Pricing: 1998* (Washington, D.C.: The College Board, 1998), fig. 7.
5. See, for example, Dominic J. Brewer, Eric R. Eide, and Ronald G. Ehrenberg, "Does It Pay to Attend an Elite Private College?" *Journal of Human Resources* 34 (Winter 1999): 123, and Ronald G. Ehrenberg, "An Economic Analysis of the Market for Law School Graduates," *Journal of Legal Education* 39 (1989): 627–654.
6. Gordon Winston, "Subsidies, Hierarchy, and Peers: The Awkward Economics of Higher Education," *Journal of Economic Perspectives* 13 (Winter 1999): 13–36.
7. Robert Zemsky, "Faculty Discretionary Time: Departments and the Academic Ratchet," *Journal of Higher Education* 65 (January/February 1994): 1–22.
8. Robert H. Frank and Philip J. Cook, *The Winner-Take-All Society: How More and More Americans Compete for Ever Fewer and Bigger Prizes, Encouraging Economic Waste and Income Inequality and an Impoverished Cultural Life* (New York: Free Press, 1995).
9. One of the reasons for the short-term balances is that students pay their tuition and fees at the beginning of each semester, but the university incurs costs throughout the semester. So it invests the balances in money market instruments and uses the revenue so generated to help support its operations.

2. Who Is in Charge of the University?

1. This attitude ignores the possibility that accessibility can also be maintained the way selective private institutions maintain it, with a high tuition policy and the

provision of need-based financial aid. Many supporters of low public tuition levels worry that once public tuition levels are raised, there is no guarantee that state funding will always be sufficient to maintain accessibility. They also worry that high public tuition levels will lead to a loss of support from the middle class for these institutions.

2. Michael D. Cohen and James G. March, *Leadership and Ambiguity: The American College President,* 2nd ed. (Boston: Harvard Business School Press, 1986).

3. John Strauss, John Curry, and Edward Whalen, "Revenue Responsibility Budgeting" in William Massey, ed., *Resource Allocation in Higher Education* (Ann Arbor: University of Michigan Press, 1996).

4. Alison Schneider, "Columbia U. President Hires Back a Dean He Forced Out," *Chronicle of Higher Education,* July 18, 1997, p. A38.

5. Katherine Mangan, "An Unfair Tax? Law and Business Schools Object to Bailing Out Medical Centers," *Chronicle of Higher Education,* May 5, 1988, pp. A43–44.

6. Robert B. Reich, *Locked in the Cabinet* (New York: Knopf, 1997), pp. 150–151.

3. Endowment Policies, Development Policies, and the Color of Money

1. A survey of 467 academic institutions undertaken by NACUBO, the National Association of College and University Business Officers, indicated that in 1996 the mean payout rate on these endowments was 4.3 percent and the median was 4.1 percent.

2. These numbers come from the 1996 NACUBO endowment study and were reported in "Payout Rates of College Endowments, 1996," *Chronicle of Higher Education,* November 14, 1997, p. A41.

3. Julie Nicklin, "Bull Markets Helped Endowments Earn an Average of 17.2% in 1996," *Chronicle of Higher Education,* February 14, 1997, p. A34.

4. Kit Lively, "College Endowments Earned 18.2% Return in Fiscal 1998," *Chronicle of Higher Education,* November 27, 1998, p. A33. Other assets included risky assets such as venture capital investments, hedge funds, high yield ("junk") bonds, oil and gas partnerships, and the like.

5. The HEPI has been calculated only since 1961. Between 1961 and 1998, the average annual percentage increase in the HEPI was 5.5. This contrasts to an average annual percentage of 4.7 in the CPI during the period. See *Inflation Measures for Schools, Colleges, and Libraries: 1998 Update* (Washington, D.C.: Research Associates of Washington, 1998).

6. Kim Stosnider, "Booming Economy Spurs Many Colleges to Trim Rates for Endowment Spending," *Chronicle of Higher Education,* November 14, 1997, p. A41.

7. See, for example, Ben Gose, "8 Months behind Its Rivals, Harvard Increases Financial Aid," *Chronicle of Higher Education,* September 17, 1998. Subscribers to the daily *Chronicle* can retrieve this article from <http://chronicle.com/weekly/sitesearch.htm>.

8. Julie Nicklin, "Revolving Doors in Development Offices," *Chronicle of Higher Education,* September 25, 1998, p. A45

9. *Expenditures in Fund Raising, Alumni Relations, and Other Constituent (Public) Relations* (Washington, D.C.: Council for Advancement and Support of Education, 1990), table 1. Although lower than the costs reported by many charitable organizations, these costs were close to the mean and median costs of each dollar raised by twenty-five major noneducational charities in the mid-1990s. The latter costs are reported in Ellen Stark, "Which Charities Merit Your Money: Follow These Steps to Learn Where You Can Give Money Most Effectively Beginning With Our Charity of the Year, the American Red Cross," *Money* 25 (November 1996); available on the World Wide Web at <http://www.pathfinder.com/money/archive/magsearch/>.

10. Frank H. T. Rhodes and Inge T. Reichenbach, "Successful Fund Raising at a Large Private Research University," in Frank H. T. Rhodes, ed., *Successful Fund Raising for Higher Education: The Advancement of Learning* (Phoenix: Oryx Press, 1997), pp. 1–22.

4. Undergraduate and Graduate Program Rankings

1. James Monks and Ronald G. Ehrenberg, "*U.S. News & World Report*'s College Rankings: Why Do They Matter? *Change* 31 (November/December 1999): 42–51.

2. Amy E. Graham and Robert J. Morse, "How U.S. News Ranks Colleges: An Explanation of Our Methodology," in *1999 America's Best Colleges* (Washington, D.C.: *USNWR,* August 1998), pp. 33–35.

3. Marvin Goldberger, Brendan A. Maher, and Pamela Ebert Flattau, ed., *Research-Doctorate Programs in the United States: Continuity and Change* (Washington, D.C.: National Academy Press, 1995).

4. Ronald G. Ehrenberg and Peter J. Hurst, "The 1995 Ratings of Doctoral Programs: A Hedonic Model," *Change* 28 (May/June, 1996): 46–55. Interested readers should consult this article for the details of our research.

5. Admissions and Financial Aid Policies

1. One can also infer the fraction of the accepted applicants who enroll at each institution by dividing the numbers in Table 5.1 by those in Table 5.2. So, for example, roughly 77 percent of Harvard's accepted applicants (10/13) enrolled. In contrast, Tufts, which had the same enrollee to applicant ratio as Harvard (.10), enrolled only about 31 percent of its accepted applicants (10/32).

2. Parts of this section draw on material first presented in Ronald G. Ehrenberg and Susan H. Murphy, "What Price Diversity? The Death of Need-Based Financial Aid at Selective Private Colleges," *Change* 25 (July/August 1993): 64–73.

3. Philip J. Cook and Robert H. Frank, "The Growing Concentration of Top Students at Elite Schools," in Charles T. Clotfelter and Michael Rothschild, ed.,

Studies of Supply and Demand in Higher Education (Chicago: University of Chicago Press, 1993).

4. Ben Gose, "Changes at Elite Colleges Fuel Intense Competition in Student Aid," *Chronicle of Higher Education,* February 5, 1999, pp. A42–43.

5. Meg Lindstrom, "Introduction to Haggling," *BW,* March 15, 1999, pp. 104–106.

6. Maia Werner "Wells Cuts Costs, Gets Surge," *Ithaca Journal,* March 9, 1999.

7. Ronald G. Ehrenberg and Daniel S. Sherman, "Optimal Financial Aid Policies for a Selective University," *Journal of Human Resources* 19 (Spring 1984):202–230.

8. Ben Gose "Colleges Turn to 'Leveraging' to Attract Well-Off Students", *Chronicle of Higher Education,* September 13, 1996, p. A45.

9. Michael S. McPherson and Morton Owen Schapiro, *The Student Aid Game* (Princeton: Princeton University Press, 1998).

10. Harvard, and several other institutions, have early-action programs in which an applicant is informed by mid-December of the admission decision, but is not required to accept the offer until April. Virtually all of Harvard's early-action admissions do enroll there.

11. Christopher Avery, Andrew Fairbanks, and Richard Zeckhauser, "An Assessment of Early Admissions Programs at Highly Selective Undergraduate Institutions" (Cambridge, Mass.: John Fitzgerald Kennedy School of Government, Harvard University, May 1998, mimeograph).

6. Why Relative Prices Don't Matter

1. See Donald Kennedy, *Academic Duty* (Cambridge, Mass.: Harvard University Press, 1997), pp. 164–175, for an insider's view of the episode. Kennedy was president of Stanford when this case occurred.

2. Interestingly, the only empirical study on the topic found no evidence that the public institutions or their faculty benefit from keeping their indirect cost rates low. See Ronald G. Ehrenberg and Jaroslava K. Mykula, "Do Indirect Cost Rates Matter?" National Bureau of Economic Research Working Paper 6976 (Cambridge, Mass., March 1999).

3. Alex Cukierman and Mariano Tommasi, in "When Does It Take a Nixon to Go to China? *American Economic Review* 88 (March 1998): 180–197, present a formal treatment of why substantial policy changes may be implemented by "unlikely" parties.

7. Staying on the Cutting Edge in Science

1. David Brand, "CU trustees' budget action helps Duffield Hall take planned shape," *Cornell Chronicle* 31, March 23, 2000, p. 1.

2. Cornell University News Service, "National Science Foundation funding Launches Nanobiotecnology Center at Cornell." Available on the World Wide Web at <http://www/news.Cornell.edu/releases/July30/1999/nanobiotech.hrs.html>.

8. Salaries

1. In NLRB V. Yeshiva University, 944 U.S. 672 (1980), the U.S. Supreme Court held that Yeshiva University's full-time faculty members were managerial employees because they determined the curriculum, grading systems, admission and matriculation standards, academic calendars and course schedules, and also played influential roles in faculty hiring, tenure, and promotion decisions. As such, under the National Labor Relations Act they were precluded from bargaining collectively. This decision has effectively barred collective bargaining by faculty members at most private colleges and universities.

2. Data are also collected each year by the AAUP on the cost to each institution of providing health, retirement, and other benefits to the faculty. These costs also enter into the discussion of what the appropriate level of faculty salaries should be.

3. The institutions often also collect comparative data on discipline-specific faculty salaries, for disciplines that exist at a number of institutions. Unlike the AAUP data, these data are collected and shared under conditions of strict confidentiality and are typically judged to be too sensitive to be shared with faculty committees.

4. See Amy E. Graham and Robert J. Morse, "How U.S. News Ranks Colleges: An Explanation of Our Methodology," in *1999 America's Best Colleges* (Washington, D.C.: *USNWR*, August 1998), pp. 33–35.

5. There is a useful analogy here to the model of union behavior developed by Orley Ashenfelter and George Johnson in, "Bargaining Theory, Trade Unions, and Industrial Strike Activity," *American Economic Review* 59 (March 1969): 35–59. In their model the objectives of union leaders and union members are assumed to diverge. The union members care about their salaries, while the leaders also care about the survival of the union and their personal political survival. Suppose that the union leaders, after negotiating with management, realize that the "best" settlement likely to be obtained will not satisfy the union members' expectations. The leaders can try to "sell" this settlement to the members, or they can take a militant stance and lead them out on a strike. Since the former strategy leaves union leaders open to the charge of "being in bed" with management, the latter is often the preferred strategy for leaders who want to remain in office. Substitute the word "professor" for "union member," "faculty leader" for "union leader," and "university administration" for "management," and the analogy is clear.

6. Ronald G. Ehrenberg, Hirschel Kasper, and Daniel Rees, "Faculty Turnover at American Colleges and Universities," *Economics of Education Review* 10 (1991): 99–110.

7. The practice of routinely providing relatively small salary increases for senior faculty members but offering larger amounts to professors who present the administration with outside offers may differentially affect male and female faculty members. A recent study of full professors at MIT suggested that a major reason

that female full professors tend to be paid less than male full professors at MIT was that female full professors were much less likely to present the administration with job offers from other universities. "A Study on the Status of Women Faculty in Science at MIT," available on the World Wide Web at <http://web.MIT.edu/faculty/reports>.

9. Tenure and the End of Mandatory Retirement

1. See Mathew Finkin, ed., *The Case for Tenure* (Ithaca: ILR Press, 1996), for a more complete discussion of what tenure is and is not.

2. Ronald G. Ehrenberg, *The Regulatory Process and Labor Earnings* (New York: Academic Press, 1979), pp. 147–48, contains a discussion of other actions that Cornell took, in the face of political pressures, to defend my academic freedom.

   Other institutions have not always been so forthright. For example, in a very famous case involving Iowa State University in the early 1950s, the university bowed to political pressure and dismissed an extension associate who had discovered that margarine was just as nutritious as butter. This discovery came at a time when the dairy industry was fighting to keep margarine off the shelves of American stores and it did not go over well in Iowa, which is a heavily agricultural state. In response to the dismissal of the extension associate, a number of prominent economists on the faculty resigned, including Theodore Schultz, a future winner of the Nobel Prize.

3. "On Post-Tenure Review," *Academe* 83 (September/October 1997): 44–51.

4. In 1997–98, about 20 percent of the full-time faculty at Cornell were in non–tenure-track positions. These positions most often carried the titles of instructor, lecturer, senior lecturer, and teaching associate. Non–tenure-track faculty were most often found in fields in which there was not a strong research tradition (such as freshman writing and stage combat in theater arts), in which courses were offered primarily because of the availability of federal funding whose future was highly uncertain (many language courses in "minor" languages that were connected to federally financed area research centers), in which many freshmen were enrolled (such as calculus and introductory biology), and, in a few cases, in fields in which state budget cutbacks made hiring a tenure-track faculty member prohibitively expensive (fields such as introductory statistics and accounting).

5. John Pencavel, "The Response of Employers to Severance Incentives: The University of California Faculty, 1991–94" (Palo Alto: Department of Economics, Stanford University, April 1998, mimeograph).

6. An extensive discussion of the importance of enhancing the status of emeritus professors appears in Ronald G. Ehrenberg, "No Longer Forced Out: How One Institution Is Dealing with the End of Mandatory Retirement," *Academe* 85 (May/June 1999): 34–39.

7. It is also worth noting here that in a typical year the annual contribution that the university makes to the retirement account of senior faculty members is

dwarfed by the earnings generated by the assets already in the account. For a professor earning $90,000 a year, the university's 10 percent contribution rate would augment the professor's retirement assets by $9,000. If the professor's retirement account assets were $1,000,000 (not an uncommon amount for Cornell faculty members retiring in the late 1990s) and the assets generated a 10 percent return, the investment earnings would be $100,000. Hence the university's contribution would be responsible for less than 9 percent (9/109) of the account's growth in the year.

10. Deferred Maintenance, Space Planning, and Imperfect Information

1. Julia Nicklin, "A University Tries to Repair Its Aging Buildings," *Chronicle of Higher Education,* November 8, 1996, p. A35. See also Harvey H. Kaiser, *A Foundation to Uphold* (Alexandria, Va.: Association of Higher Education Facilities Officers, 1998).
2. Harvey H. Kaiser, *Crumbling Academe: Solving the Capital Renewal and Replacement Dilemma* (Washington, D.C.: Association of Governing Boards of American Universities and Colleges, 1984); Steven Glazner, ed., *Critical Issues in Facility Management, 4: Capital Renewal and Deferred Maintenance* (Alexandria, Va.: Association of Physical Plant Administrators of Universities and Colleges, 1989), and Sean C. Rush and Sandra L. Johnson, *The Decaying American Campus: A Ticking Time Bomb* (Alexandria, Va.: Association of Physical Plant Administrators of Universities and Colleges, 1989).

11. The Costs of Space

1. Like most general statements about Cornell, or any other academic institution, this statement must be qualified. The designated colleges are billed directly for the operating and maintenance costs of their space (although planned maintenance is undertaken at their discretion). Statutory college costs are paid by state appropriations, which to date have risen automatically when new construction or renovations are undertaken. Hence the statement applies primarily to the endowed general-purpose colleges and to individual departments and faculty members within each of the colleges. Faculty members with external research grants that provide for indirect cost recoveries are also implicitly billed for their space costs, and the College of Agriculture and Life Sciences explicitly bills faculty for using some specialized facilities, such as greenhouses.
2. Jean Baptiste Say, *A Treatise on Political Economy* (Boston: Wells and Lilly, 1821).
3. Lest the reader become confused because different numbers appear to be given in different chapters, this 1.5 percent figure refers only to planned maintenance. The 4 percent figure used in Chapter 7's discussion of Duffield Hall includes the expected annual costs of utilities and custodial and routine maintenance costs, as well as the costs of planned maintenance for that building.

4. William J. Boyes and Stephen K. Happel, "Auctions as an Allocation Mechanism in Academia: The Case of Faculty Offices," *Journal of Economic Perspectives* 3 (Summer 1989): 37–41.

5. One way that economists would address the problem of spaces' differing in their energy efficiency, or in other characteristics, would be to develop what is called a hedonic model of space costs. In such a model, the cost of different spaces is statistically related to the characteristics of each, for example their size, whether there is air conditioning, whether their are wet labs, whether there are double-pane windows, and the like. The coefficient weights that are estimated for each characteristic are the implicit prices, or value, of those characteristics. One can then use these coefficients and knowledge of the actual characteristics of each space to obtain an estimate of the implicit price of the space as a whole. Such an effort was far beyond the capabilities of Cornell's data systems at the time. Readers interested in learning more about the hedonic pricing models can consult Ronald G. Ehrenberg and Robert S. Smith, *Modern Labor Economics*, 6th ed. (Reading, Mass.: Addison Wesley, 1997), chap. 8, to see how such models are used to determine the value of nonpecuniary job characteristics.

13. Enrollment Management

1. See *1999 America's Best Colleges* (Washington, D.C.: USNWR, August 1998), p. 36.

2. As will be discussed in Chapter 18, during the spring of 1998 Cornell's president announced an ambitious plan to construct new residential units on campus and to guarantee on-campus housing for any sophomore student who wanted it.

3. In the short run, roughly $500,000 of the funds needed annually came from other sources, including the reserves of the graduate school.

4. First-year enrollments of engineering and physical science doctoral students rose dramatically in the fall of 1998. The fact that this increase was double the number of new fellowships created suggests that some other forces were at work. Whether the Cornell faculty will be able to respond by increasing the number of students that it supports externally on research grants will not be known for a number of years.

5. Goldie Blumenstyk, "Some Elite Private Universities Get Serious about Distance Learning," *Chronicle of Higher Education*, June 20, 1997, pp. A23–24.

6. Ben Gose, "U. of Chicago President to Resign, but the Battle over His Policies Lives On," *Chronicle of Higher Education*, June 7, 1999; available to subscribers to the daily *Chronicle* at <http://chronicle.com/weekly/sitesearch.htm>.

14. Information Technology, Libraries, and Distance Learning

1. This may be an overestimate of the cost because the underground location buffers the facility from outside temperature changes and may have reduced its heating and cooling costs.

2. William Honan, "Latest Discovery in Scholarly Journals Is Runaway Subscription Costs", *New York Times,* March 3, 1999, p. B10.

3. *ARL Statistics, 1996–97* (Washington, D.C.: Association of Research Libraries, 1998), p. 8.

4. Intellectual honesty impels me to alert the reader to the fact that I am the recipient of funding from the Andrew W. Mellon Foundation. I believe that my admiration for the activities of the foundation is not colored by this relationship.

5. A detailed description of JSTOR can be found on the World Wide Web at <http://www.jstor.org.>.

16. Cooling Systems

1. Although I highlight the role of Lanny Joyce in the text, kudos are also due to three other Cornell employees who were active participants in the development of the Lake Source Cooling Project: Henry Doney, Robert Bland, and Stephen Little.

2. Students would not reap the full financial benefits from Lake Source Cooling or pay all of the extra cost if it was not undertaken. At Cornell, the utilities division is an enterprise that is expected to break even. The savings that it would accrue from Lake Source Cooling would be reflected in the lower utility rates charged all of the units on campus through the administrative cost mechanism discussed in Chapter 12. Money that the colleges saved could be used to fund other activities or to lower planned tuition increases. Savings achieved by student service units that behave as enterprises, for example the housing and dining services, would allow them to lower their charges. This in turn would benefit students directly and would indirectly benefit the university inasmuch as the costs of financial aid would be reduced for those students receiving grant aid, because their financial need would be reduced owing to the lower housing and dining rates.

   The federal government would also benefit. As noted above, major users of cooling on campus are research laboratories, computer rooms, and libraries. The share of utility costs for these facilities that is attributable to sponsored research is built into the university's indirect cost rates. Hence any reduction in utility rates would reduce the indirect cost revenue that the university could recover from the federal government.

   To encourage the state-assisted units at Cornell to take energy-conservation actions, the central SUNY administration and New York state have allowed them (and other SUNY units) to retain for other purposes any utility cost savings that they achieve. However, the federal government has not built energy-conservation incentives into the indirect cost mechanism.

17. Intercollegiate Athletics and Gender Equity

1. The NCAA classifies institutions into three divisions by the number of intercollegiate sports programs in which they compete and the types of schools with

which they compete. Division I is the highest classification and requires an institution to have at least fourteen varsity athletic programs. Division I schools are further divided in football into those whose average home attendance in football exceeds 20,000 (Division IA) and those with lower average attendance (Division IAA). Division I schools also must meet a number of other conditions that pertain to financial aid for athletes, the proportion of games played at home, and the proportion of games scheduled against other Division I schools.

2. The data cited in the next two paragraphs come from Michael Todd, "Sports: A Great Calling Card to Present to Potential Students," *USA Today,* July 11–13, 1997.

3. See, for example, Robert A. Baade and Jeffrey O. Sundberg, "Fourth Down and Gold To Go? Assessing the Link between Athletics and Alumni Giving," *Social Science Quarterly* 77 (December 1996):789–803, and Franklin Mixon, Jr., "Athletics vs. Academics? Rejoining the Evidence from SAT Scores," *Education Economics* 3 (December 1995): 277–283.

4. *1998 NCAA Graduation Rates Summary,* available on the NCAA Web page at <http://www.ncaa.org/graduation_rates.html>.

5. In March of 1999, a federal district court judge in Philadelphia ruled that the NCAA could not enforce its minimum test score requirement for athletic scholarships because the requirement had a disparate impact on African-Americans (Karla Haworth, "Federal Judge Bars NCAA from Using Eligibility Rules Based on Test Scores," *Chronicle of Higher Education,* March 19, 1999, pp. A46–47). The NCAA is appealing the decision.

6. Joshua Rolnick, "Financing of Big-Time College Sports Takes a Sharp Turn for the Worse," *Chronicle of Higher Education,* October 23, 1998, p. A59.

7. Andrew Zimbalist, *Unpaid Professionals: Commercialism and Conflict in Big-Time College Sports* (Princeton: Princeton University Press, 1999), pp. 149–172.

8. Varsity athletes' graduation rates are not an issue for schools in the Ivy League. Indeed, varsity athletes who first enrolled as freshmen at Cornell in the fall of 1991 had a slightly higher six-year graduation rate (90.3 percent) than all Cornell students who first enrolled as freshmen that fall (90.2 percent).

9. The next few paragraphs draw on Dmitry Kotlyarenko and Ronald G. Ehrenberg, "Ivy League Varsity Athletics Performance: Do Brains Win?" *Journal of Sports Economics* 1 (May 2000), forthcoming.

10. See, for example, "Princeton Plans Major Increase in Aid for Middle- and Low-Income Students," *Chronicle of Higher Education,* January 30, 1998, p. A35.

11. Jim Naughton, "Supreme Court Denies Brown's Appeal on Gender Equity in Sports," *Chronicle of Higher Education,* May 2, 1997, p. A45.

12. *Cornell University NCAA Athletics Certification Self-Study* (Ithaca: Cornell University, February 10, 1999), p. IV-5.

13. Peter Monaghan, "Dropping Men's Teams to Comply with Title IX," *Chronicle of Higher Education,* December 4, 1998, p. A4.

14. Table 17.1 lists Cornell as having thirty-four sports in 1998–99. The difference is that indoor and outdoor track, which are considered separate sports by Cornell, are counted as one sport for men and one for women in Table 17.1.

15. In March 1999, a federal district court judge prohibited California State University at Bakersfield from cutting the number of men on its wrestling team to help achieve gender equity. Believing that this ruling was inconsistent with at least six previous federal court decisions, the university quickly appealed the decision, and the federal appeals court overturned the decision in December 1999.

    See Welch Suggs, "2 Appeals Courts Uphold Right of Universities to Reduce Number of Male Athletes," *Chronicle of Higher Education*, January 7, 2000, p. A64.

18. Dining and Housing

1. See, for example, Edward Fiske, *The Fiske Guide to Colleges, 1999* (New York: Random House, 1998), p. 196.
2. Faculty clubs all around the nation are declining in popularity for a variety of reasons. See Allison Schneider, "Empty Tables at Faculty Club Worry Some Academics," *Chronicle of Higher Education*, June 13, 1997, p. A12.
3. Details of the calculation of the livable wage are available from the Web page of the Ithaca Alternatives Federal Credit Union, <http://www.alternatives.org>.
4. "U.S. Civil Rights Office Dismisses Complaint over Program Houses", *Cornell Chronicle*, September 26, 1996; available from the World Wide Web at <http://www.news.cornell.edu/Chronicle2.html>.
5. Ben Gose, "Duke Students Say New Intellectualism Will Ruin Campus Culture," *Chronicle of Higher Education*, March 8, 1996, p. A33.

19. Looking to the Future

1. Williams College announced on January 5, 2000, that it would freeze its tuition and fees for the next academic year at their current levels and would finance its increased costs out of increased endowment payout. Williams has one of the highest endowments per student among the selective private colleges, and time will tell if other selective private colleges will follow Williams's lead. See "Williams College Freezes Tuition at $31,520," *Chronicle of Higher Education*, January 14, 2000, p. A52.
2. A contrary view is expressed by my colleague Robert Frank in *Luxury Fever: Why Money Fails to Satisfy in an Era of Excess* (New York: Free Press, 1999).
3. *National Commission on the Costs of Higher Education, Straight Talk about College Costs and Prices* (Washington, D.C., January 21, 1998), p. 4.
4. Welch Suggs, "IRS Challenges Deductions for Suites at College Stadiums," *Chronicle of Higher Education*, September 29, 1995, p. A5.
5. Patrick Healy, "Pa. Court Voids Ban on Private College Tax Exemption," *Chronicle of Higher Education*, September 29, 1995, p. A5.
6. Roger G. Noll and William P. Rogerson discuss the details of such a proposal in "The Economics of Indirect Cost Reimbursement in Federal Research Grants," in Roger G. Noll, ed., *Challenges to Research Universities* (Washington, D.C.: Brookings Institution, 1998).

7. Jeffrey Brainard, "Clinton Tells Agencies to Adopt Reforms to Let Scientists Work More Efficiently," *Chronicle of Higher Education*, May 7, 1999, p. A40.

8. Judy Zellio, "State Payments in Lieu of Taxes in Connecticut" (Denver: National Conference of State Legislatures, January 22, 1999, memo).

20. A Final Thought

1. Ronald G. Ehrenberg, ed., *The American University: National Treasure or Endangered Species?* (Ithaca: Cornell University Press, 1997).

Appendix

1. I simplify greatly here. Annual benefits are actuarially reduced if the faculty member retires before the age of 65 and are also reduced if annual benefits are guaranteed to the faculty member's spouse.

Acknowledgments

During my years at Cornell, the institution has been guided by a series of great presidents and provosts: Dale Corson, Frank H. T. Rhodes, Hunter R. Rawlings III, David Knapp, W. Keith Kennedy, Robert Barker, Mal Nesheim, and Don Randel. I have learned an enormous amount about leading a university from watching and working with each of them.

While I was a Cornell vice president, I was fortunate to work with a fine group of college deans and senior administrative colleagues including Glen Altschuler, Walter Cohen, Hal Craft, Hank Dullea, Tom Dychman, Francille Firebaugh, John Hopcoft, Ed Lawler, Phil Lewis, Dave Lipsky, Daryl Lund, Alan Merton, Jim Mingle, Susan Murphy, Mary Opperman, Russell Osgood, Inge Reichenbach, Yoke San Reynolds, Fred Rogers, Norm Scott, Don Smith, Bob Swieringa, and Tony Vidler. The devotion of each to the part of the university for which he or she was responsible helped me to better understand all parts of the institution. Carolyn Ainslie, Nathan Fawcett, Michael Matier, and Michael Whalen were wonderful colleagues in the budget, institutional research and planning, and statutory affairs offices of the university. Working with the four of them on a daily basis was among the most enjoyable parts of my job.

Since the late 1980s I have focused my research on the economics of higher education. While I had a long-standing interest in this subject, my interest was deepened by an invitation from Charlie Clotfelter to join him, Malcolm Getz, and John Siegfried in writing the book *Economic Challenges in Higher Education*. As I continued to study higher education issues and participated in the Higher Education Working Group of the National Bureau of Economic Research (NBER), I interacted with many talented economists who have also devoted time to thinking about issues of higher education. At the risk of omitting numerous names of friends and colleagues from around

303

the country, I want to especially stress how important the contributions of Mortie Schapiro, Mike McPherson, Gordon Winston, David Breneman, and Bill Massy have been both to the profession and to my thinking.

This book grew out of my experience as a Cornell administrator, but the idea for it has been in the back of my mind for years. My close friend and former jogging partner James Jacobs from the NYU law school has regularly urged me to write this book. Jim kept the idea of the book alive until I realized that it was time to write it.

A large number of scholars and administrators from around the country have generously spent time talking to me about higher education issues and providing me with feedback and advice on specific chapters of this book. I especially appreciate the people who took the time to read a complete draft of the book during the late spring and summer of 1999. They include Michael Baer, Derek Bok, Charlie Clotfelter, Henry Rosovsky (whose own wonderful and humorous book *The University: An Owner's Manual* every reader of this book should read), Michael Rothschild, Frank H. T. Rhodes, and Myra Strober. The book is more focused and readable because of their comments.

I agreed to have Harvard University Press publish this book primarily because my editor, Michael Aronson, expressed such enthusiasm for it while it was still a germ of an idea. At several points during the subsequent writing, Mike pushed me to sharpen my focus. Once a draft was finished, he pushed me to tighten my writing still further. He also, as he promised he would, selected the title. After the final manuscript was submitted to the Press, Nancy Clemente very ably edited it and Tobiah Waldron prepared the index. Larry Clarkberg expertly drew all the figures. I thank Sage Chandler for her proofreading and Andrea Dodge for guiding the book through the production process.

Bob McKersie, now at MIT, was the Dean who first hired me at Cornell. Bob gave me two important pieces of advice that all faculty and administrators should take to heart. First, don't make decisions based on where an institution currently is; make them based upon where you think it can be. Second, don't become an administrator because you want to be an administrator; become one because you have a set of objectives that you want to accomplish at an institution.

My greatest debt is to two great academic leaders and scholars. Frank H. T. Rhodes served as President of Cornell University for eighteen years. By his example, he taught me that great academic leaders never compromise their academic values. He also showed me, again by example, how important it is to involve faculty in the decisions that great universities have to make and to mentor them to be the next generation of academic leaders. Frank's presidency coincided with much of my career at Cornell and I feel very fortunate to have had him as a friend and a colleague for almost twenty-five years.

After a distinguished career as President of Princeton University, William G. Bowen became the President of the Andrew W. Mellon Foundation. In this position, he has continued to conduct research and has co-authored several extremely important books on higher education. He has used resources of the Mellon foundation to support research by foundation staff and others that is aimed at improving higher education. The JSTOR project, which I discussed in chapter 14, is but one example of the foundation's initiatives. Among the recipients of support from Mellon are the NBER higher education research group and the Cornell Higher Education Research Institute, which I direct. I am, of course, most grateful to the Andrew W. Mellon Foundation for its support

When I knew I was stepping down from my position as a vice president at Cornell, I paid Bill a visit to discuss my future plans. He urged me not to consider leadership positions at other academic institutions, arguing that I could have a greater influence on higher education through my writings than I could through leading any single institution.

I decided to take Bill's advice, at least for the short-run. This book is the result.

Index

Ability-to-pay, 122

Academic Duty (Kennedy), 294

Academic environment, 21–22; internal transfer prices and, 157–170; enrollment management and, 171–186; information technology and, 187–193; libraries and, 193–201; distance learning and, 201–206; rising costs and, 265–266; society and, 266–269; government and, 269–277; institutions and, 277–282

Academic quality, 50, 53–54, 61

Academic ratchet, 12

Accessory instruction, 158–165

Accounting standards, 60–61

Administration: cost control and, 11–14; shared governance and, 19–23; budgets and, 23–26; internal structure and, 26–31; endowments and, 46–47; rankings and, 51–69; research facilities and, 104–109; salary and, 113–125; tenure and, 126–136; maintenance and, 141; space planning and, 143–145; space costs and, 148–153; internal transfer prices and, 157–170; charges of, 165–170; enrollment management and, 171–186; information technology and, 187–193; libraries and, 193–201; distance learning and, 201–206; parking and, 209–217; cooling systems and, 218–230; dining and, 249–255; housing and, 256–261; rising costs and, 265–266; society and, 266–269; government and, 269–277; institutions

and, 277–282; compensation structures and, 280; retirement and, 287–289

Admissions, 294; standards of, 3; rates of, 8–9; rankings and, 50, 53, 62; early-decision process and, 55–56, 88–90; recruiting/enrollment costs and, 70–75; need-blind, 84–88, 268; preferential packaging and, 84–88; enrollment management and, 171–186; athletics and, 234

Age Discrimination in Employment Act, 126

Ageism, 133

Agriculture, 29, 48, 67, 144, 297; internal transfer prices and, 159–161, 164; Experimental Station and, 193; book prices and, 197

Air conditioning, 219

Akwe:kon (American Indian House), 257

Allocation: endowments and, 40; rankings and, 64–65; maintenance and, 141; space costs and, 153; internal transfer prices and, 157–158; administrative charges and, 167

Alumni: private cost pressures and, 15; salaries and, 24–25; dean appointments and, 30–31; endowments and, 44; rankings and, 52, 54; satisfaction and, 58–60, 62, 64; admissions and, 71, 75; administrative charges and, 167; distance learning and, 206; athletics and, 233–234; gender equity and, 246

American Association of University Professors (AAUP), 115–117, 295